FORTS IN AMERICA

FORTS

SENTRY TOWER AT
THE CASTILLO DE SAN MARCOS

Illustrated by DANIEL D. FEASER

HAROLD L. PETERSON

IN AMERICA

CHARLES SCRIBNER'S SONS, NEW YORK

PRINTED IN THE UNITED STATES OF AMERICA

Library of Congress Catalog Card Number 64-17210

PENTAGONAL BRICK AND STONE REDOUBT
AT FORT PITT, 1765

Introduction

For almost four hundred years forts played a key role in American history. They were the first structures in each new colony along the Atlantic coast. This was often a hostile shore, and forts were needed for protection against both Indians and European rivals. As the frontier spread inland, the forts moved westward too. The selection of a defensible site often decided the location of settlements which have continued to the present day. Fort Pitt is now called Pittsburgh, but a large number of other cities and towns across the United States still carry the word "fort" in their names to indicate their origin.

Many kinds of forts have contributed to the growth of America. There have been fortified houses and missions, converted barns, factories or other buildings, and temporary field fortifications erected for a single campaign or perhaps even a single battle. Above all there have been the permanent forts. Designed specifically for defense and built to last, these permanent forts mirrored the growing knowledge and skill of their builders.

Literally hundreds of historic American forts still survive. They can be found in every state, and in most areas a short trip can include several that are open to the public as historic shrines. Visiting them can be a thrilling experience in reliving history. It can also lead to an appreciation of craftsmanship and of building techniques and to an insight into military science. The following pages trace the major developments in the design and construction of permanent forts in the United States.

STONE REDOUBT
INSIDE FORT NIAGARA, 1771

Contents

The Transition Period

The 1500's were years of change. The world had just been proved to be round. New continents had been discovered and awaited exploration and settlement. New trade routes to Africa and the Orient were bringing forth exotic materials and products. The last traces of feudalism were disappearing. Cities were growing larger and more important, and ways of life were altering rapidly.

Forts were changing too. The old castles were no longer safe strongholds against attack. Cannon had made them obsolete. These new and powerful guns could strike from a safe distance beyond the range of the archers or handgunners on the battlements. Castle walls were much too

Fort Caroline

high and thin to withstand the shattering impact of the cannon's solid iron balls. And castles were not designed to mount cannon of their own to help hold the attackers at bay. In 1494 King Charles VIII of France invaded Italy with a fine train of artillery, capturing cities almost at will. Castles that previously had held out for months fell in a few hours to the superior weapons. So complete was the domination of cannon over castle that for a time many people believed fortifications were no longer of any use.

Cooler heads, however, argued that although castles were indeed useless, new kinds of forts might be built which would offer efficient protection. During the 1500's engineers began to design such forts with lower, thicker walls made of soft materials that would not shatter easily. They put obstructions in front of the walls to prevent the enemy from getting a clear shot at the fort, and they added projections to the walls called bastions, so designed that cannon could be mounted in them to hold off the enemy in all directions.

These changes took time. For more than a hundred years engineers experimented with different designs and materials. During this period, which has been called the age of transition in fortification, the first forts in what is now the United States were built. They reflect the spirit of the times, for the settlers used available materials and sought to adapt the new designs to local situations.

One of the first American forts was Fort Caroline, near present-day Jacksonville, Florida. There a small colony of French Huguenots decided to establish a new home in 1564. The neighboring Indians seemed friendly at first, but the colonists were not sure how long this would last. Also, Spain claimed the territory they had selected. The Spaniards would look upon the French as trespassers and regard the settlement as a possible base for attacks against the treasure fleets which sailed up along the

FORT CAROLINE

Florida coast on their way back to Spain. Thus the French knew they would need a strong fort for protection against either Spaniard or Indian, and it had to be big enough for the whole colony to live in.

The leader of the French settlement was René de Laudonnière. He was noted primarily as a mariner and ship captain, rather than as an expert in fortification, but the fort his men built was a good one. The site selected was a meadow suitable for a landing place on the banks of the St. Johns River. The fort itself was shaped like a triangle with its base on the river bank and its apex pointed inland.

To start, the colonists dug a deep ditch along the two land sides of the triangle and let water from the river flow in to form a moat. Curious Indians helped in the labor. The dirt from the ditch was piled along its inside edge to make a wall or rampart 9 feet high along the land sides of the fort. Military engineers had learned that dirt was one of the most effective defenses against cannon. Balls that could shatter a stone wall simply buried themselves in the dirt.

Dirt, however, would erode and wash away in heavy rains, and so it had to be faced with something to hold it in place. For the inside facing the French tied bundles of sticks together to make fascines. These they fastened to the dirt walls by driving stakes through them. They also put a layer of fascines crosswise through the dirt wall every 2 or 3 feet to help hold it together. For the outside facing they used sod. Turf was cut into blocks and laid up along the outside wall in much the same manner as a mason would lay bricks, except that stakes were used to fasten the blocks in place instead of mortar. In laying sod, the grass side was always placed down. This kept the dirt from shaking out, and soon the grass would grow out and up the sides of the wall, holding the dirt firmly in place to make a strong defense.

The side of the fort towards the river was different. There the French built a stockade wall of sawn planks, heavily braced and probably pierced with loopholes so they could shoot through it. Apparently Laudonnière planned to rely on his ships to prevent an attack on the fort from this direction, for this was the weakest wall. The strong sides faced the land.

Along the inside of the dirt walls the French built a wide ledge to stand on. In the event of an attack they could fire over the thin upper part of

the wall or parapet. At each of the three angles of the walls they built a bastion. These were also roughly triangular in shape, with widened ledges to provide room for mounting cannon. Because of the way these ledges were designed, the cannon could only be placed to cover the land faces of the fort, another indication that this was the direction from which Laudonnière expected an attack. Later bastions would offer much wider and more versatile coverage, but Fort Caroline was an early experiment with such devices. Improvements came with time and experience.

13

On the land wall to the right the French built the only entrance to the fort. They made a dirt bridge or causeway across the moat, and over the heavy wooden doors they erected a tall archway with the arms of France carved proudly at the top. It was the only handsome decoration in the simple fort.

Inside the walls were the necessary structures for daily living. This was to be a permanent colony with men, women and children from all walks of life—nobles, artisans, scholars, and the artist Jacques Le Moyne who painted pictures of the colony. There were simple houses thatched with palm leaves for the citizens and the soldiers and a bigger house for

The Spanish attack

Laudonnière. Because they had never seen a Florida hurricane, the French built one of the houses too tall, and it was promptly blown down. Thereafter the houses were made lower and stronger. Fort Caroline also contained a guardhouse, a granary, an arms magazine and other storehouses. And there was a well for water. There were some buildings outside the fort too, including a bake oven which was placed away from the houses to avoid the danger of fire. In an emergency, however, all necessary cooking could be done inside the fort, and the outer buildings could be abandoned.

Except for the river front, Fort Caroline was strong; yet it did not survive. On a rainy night in September, 1565, the Spanish struck. Most of the French fighting men were away on an expedition against the Spanish settlement of St. Augustine. Because of the wet weather the sentries had foolishly been allowed to stay inside where it was warm and dry. In the confusion of the sudden attack, someone opened the gate, and the Spaniards poured in to overwhelm such resistance as Laudonnière could organize among the remaining French. A few men and women managed to escape, but most were either captured or killed. The Spanish conquerors strengthened the fort and renamed it Fort San Mateo, but in 1568 the French took revenge and destroyed it completely. Today even the site is gone, washed away by the St. Johns River. Fort Caroline National Memorial on the present river bank commemorates its dramatic history.

JAMESTOWN

In 1607, within fifty years of the destruction of Fort Caroline, English colonists built a triangular fort at Jamestown, Virginia. Unlike the Indians near Fort Caroline, those in Virginia were definitely hostile. When the English first set foot ashore, the Indians attacked and wounded several of them. Thus the new colonists' immediate project, after they had selected the site for their settlement, was the building of a fort. They anchored their ships late on May 13, began work on the fort the next day and finished it by mid-June. It was quick work, but they knew they needed protection against both the Indians and the Spanish who also claimed Virginia as their own.

No one knows who designed the fort at Jamestown. Captain John Smith arrived as a prisoner in irons because of an argument on board

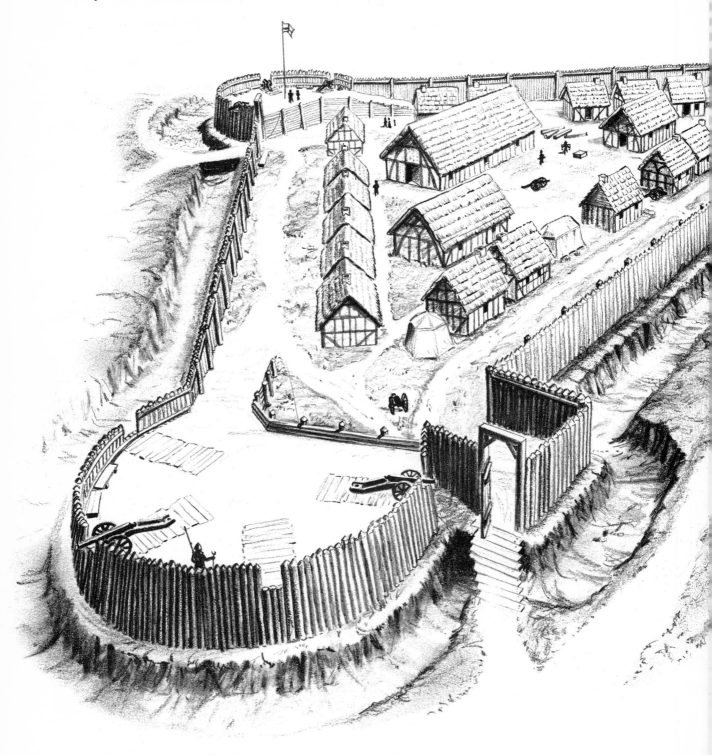

The fort at Jamestown, 1607

16

ship and he was not freed until the fort was almost finished. Thus in all probability he had little or nothing to do with it. The designer may have been Edward Maria Wingfield since he was the only other leader of wide military experience and since he also was president of the council that governed the colony. In any event, the new fort was similar to Fort Caroline in two ways. It was built on a river bank to protect the ship anchorage, and it was triangular in form with its base towards the river and its apex pointed inland.

There the similarities ceased. A ditch was dug all around the fort at Jamestown, even on the river front; but because the river bank was high, it was a dry ditch rather than a wet moat. In fact, a dry ditch was almost as good a protection as a wet one. It was made so wide that an attacking party could not reach the actual wall from the outer rim. If the enemy did manage to get down into the ditch, he found the top of the wall that much higher above his head, and the time it took him to climb in or out of this obstacle exposed him that much longer to the fire of the defenders.

The English built all of the walls at Jamestown of wood. A stockade of logs, planks and posts 14 or 15 feet high was erected. Not as strong as the dirt walls of Fort Caroline, but more resilient than stone, the wooden walls were probably heavy enough to withstand shots from small cannon.

At each corner of the triangle formed by the stockade was a bastion just as there was at Fort Caroline. At Jamestown, however, the bastions were circular, much as if their designer had been thinking of the round towers of castles. These bastions were the principal defensive positions in the fort. Dirt from the ditch was probably used to raise the floor level of the bastions to within 5 or 6 feet of the top of the stockade. Here most of the cannon were mounted, and a firing step would have been built between the openings for the big guns so that the soldiers could shoot over the top of the wall. From these

Cannon were hauled up dirt ramps to the bastions

positions the men could cover the long "curtains" as the walls between the bastions were called.

The English built several gates at Jamestown. The main gate was in the center of the wall towards the river, and there were smaller ones on the land sides right next to the bastions. Each entrance was defended by a cannon mounted inside directly facing the gate. There were probably loopholes for small arms too, although the records are not clear about this.

This was a big fort. The river front was 140 yards long, and each of the other sides was 100 yards. Like Fort Caroline, Jamestown contained all the buildings necessary for survival in case of attack: a storehouse, guardhouse and market place and, perhaps most important, the well for water. Even the bake oven was inside, and this may have been a mistake for there were a number of fires. Along each land wall was a row of small thatched houses, and in the center of the fort was a big church which John Smith described as "a homely thing like a barne."

Within the walls of Jamestown the first permanent English settlement in America eked out its early years. Life in the fort was harsh, and survival was a matter of luck. Most of the settlers were men. There were very few women in the beginning and almost no comforts. Disease, crop failures and hostile Indians plagued the little band. The winter of 1609–1610 brought the "Starving Time" when all of these ills reached their peak. In a few short months death reduced the population from about 500 to 60, and the few survivors were so weak they could hardly care for themselves.

Spring brought some relief. More settlers arrived under the leadership of Sir Thomas Gates. He was shocked at the appearance of the fort. It looked, he wrote, "rather as the ruins of some ancient fortification, then that any people living might now inhabit it." The stockade posts and some of the houses had been used for firewood by colonists too weak to gather fuel in the forest or too fearful of the Indians who lurked nearby. Indeed the Indians could have captured the village at almost any time, so poorly was it protected. For some reason they never tried, perhaps believing that it was to their advantage to wait until starvation and disease had claimed even more defenders. Within a month of Gates's arrival another group of colonists came with the new governor, Lord Delaware. The crisis was past, and the settlement was firmly established.

The fort at Jamestown was never attacked although Spanish spies quickly provided their king with a map and a description. Still, its life was almost the same length as Fort Caroline's. From 1607 until 1610 it was the heart of the colony. Then with the increase of population the settlement began to spread out. Newer defenses were built further away, and the first fort disappeared. Its timbers rotted, and the colonists undoubtedly leveled the bastions and filled the ditches. Today the original site has been washed away by the James River, but there is an excellent model of it in the visitor center of Colonial National Historical Park at Jamestown. Nearby, the State of Virginia has erected a full-scale reconstruction which gives a very accurate impression of this early fort if one remembers that the ditch should be larger and the stockade higher.

PLYMOUTH   More relaxed militarily than either of their southern neighbors were the Pilgrims who landed at Plymouth, Massachusetts, in December, 1620. They were primarily tradespeople, farmers and artisans with little military experience or inclination. The Indians were few, and the Spanish were far away. It was up to doughty little Miles Standish, their military adviser, to take charge of such matters. Under his direction, the Pilgrims' first effort for defense was a simple but stout stockade enclosing the houses and gardens which were given primary attention. The palisade with three gates was completed in March, 1621. It had no bastions but would have afforded some protection against a surprise Indian attack. Standish was careful to see that a watch was kept at all times and that the gates were locked at night.

This first stockade was a simple wall of logs about 8 feet tall. A few years later a more complicated wall was built. It was made of planks 9 feet long, sharpened at the top and fastened to a framework of stout posts, 10 inches in diameter, set 19 feet apart and connected with three cross rails.

Plymouth with its fortifications complete

20

Both walls were well built. They might be climbed, but it would take a heavy blow to knock them down. John Pory of Jamestown, who visited Plymouth in 1622, described the first one as "stronger than I have seene anie in Virginia."

At the time of Pory's visit, the Pilgrims were also at work on their first true fort. This was a square blockhouse of heavy oak timbers with a flat roof and battlements for mounting four heavy cannon. The ground floor of the building, which was pierced with loopholes for small arms, was used as a church and meeting house and also provided sleeping quarters for the guard. The site selected for the fort was the top of a hill, the highest ground in the vicinity. From it the cannon could cover the entire harbor and keep enemy ships away. Since the village itself was further down the slope of the hill, the stockade was extended to the fort and then back, making a wall 2,700 feet long. The building thus became a form of bastion or redoubt at the angle of two curtain walls. In a sense it was the ancestor of a whole host of later frontier forts composed of blockhouses and a stockade.

Defensive arrangements were completed with the erection of a small square stockade in the center of the village where the two streets crossed. Four little swivel guns mounted there could cover the streets and gates in every direction.

Planks for the fort were cut in a saw pit

The fort at Plymouth

The Plymouth fortifications were not particularly strong even when complete. They would have withstood a short attack, but a siege would quickly have captured them. There was only one blockhouse. Two or more would have offered protection to each other. The stockade, though stout, was too long and too low to be defended adequately, and as far as surviving records show, there were no loopholes or other provisions for shooting through or over it. All it offered was an obstacle that would slow an attacking force and perhaps allow the colonists time to run to the fort where they might huddle together with some safety until their food and water ran out.

Fortunately for the Pilgrims, the defenses were never tested. With periodic repairs the fortifications stood until they were no longer needed and the timber was used to build houses. The site of the original Pilgrim fort remains in the center of the burial ground at Plymouth while the modern city covers the area within the stockade. On a similar site just outside the city, however, Plimoth Plantation, Inc. has reconstructed the original village and its fortifications so that it is still possible to see and test the strengths and weaknesses of a pioneer blockhouse and stockade system.

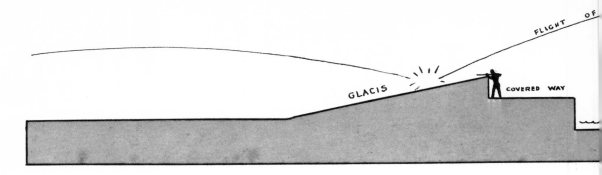

The Bastioned System

While colonists from England, France and Spain built simple forts in the wilds of North America, military engineers of Europe worked at perfecting a whole system of fortification. Each nation developed slightly different versions of its own, but two men are generally recognized as having brought the new system to its highest development. One was a Frenchman, Marshal Sebastien le Prestre de Vauban (1633–1707); the other a Hollander, Baron Menno van Coehoorn (1641–1704). Each of them published a set of general principles for fortification, and each supervised the construction of great defensive systems within his own country. For over a hundred years almost every other military engineer in Europe described his own ideas about fortification by comparing them with the work of these two men.

The key features of the new system were the perfection of the bastions of the main fort and the development of a series of outerworks designed to keep the enemy and his cannon balls away from the fort itself. It was the bastion which gave the system its name, but the outer defenses were just as important.

There had been bastions at Fort Caroline, at Jamestown and at other forts in America during the 1500's and early 1600's, but they were largely experimental and inefficient. In the new system the fort was usually a four- or five-sided structure with a pointed bastion at each corner designed so that every foot of ground immediately surrounding the fort could be covered by the fire of the defenders. There was no "dead space" where an attacker would be safe from harm because the guns of the fort could not be pointed at him.

The outerworks began at the ditch. Instead of throwing all of the dirt along the inside edge of the ditch to form the fort walls, the builders put some on the outside as well. Thus they created a bank with a steep inner

24

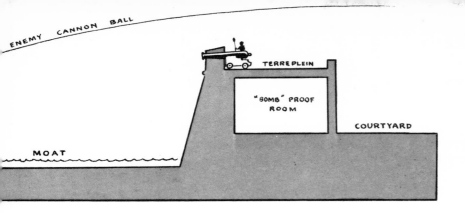

ENEMY CANNON BALL

TERREPLEIN

"BOMB" PROOF ROOM

COURTYARD

MOAT

Cross section of the wall and outworks of a typical bastioned fort

face and an outer surface that sloped gradually away. This slope was called the glacis, and it had several purposes. First of all, it was high enough to protect the lower part of the fort's rampart from enemy fire. Cannon balls striking the sloping surface might even bounce right over the fort, missing it entirely. Second, it created a smooth field all around with no bumps or gullies in which an attacker might hide. Finally, it afforded protection for an advanced line of defenders. This was done by leaving a ledge between the ditch and the steep inner bank of the glacis. Soldiers could stand on this ledge, or covered way as it was called, and use the bank as a breastwork. An attacking force would have to drive them out of this advanced position before it could even think of assaulting the main fort.

There were more formal outworks also. The most important was a triangular defense called a ravelin or demilune. These ravelins were built at the outer edge of the ditch and were designed to protect a gateway by cutting off enemy fire. They might also be used to cover the curtain wall between the bastions on those sides of a fort from which an attack was most likely.

Other outworks included separate small forts called redoubts. Sometimes these were actually blockhouses, sometimes just dirt embankments erected outside the glacis, perhaps as much as a musket shot away. Redoubts were designed to slow up the advance of an enemy and give the defenders of the main fort as much time as possible to get ready. There were defenses with jagged outlines called horn works and crown works and many more besides. In Europe whole cities and harbors were ringed with miles of such fortifications, but in America there was seldom more than the principal fort with its bastions, ditch, glacis, one or two ravelins and perhaps a redoubt. For the wild new country this was usually enough.

25

THE CASTILLO DE SAN MARCOS

One of the most beautiful early examples of the bastioned system in America is the Castillo de San Marcos or Castle of Saint Mark built by the Spanish at St. Augustine, Florida. The little outpost that guarded the route of the treasure ships needed a stout defense. France and England both envied the wealth Spain received from her colonies. Free-

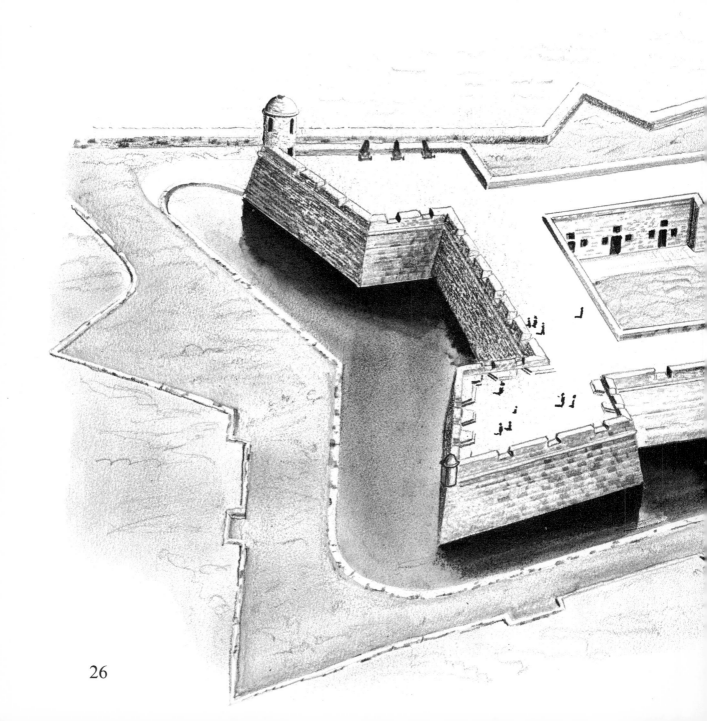

booters, pirates and privateers delighted in capturing the gold, silver and gems carried by Spanish ships or stored in Spanish warehouses. St. Augustine itself was a poor town with no wealth to tempt the pirates, but it offered a haven for the ships, and so it was raided time and time again, once by Sir Francis Drake. Nine wood and dirt forts were built one after

The Castillo de San Marcos as it appears today

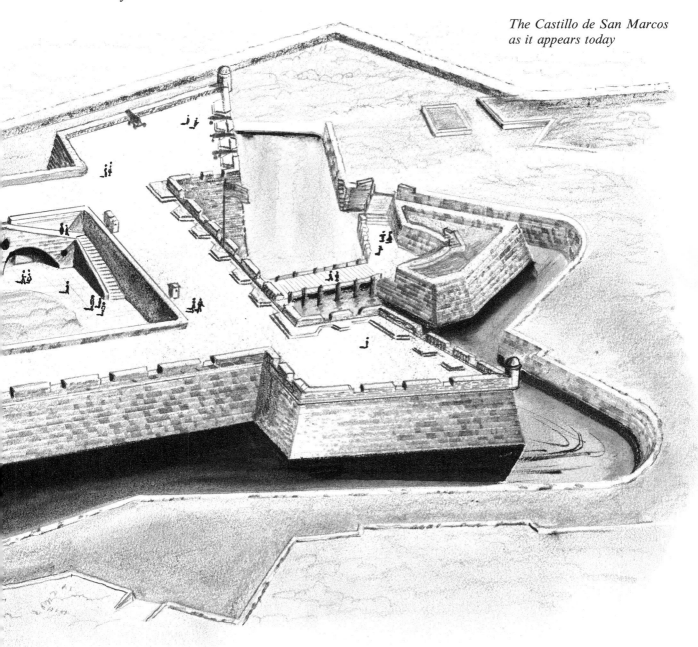

another to protect the town, but the soil was sandy and eroded easily and wood rotted quickly in the damp climate. Indians burned one fort, the English destroyed another, and the rest fell apart by themselves. Something more permanent was needed.

On October 2, 1672, Don Manuel de Sendoya, governor and captain general of the province, turned the first shovelful of earth to mark the beginning of a new stone fort. Ignacio Daza, a military engineer, had designed it in the latest fashion. It was to be a stout defense with four bastions, a moat, covered way and glacis. There would be a ravelin too,

The soft coquina was quarried with pick and crowbar

Sentry tower at the Castillo de San Marcos

directly in front of the gate, and anyone who wanted to enter would have to cross the moat twice. One drawbridge would lead him to the ravelin; a longer one would take him to the fort itself. Even then he would be faced by heavy doors and a portcullis—a grating of stout timbers shod with iron that could be raised and lowered to form a second door. A surprise assault would be all but impossible if the garrison was alert, and to provide shelter for the sentries, little watchtowers were built on the point of each bastion. Inside the fort there were quarters for the soldiers, store-rooms for provisions and ammunition, a well, a prison and a chapel.

Daza and the Governor selected the site for the fort carefully. Built on the shore of Matanzas Bay, it could defend the harbor; and a shallow sand bar kept big ships far enough away so that their heavy guns could not reach the fort. Swamps, arms of the bay and a creek protected the other sides of the Castillo, making it difficult for an enemy to bring siege guns against it.

The Castillo de San Marcos took many years to build. Spanish workmen, Indians and prisoners quarried the soft native shell rock called coquina and built the walls 30 feet high and up to 12 feet thick for wages that ranged from 12½¢ a day for a laborer to $3 a day for the engineer. Daza died, and new governors replaced Sendoya, but the work continued for almost twenty-five years before the fort was completed. Even then there were improvements to follow as new engineers added bombproof rooms and strengthened some of the outworks. Finally the fort was finished, a massive structure, impregnable in its day—and handsome. The white plaster which covered all its walls reflected the strong Florida sun and contrasted with the red watchtowers and the painted decorations inside, while the waters of the moat mirrored the sculptured arms of Spain above the entrance.

The Castillo needed all its strength. Pirates, Indians, English soldiers and American colonists all attacked it. There were raids in 1683, 1704, 1728 and 1743 and actual sieges in 1702 and 1740.

General James Oglethorpe, governor of the new English colony of Georgia, conducted the second siege and gave the Castillo its severest test. Because the fort was so well-placed, the English could get their artillery no closer than the far side of the bay. From that distance their big guns thundered at the fort for twenty-seven straight days. But the soft shell rock did not splinter under the impact of the heavy iron balls. Instead, it absorbed them as one Englishman remarked, "as though you would stick a knife into cheese." Only two Spaniards in the fort were killed. Discouraged, Oglethorpe quit the bombardment. He thought about a direct assault but abandoned that idea and decided to starve out the garrison. Finally he gave that up too, and on the thirty-eighth day of the siege he sailed back to Georgia.

After the raid of 1743, the rest of the Castillo's days were relatively peaceful. England gained control of the fort by treaty in 1763, kept American prisoners there during the Revolution, and by the treaty ending that war returned it to Spain in 1783.

In 1821 the United States acquired Florida from Spain, and the Castillo was renamed Fort Marion after General Francis Marion. In 1924 it became a National Monument, and it still stands today for all who wish to see this fine original example of the early bastioned system of fortification.

One of the principal teachings of Marshal Vauban was that a fort should not be built according to rigid rules. He believed that the theories of fortification should be modified and adapted to the nature of the ground and the place to be defended. Canadian-born Lt. Michel Chartier, Sieur de Lotbinière, studied military engineering in France and had Vauban's instruction clearly in mind when he set out, in 1755, to build one of America's great bastioned forts in the wilderness along the shores of Lake Champlain. He named his project Fort Vaudreuil at first, then Fort Carillon. Later the English called it Fort Ticonderoga. De Lotbinière selected the crest of a rocky ridge at the base of a peninsula that jutted out into the lake. From this position he could command a key point—the main route to Lake George. The steep slopes to the lake protected the

*Plan of Fort Ticonderoga
and its outworks*

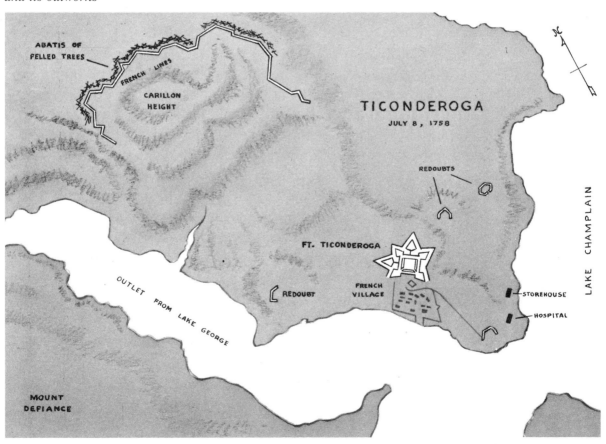

fort from attack on two sides, but made ditching in the usual manner impossible. The solid rock just beneath the earth's surface hampered ditching on the other sides. De Lotbinière had to do something different.

The first year he could do little more than clear the land and make a modest start. He outlined a typical four-bastioned fort with ravelins or demilunes protecting the curtain walls on the two sides from which an enemy might attack. His men raised the walls to a height of 7 feet before most of them had to leave for winter quarters.

This was not a stone-faced fort in the beginning. De Lotbinière had no stonemasons and few tools. Thus he built the walls of horizontal logs and dirt. To do this he constructed two log walls about 10 feet apart, fastened together by crosspieces. The space between was filled with rubble and dirt. It was an ancient technique and many American forts were built in this manner, including Fort William Henry at the southern end of Lake George. There the English and Americans were establishing a base hoping to drive the French back to Canada.

One advantage of the log and dirt construction was that it could always be faced with stone at a later date. This was exactly what the French did in 1756 and 1757 as they continued work on the fort. Stone facings helped make a fort stronger and more durable. Even if the stone shattered even-

Fort Ticonderoga as it appears today

tually under cannon fire, the dirt behind remained as a solid protection. And the stone held the dirt in place, preventing erosion and simplifying maintenance. At this time the French also raised the height of the walls, and then started on the outworks.

A wall was built along one steep slope a little way from the fort to provide a breastwork and a place to mount cannon. A covered way was planned for the other steep side, but it was never completed. Instead, the French concentrated on the two exposed sides. They completed two large demilunes and dug a ditch around them. It was a most unusual ditch. The workmen just cut away part of the low hillside in front of the fort, blasting out rock to clear the way. Thus the bottom of the ditch was on the same level as the parade ground inside, and the main entrance opened right into it. The natural hill made a perfect glacis. De Lotbinière had obeyed the master Vauban well in changing his plans to fit the ground. Out towards the end of the point the young French engineer built a redoubt. Other small works to protect approaches to the fort and to guard important places were added later.

Inside the fort were the usual necessary storerooms and living quarters. Interestingly, the barracks towered over the walls, and other engineers were critical of this for the buildings thus became targets for enemy cannon. The well was outside the fort too. Set on one of the protected sides, it probably would have been accessible even during an attack. Just to be sure, however, the French built a big cistern to collect and store rainwater so that they would have a supply even if the well were cut off.

Ticonderoga was an excellent fortification, well designed and well built. But it took more than that for a fort to be impregnable. Much depended upon the skill and determination of the attackers and defenders—and upon the number of men available. The history of Fort Ticonderoga —one successful defense and three captures—points this out very clearly. In none of the encounters was the strength of the fort itself questioned.

*Building a horizontal log
and dirt wall*

Redoubt No. 10 at Yorktown,
a dirt fortification
with horizontal log fraises

The first attack against Ticonderoga was launched by a British and American army in 1758. The French, commanded by the renowned Marquis de Montcalm, met them at an entrenched line well in front of the fort and defeated them decisively. Then the fortunes of war changed. When a new British-American army returned the next year, Montcalm and most of the French army were away. The remaining garrison resisted the attackers for a few days, then blew up the powder magazine, set fire to the fort and retreated without really trying to defend it.

The British rebuilt the fort, officially named it Fort Ticonderoga, and then proceeded to lose it just as quickly and ignominiously as the French had. The American Revolution broke out in April, 1775, but news traveled slowly in such remote areas. Ethan Allen and Benedict Arnold with only eighty-three Green Mountain Boys were able to surprise and capture the great fort because its commander did not even know there was a war.

This victory gave the Americans their chance to make a mistake. They failed to fortify a steep hill overlooking the fort because they did not believe an enemy could possibly haul cannon up its slopes. In 1777, however, a British Army under General John Burgoyne mounted guns on the hill and 3,000 American troops had to flee for their lives, leaving the fort to the British. Later that year a surprise raid by the Americans under Colonel John Brown captured most of the outworks but failed to retake the fort.

At the end of the American Revolution the British abandoned Fort Ticonderoga, and it was never again occupied by a military garrison. Today the great fort has been restored through the efforts of the late Stephen H. P. Pell and the Fort Ticonderoga Association, and it is possible once more to see just how the young de Lotbinière adapted a bastioned fort to fit a special situation.

There were many bastioned forts built in America. Some were stone like the Castillo de San Marcos or dirt faced with stone like Fort Ticonderoga. Some had only dirt walls. Others like Fort William Henry used the horizontal log and dirt wall construction, and some combined that with the vertical palisade. Many used the palisade alone. The design of a fort was determined by its strategic importance, the speed with which it had to be built, the materials and skilled labor available to the engineer.

Most forts were four-sided, but there were also some with five sides and five bastions. Fort Pitt was one, Fort Ontario at Oswego, New York,

Fort McHenry, 1814

36

was another, and Fort McHenry in Maryland was a third. All had similar outlines, but there the likeness ceased. Fort Ontario was of log and dirt construction. Fort Pitt, with one of the finest systems of outworks ever built in America, was primarily a dirt fort except that the two most exposed sides were faced with masonry.

Fort McHenry, much the latest of the three, had all of its dirt walls faced with brick both inside and out. This famous fort guarding Baltimore harbor was built between 1794 and 1805 and named for James McHenry, Secretary of War. Later years brought modifications designed to increase its strength. It had one ravelin opposite its entrance and a ditch all the way around. Since its main purpose was to protect the harbor, additional batteries of cannon with dirt embankments for protection were erected close to the shore. These could be abandoned if necessary, and the artillerists could flee into the main fort.

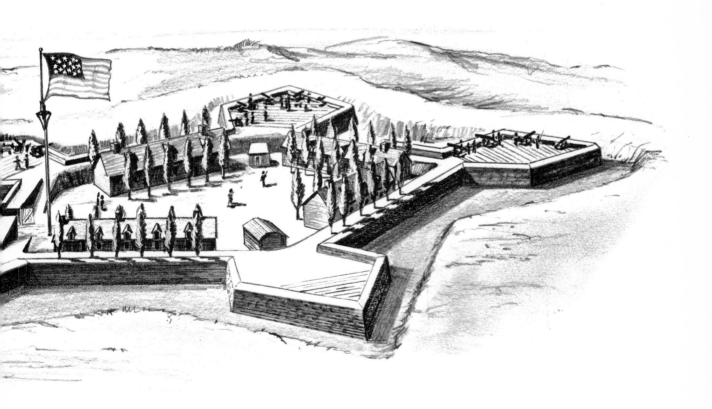

Fortunately Fort McHenry was solidly built. When the British attacked Baltimore in September, 1814, their ships had guns with a longer range than those in the fort. They stopped out of range of the Americans and bombarded them with rockets and huge mortar shells. Major George Armistead and his garrison in the fort were helpless to reply. All day long the British kept up their fire. Then, at night, they tried to send a party upriver past the fort to land behind it. At last the Americans could shoot back, and they did so with vigor, aiming at the flashes of the British guns. They shot well and the British fell back.

On the deck of a British ship in the harbor Francis Scott Key watched the shelling. He had come aboard to seek the release of a prominent Baltimore physician and was detained by the British for the duration of the battle. Keeping an anxious vigil through the night, Key wondered if his countrymen could possibly stand the pounding. When dawn broke and he saw the huge flag still flying over the fort, he took a letter from his pocket and wrote a few lines of a poem to express his joy and gratitude. Later that day the British gave up their attack, and Key went ashore. He completed his poem, and it was printed as a handbill in Baltimore on September 15, 1814. He called it "Defence of Fort McHenry," but it soon became known as "The Star-Spangled Banner."

Fort McHenry weathered the bombardment well. Major Armistead estimated that perhaps as many as 1,800 shells had been fired by the British and that about 400 had actually landed within his defenses. One gun had been disabled; two buildings had been damaged; four Americans had been killed and twenty-four wounded. But the strong fort walls had survived, and so had the nerves of the defenders. Today the ditch and the water batteries are gone and some heavy gun emplacements of the Civil War era are scattered about, but Fort McHenry itself, now a unit in the National Park System, still stands solidly at the edge of Baltimore harbor.

Erecting a log stockade

The Forts Move West

Big bastioned forts like Ticonderoga, McHenry and the Castillo de San Marcos were designed to withstand attacks by European enemies with heavy artillery. They guarded important cities and transportation routes such well-equipped foes might attack. In the back country where big bodies of troops and heavy guns could not move so readily, forts could be simpler. Here the principal enemies were Indians and perhaps a few hostile white men. There would probably be no artillery to worry about, and the chances of a long siege would be slight. Indians did not normally fight that way.

Blockhouse with octagonal top,
Fort Vancouver, Washington, c. 1846

For the remote hamlet, the trading post or the frontier Army garrison, blockhouses and stockades were the standard defenses. Occasionally such fortifications were made of stone. Sir William Johnson had two stone blockhouses to protect his estate at Johnstown, New York, and Fort Snelling, Minnesota, boasted stone walls as well as a blockhouse and tower. But these were exceptions. Wood was the usual material. In most places there was plenty of timber waiting to be cut. It was easier to use than stone, and it was strong enough to withstand the type of attack that could be expected.

The Pilgrims had made their second stockade of sawn plank, but most American frontier forts were built of whole logs. If there was time, the pioneers would square the logs with axes so that they would fit together more tightly, and the War Department recommended in 1803 that logs used in Army forts be peeled and burned slightly so that they would last longer.

Some of the frontier forts were extremely simple. For the smallest a single blockhouse was sometimes thought to be enough. Many others were only a little more elaborate. When the men of the famous Lewis and Clark expedition reached the Pacific coast in 1805 and realized that they would have to spend the winter in what is now Oregon, they built a little fort for protection against both Indians and the weather. On December 8 they began construction of two long low buildings facing each other and about 20 feet apart. By Christmas day the roofs were on, and the men celebrated by firing a volley from their guns, singing, exchanging simple gifts and feasting on lean elk meat, spoiled dried fish and roots. Then they went back to work and built stockade walls connecting the ends of the buildings. It was not much of a fort, but it was all they needed in that far-off place. They named it Fort Clatsop after a friendly Indian tribe.

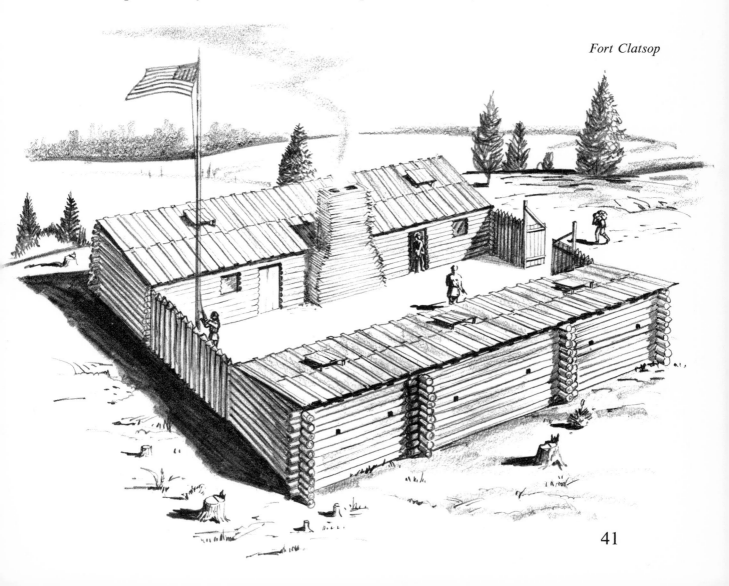

Fort Clatsop

The bigger and better forts usually had two blockhouses, tall stockades and several buildings inside. When these blockhouses were placed on diagonal corners of the walls and projected out beyond them, they served much the same functions as bastions in permitting the defenders to shoot along the outside of the stockade. Each blockhouse would cover two of the walls.

FORT
DEARBORN

Fort Dearborn was an excellent example of a fully developed frontier Army fort of the type preferred by the War Department about 1800. It was built by Captain John Whistler in 1803 at the foot of Lake Michigan. The site is now the city of Chicago, but at the time was occupied by only four huts.

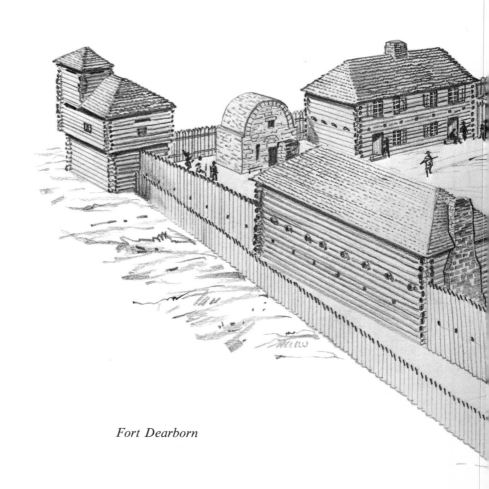

Fort Dearborn

42

The gallant captain had come to America with the British Army in 1777 to help subdue the rebellious colonies, but he had been captured at Saratoga and had grown to like the new land. When the war was over, he joined the American Army and proved a loyal and dependable soldier. Whistler built his fort in the wilderness precisely according to instructions from the War Department and even named it after Secretary of War Henry Dearborn. It had two blockhouses on diagonal corners and four large two-story buildings that formed a square. The space between these buildings was filled in with a stockade, and there were loopholes in both the back walls of the buildings and the stockade for the soldiers to shoot through. There were even two low stockade walls somewhat like bastions outside the main fort on the corners opposite the blockhouses to give the defenders more of a chance for a flanking fire along the walls. A special feature was a brick powder magazine, which Whistler's instructions had suggested he erect.

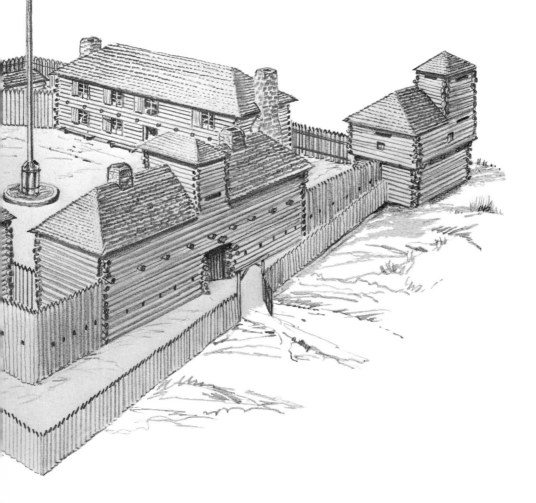

Fort Dearborn was everything that a frontier fort should be. Army specifications had been followed to the letter. But when the War of 1812 broke out, there were not enough supplies to maintain the fort and the commandant was ordered to abandon it and move the garrison and their families to Detroit. It was a sad mistake. Hostile Indians fell upon the departing residents, killed or captured almost all of them, and destroyed the fortification.

Fort William

FORT
LARAMIE

One of the most famous of all Western frontier outposts was Fort Laramie. Located on the great Oregon Trail in what is now Wyoming, it was a depot for fur traders and trappers, a haven for emigrants and forty-niners, a station for the Pony Express and the Overland Stage, and an Army post. Jim Bridger, the famous mountain man, was a part-owner for a time. Kit Carson visited it. So did Calamity Jane and a host of other famous Westerners. Its history is a fine illustration of the evolution of America's Western forts.

Two fur traders, William Sublette and Robert Campbell, built the first Fort Laramie in 1834. They named it Fort William in honor of Sublette, but because of its position on the banks of the Laramie River, almost everyone called it Fort Laramie. Sublette and Campbell were experienced mountain men, and they built a good fort. They squared the timbers for the stockade and put blockhouses on diagonal corners. Over the gate they put another large blockhouse and mounted a cannon in it. In-

side they built rows of small cabins right up against the stockade so that their roofs formed a platform that defenders could stand on to shoot over the walls. Indians camped outside the walls in large numbers when they came to trade their furs for white men's goods. At such times the traders demonstrated their cannon with good effect. The artist Alfred Miller, who visited the fort in 1837, reported: "The Indians have a mortal horror of the 'big gun' which rests in the blockhouse, as they have had experience of its prowess and witnessed the havoc produced by its loud 'talk.'

Inside Fort William
(from a painting by Alfred Miller)

They conceive it to be only asleep and have a wholesome dread of its being waked up."

By 1841 the wooden walls of Fort William had decayed. A new fort was needed, and the Pierre Chouteau, Jr. and Company, which had bought the old fort, built a new one. Instead of logs they used adobe, a kind of sun-dried brick. Fort John, as they called it, also had two blockhouses, and its walls were 15 feet high with a little wooden palisade set on top for additional protection. Inside, the tops of the cabins still formed a firing platform. Trade with the Indians was good, and the Company also made a handsome profit selling supplies to westward-moving emigrants at exorbitant prices. The price for a cup of sugar, for instance, was $2, and bullets brought 75¢ a pound.

Fort John

Fort Laramie, 1876

As the emigrants moved West in greater numbers, the Army began to build forts to protect their routes of travel. In 1849 the War Department bought Fort John, and it became officially Fort Laramie. The old adobe fort was used for shelter at first, but almost immediately the soldiers began to erect buildings outside it in a square around an open parade ground. This became the Army post proper and the real Fort Laramie. By 1863 the old fort had vanished completely, and eventually even the minor defenses and outworks disappeared. Fort Laramie was a fort in name only. There were no walls or defenses of any kind.

These were active years for Fort Laramie. The Indians had become increasingly hostile. Councils were held in efforts to obtain peace, and when these failed and open warfare broke out in the territory, the fort—which was never attacked—became a base for expeditions to subdue the hostile tribes. Then the frontier passed. The Plains Indians were sub-

dued, and in 1890 Fort Laramie was abandoned. Today it is a unit in the National Park System. Fort William and Fort John have completely disappeared, but the visitor can still see many of the buildings of the Army's Fort Laramie and visualize through them the appearance of a typical unfortified "fort" of the West.

Defending the Coasts

Hostile Indians in the West were not the only problem facing the American Army. There was also the long coastline to defend against possible attack by an unfriendly European power. In the years immediately following the Revolution the new nation did not worry greatly about a threat from abroad. Then the troubles leading to the War of 1812 made Americans aware of the need for seacoast protection.

Coastal fortification was quite different from inland defense. For one thing, the enemy would probably be on shipboard. Most of the time the ships would be moving, and usually they would stay a long distance off. If the fort was on the mainland, an enemy might be able to land some distance away and attack on foot. Thus the land face of a seacoast fort might need a ravelin and bastions or some other device for a flanking fire

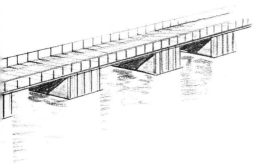

Castle Clinton

against assaulting troops. But the sea faces could be designed specifically to fight ships. This meant long rows of heavy cannon that could be swung in wide arcs to follow a moving vessel. Bastions would get in the way for such work, and so they were usually omitted. And since guns on moving ships could seldom hit twice in exactly the same spot, the solid walls of the land forts could be lightened. Indeed they could be hollowed out to make a series of rooms called casemates for mounting more cannon. Thus, instead of just having cannon on top of the ramparts like the old bastioned forts, new seacoast defenses might have two or even three tiers of guns.

Some of the earliest of these specialized seacoast forts were round or almost round. Castle Clinton, on a little man-made island 200 feet from the tip of Manhattan, had red sandstone walls 8 feet thick with one tier of casemates for guns. A timber causeway with a drawbridge connected it to the shore. Opposite, on Governors Island, stood another round tower, Castle William, with three tiers of guns. Both forts were begun as tension mounted with England, and were finished just before the War of 1812 actually broke out. Both are standing today. Castle William is still in use by the Army. Castle Clinton served as headquarters for the defenses of New York City and vicinity until 1821. Then it became in turn a place of amusement called Castle Gardens, an emigrant landing depot, the New York City Aquarium, and now Castle Clinton National Monument. Restored to its appearance as a fort, it stands in Battery Park surrounded by land reclaimed from the harbor.

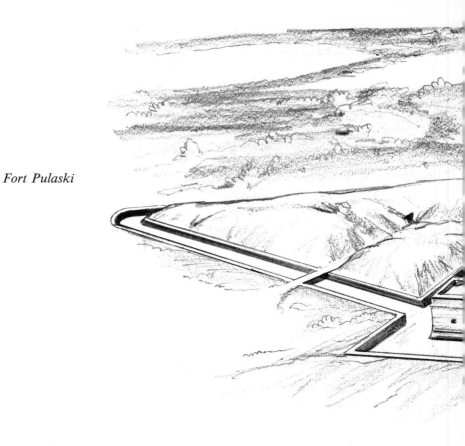

Fort Pulaski

FORT PULASKI   After the War of 1812 the building of coastal forts began in earnest. Experience in the war had shown how weakly the shoreline was defended. At the direction of Congress a military board of engineers surveyed the entire coast and planned a series of forts from Maine to Florida and along the Gulf Coast to the mouth of the Mississippi River. For more than thirty years soldiers and civilians, masons and carpenters worked to complete the plan. The forts were excellent but while they were being built, weapons improved, and their first major tests found them obsolete.

Fort Pulaski was a prime example. Brigadier General Simon Bernard selected the site guarding the approaches to Savannah, Georgia, and made the preliminary plans for the fortifications. Bernard had been one of Napoleon's best military engineers and had come to America after the

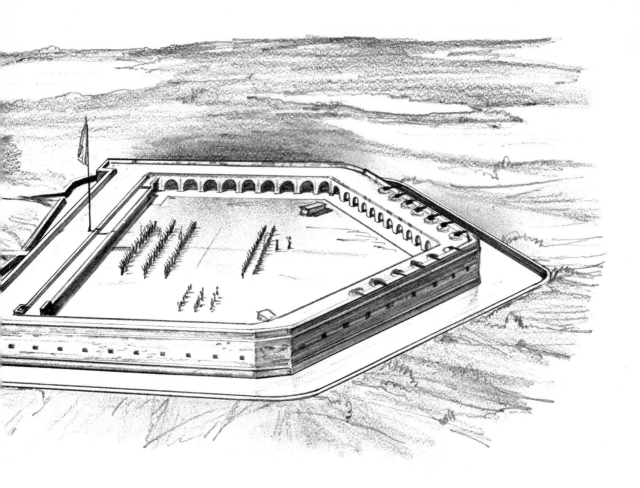

Battle of Waterloo to work on the board of engineers. Robert E. Lee, just graduated from the U. S. Military Academy at West Point, worked on the fort from 1829 to 1831 and so did other distinguished military engineers until it was finally finished in 1847.

Fort Pulaski was a big five-sided fort costing almost a million dollars to build. The land face with the drawbridge and entrance had little demibastions to provide flanking fire. There was also a ravelin and a wide wet moat on all sides. The solid brick walls were 7 to 11 feet thick and 32 feet high. There was one tier of casemates for cannon, and another tier of guns could be mounted on top. In all, plans called for 140 cannon to arm the massive masonry structure, but at the outbreak of the Civil War only 20 were in place.

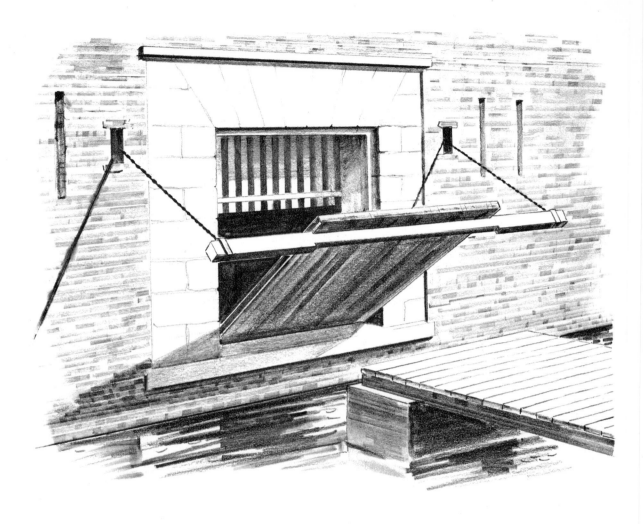

*Portcullis and drawbridge
at Fort Pulaski*

On April 11, 1862, Fort Pulaski came under fire for the first and only time. Southern troops had seized the fort just before the outbreak of war and they began immediately to prepare it for a defense. A Union force moved south to attack, but the Confederates were confident. "You might as well cannonade the Rocky Mountains as Fort Pulaski," declared one high military official. Eight hundred yards was considered the greatest distance from which cannon fire could knock down masonry walls, and the Yankees could not get that close. But the Southerners had not counted on the new rifled cannon. The Union forces set up a battery of these guns more than sixteen hundred yards away. From these guns shot weighing as much as 84 pounds apiece shattered the masonry. Within two days great holes had been punched in the massive walls, forcing the Confederates to surrender. Both sides were astonished at the ease with which the destruction had been accomplished. "The result of this bombardment must cause a change in the construction of fortifications," exulted Union General David Hunter. "No works of stone or brick can resist the impact of rifled artillery of heavy calibre."

Wall of Fort Pulaski after
Union bombardment

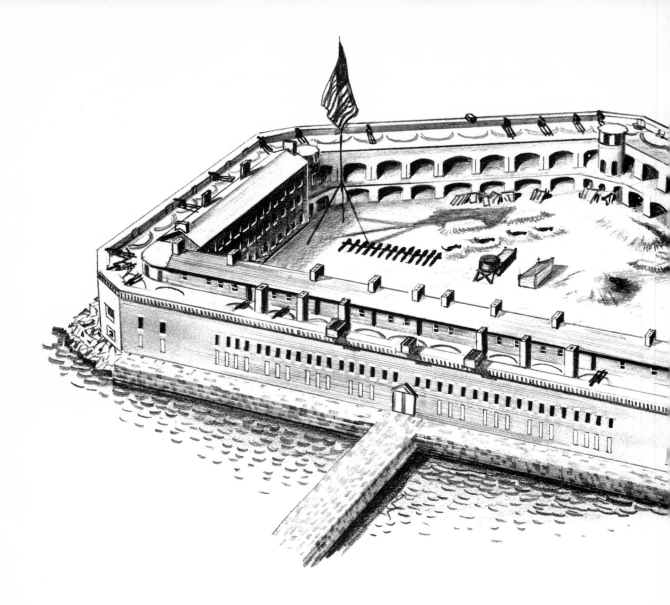

FORT
SUMTER

Fort Sumter in South Carolina reinforced this opinion and pointed the way for new developments. Like Pulaski, Sumter was a five-sided brick fort. Its walls towered some 48 feet above the waters of Charleston harbor with space for mounting three tiers of cannon. Since it stood on a man-made island and seemed to rise right out of the water, it needed no ravelin or bastions for defense against assault. It could only be attacked by artillery fire or by boats. Work on the fort had begun in 1829, and it was essentially completed in 1860.

Within a year it received its first test of battle. The very first action of the Civil War was the bombardment of Fort Sumter on April 12, 1861.

Fort Sumter just before the Civil War

Confederate forces ringing the harbor opened fire on the fort from all sides. Short of ammunition and supplies, the Union garrison surrendered the next day after sustaining a bombardment of some 3,000 shots. The fort itself was not badly damaged although several fires started by shells had destroyed the barracks and threatened the powder magazine. The Confederates quickly repaired the damage.

Two years later the real test came. On April 7, 1863, nine Union iron-clad warships steamed past the fort and battered it with their guns for two hours and twenty minutes. Sumter's walls were scarred and battered, but the attack failed. Moreover, the defenders had succeeded in sinking one of the ships and disabling 5 others.

Confederate mortar battery fires on Fort Sumter

Foiled in this attempt, the Union troops were more determined than ever to take Fort Sumter. In August, 1863, they set up a battery of rifled cannon like the one that had conquered Fort Pulaski. They even put the same man in charge of it and gave him more and bigger guns. But the Confederates were determined. They filled the casemates with sand and cotton bales, making the walls solid, and they piled more sand, dirt and cotton inside and out. As fast as the Union guns knocked down a portion of the wall, the defenders built it up again with soft materials. For twenty-two months Sumter withstood both bombardment and direct assault. Federal cannon hurled more than 3,500 tons of shot and shell into it.

As a masonry fort it was a complete ruin, but it was stronger defensively than ever. The thick piles of dirt, sand and cotton over a core of brick and stone had produced walls that were virtually indestructible.

Both Fort Pulaski and Fort Sumter are preserved as units in the National Park System. The breach in the walls at Pulaski was repaired soon after the bombardment, but great holes in the masonry still attest to the power of the rifled guns which made them. Fort Sumter also was repaired and used after the Civil War. The walls have been lowered; the dirt has been cleared away from the outside, and there is a coast defense battery of 1899 in the midst of the old fort. It is now an interesting combination of early and recent coastal defenses, but there is still much to see of one of the most gallantly defended forts in American history.

Fort Sumter pointed the way to the future. Artillery was now too powerful for exposed masonry even in seacoast defenses; but masonry protected by a heavy layer of dirt would stand up against any known

The inside of Fort Sumter in 1865

59

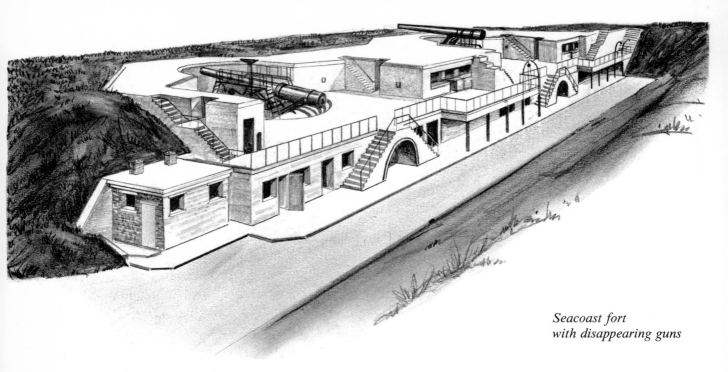

*Seacoast fort
with disappearing guns*

weapon. New forts would be dug into the ground or built as low hills. Developments in artillery helped also. Carriages were designed that could be raised and lowered so that a gun could suddenly appear over the top of the fort to fire, then drop down below thick walls of dirt and reinforced concrete for reloading. These were the famous "disappearing" guns of the late 1800's. Other cannon were designed to fire through narrow slits. The new coastal forts were hard to see from a distance, and they did not look very impressive, but they were infinitely stronger than the huge masonry structures of the years before the Civil War.

The United States built very few new coast defenses in the years right after the Civil War. Then the Spanish-American War of 1898 renewed in-

*Cross section of a seacoast fortification
of World War II*

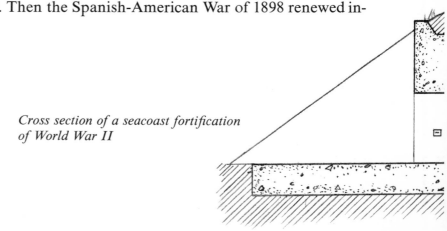

terest in seacoast forts. A widespread fear that the Spanish fleet might attack cities along the Eastern seaboard started a rush to build new dirt and concrete forts. The Spanish-American War lasted only a few months, but the building of forts continued into the early 1900's. Every important harbor had coastal defense batteries. Most of these fortifications were soon abandoned, but a few seacoast defenses were still being built just before World War II.

These newest forts usually have a thick layer of dirt on top as well as in front for protection against air attack, but the defensive theory is still the same: give the enemy as little as possible to shoot at and use a soft material to absorb the force of his projectiles. It is the same theory, in fact, that has guided military engineers ever since cannon first proved high stone walls to be vulnerable.

The French had had these thoughts in mind when they built their low dirt walls at Fort Caroline. Four hundred years had brought changes in many aspects of design and function. Intricate systems of outworks to hold an enemy at bay had been devised. New building materials such as reinforced concrete had been developed. Infinitely more powerful and longer ranging weapons had appeared to attack. But these principles had held good. America's newest forts and her oldest are united in the same tradition, a tradition that has stood the test of time and proved sound.

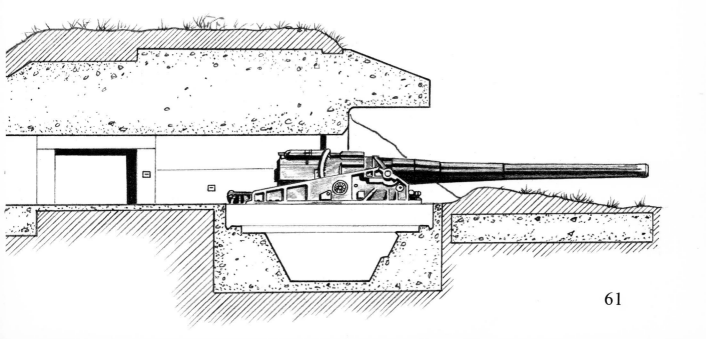

61

INDEX

Date Due			
JAN 4			

9933

HBJ SOCIAL STUDIES

COMMUNITIES

LANDMARK EDITION

Stephanie Abraham Hirsh, Ph.D.
GENERAL EDITOR

Phillip Bacon, Ph.D.
SENIOR EDITORIAL ADVISER

HBJ HARCOURT BRACE JOVANOVICH, PUBLISHERS
Orlando   San Diego   Chicago   Dallas

GENERAL EDITOR

Dr. Stephanie Abraham Hirsh is Director of Program and Staff Development for the Richardson Independent School District in Richardson, Texas. Dr. Hirsh has a B.S. degree from the University of Texas at Austin, an M.Ed. from North Texas State University, and a Ph.D. in Curriculum and Instruction from North Texas State University. In addition to her work within the school district, Dr. Hirsh has served as a consultant for social studies and staff development, has taught university courses, and has published numerous articles in several educational journals. Dr. Hirsh is a past president of the Texas Council for the Social Studies. She serves currently on the Executive Board of the Social Studies Supervisors Association and numerous committees for the National Council for the Social Studies.

SENIOR EDITORIAL ADVISER

Dr. Phillip Bacon is a professor Emeritus of Geography and Anthropology at the University of Houston. Dr. Bacon has also served on the faculties of Columbia University and the University of Washington. Formerly Dean of the Graduate School of Peabody College for Teachers at Vanderbilt University, Dr. Bacon began his career in education as a teacher of elementary and secondary social studies. He is the author or editor of more than 36 books, including the *Life Pictorial Atlas of the World*. For 18 years, Dr. Bacon served as a member of the Editorial Advisory Board of *World Book Encyclopedia*.

Among his numerous honors and awards, Dr. Bacon holds the distinguished titles of Fellow of the Explorers Club and Fellow of the Royal Geographic Society of Great Britain. He is a three-time recipient of the Teaching Excellence Award at the University of Houston. His biography appears in *Who's Who in America* and *American Men and Women in Science*.

ISBN 0-15-372903-1

SENIOR PROGRAM ADVISERS

John F. Barbini, Ed.D.
Assistant Superintendent
School District 54
Schaumberg, Illinois

Sister Marijon Binder
Global Concerns Center
Chicago, Illinois

Paul S. Hanson
Social Studies Supervisor
Dade County Public Schools
Miami, Florida

Cheryl Biles Moore
Director, Staff Development,
   Research and Evaluation
Orange County Department of Education
Costa Mesa, California

William D. Travis, Ed.D.
Curriculum Director
Pittsfield Public Schools
Pittsfield, Massachusetts

Donald P. Vetter
Supervisor of Social Studies
Carroll County Public Schools
Westminster, Maryland

Thomas Gregory Ward
Social Studies Specialist
Fairfax County Schools, Area II
Fairfax, Virginia

Alice Wells
Curriculum Consultant
Cartwright School District No. 83
Phoenix, Arizona

SENIOR CONTENT SPECIALISTS

Biliana Cicin-Sain, Ph.D.
Associate Professor of Political Science
University of California
Santa Barbara, California

Irving Cutler, Ph.D.
Chairman Emeritus, Geography Department
Chicago State University
Chicago, Illinois

Donald O. Schneider, Ph.D.
Professor and Head of
   Social Science Education
University of Georgia
Athens, Georgia

Wm. Doyle Smith, Ph.D.
Professor of Economics
University of Texas at El Paso
El Paso, Texas

Peter J. Stein, Ph.D.
Professor of Sociology
William Paterson College
Wayne, New Jersey

SKILLS DEVELOPMENT

H. Michael Hartoonian, Ph.D.
Supervisor of Social Studies Education
Wisconsin Department of Public Instruction
Madison, Wisconsin

CLASSROOM CONSULTANTS

Judith Schrage Berg
Bamber Valley Elementary School
Rochester, Minnesota

Donna M. Bosman
Emerson Elementary School
Everett, Washington

Parker Norman Call
Wake County School System
Raleigh, North Carolina

Mary L. Campbell
Harris Elementary School
Fort Wayne, Indiana

Camilla Chinn
Ruus Elementary School
Hayward, California

Lelia O. Darby
James B. Edwards Elementary School
Mt. Pleasant, South Carolina

Mary Engman
Eastwood Elementary School
Salt Lake City, Utah

Paul H. Goldman
Anson Jones Elementary School
Houston, Texas

Maria Teresa Guerrero
McAuliffe Elementary School
McAllen, Texas

Helen Howland
Irving Elementary School
Duncan, Oklahoma

Michelle Kelly
Colony Bend Elementary
Sugar Land, Texas

Diane Loughlin
Antioch C.C. School District 34
Antioch, Illinois

Cynthia V. McKinney
District 18 Schools
New York, New York

Joan Niles
Dutton Elementary School
Caledonia, Michigan

Joyce Patterson
Williamson Elementary School
Youngstown, Ohio

James R. Pohl
Chester Park School
Duluth, Minnesota

Kay Psencik
Temple
    Independent School District
Temple, Texas

Mary Lou Purpura
H.B. Whitehorne Middle School
Verona, New Jersey

Sally E. Reed
Foster Elementary School
Ludington, Michigan

Lester John Szabo
Kenmore-Town of Tonawanda
    Public Schools
Kenmore, New York

Kathy G. Walker
Highland Springs Elementary School
Highland Springs, Virginia

Mary H. Wemple
St. George School
Baton Rouge, Louisiana

Contents

Maps and Globes

Charts, Graphs, Diagrams, and Timelines

CITIZENS IN THE COMMUNITY

The pictures at the left show John Hiers. John likes to read and to take his dog for walks. These are things John can do by himself.

John also enjoys **group** activities with other people. A group is made up of people who get together because they share the same needs and interests. One special group that John belongs to is his **family.** John's family share many things.

John belongs to other groups, too. He plays on a soccer team. He sings in a choir. All the members of these groups share an interest.

John also enjoys going **downtown.** Downtown is a place where many people work and shop. John likes to spend time downtown. It makes him feel like part of his **community** (kuh•MYOO•nuh•tee).

A community is a place where people live and work together. Your community includes your family and your house and your **neighborhood.** You go to school and you play in your community. Our country, the United States of America, is also one large community. The members of this larger community are often called **citizens** (SIT•uh•zuhnz).

This book is about citizens and communities. There are many different kinds of communities. You will study about the way citizens live in communities. You will learn what it means to be a citizen. You will also read about the things good citizens must do for their communities.

Books are special tools. You need to take care of them. You should keep books clean. You should not mark in books. You should open and close books carefully so you do not tear the pages.

Open your textbook to the **Contents** in the front of your book. This table of contents shows parts of the book in the order in which they appear in the book. Each **unit** in the book tells about one large subject. Each unit has two or three **chapters.** Each chapter tells about one part of the unit subject.

Reading Your Textbook

Each chapter in your book is divided into two or more **lessons.** Each lesson has a number and a title in large capital letters.

Each lesson starts with a part called **Reading for a Purpose. Reading for a Purpose** is made up of a list of important words and questions.

The list of words is divided into **Key Words, People,** and **Places.** When you first meet these words in your reading, they appear in thick, dark type called **boldface.** Sometimes a boldface word is followed by a different spelling. An example of this is **business** (BIZ•nuhs). The spelling tells you how to say the word.

The lessons are divided into smaller parts. The smaller parts have titles, such as **Reading Your Textbook** on this page. The titles help you find the main ideas in the lesson.

Kelly looks at an atlas map of the United States.

Each lesson finishes with **Reading Check** questions. When you answer a Reading Check question, look only in that lesson for the answer.

Special Parts of Your Textbook

The back part of your textbook has places where you can find information. A quick way to find information is to look at the **Index** on pages R18–R24. The Index lists things in the book in ABC order. After each item, the Index gives the page numbers where there is information.

While you are reading your book, you may come across a Key Word you do not know. Look in the **Glossary** at the back of the book to find its meaning and how to pronounce it. The Glossary lists important words in ABC order.

Throughout your reading, you will be learning about different communities. You will look at a lot of maps in the book. You can also look at pages R4–R9 in the back of your book. Here you will find the **Atlas.** The Atlas has maps of the United States and of the world.

GEOGRAPHY: REVIEW AND PRACTICE

There are many ways to find out about different communities. You read about John and looked at pictures of his community. Reading and looking at pictures are good ways to find out about a person or a place.

Look at the picture below. It shows a **model** of a place. A model is a small copy of something. What things can you see in this model?

The model below shows part of a community. There are houses, streets, trees, a mountain, and a railroad.

Now look at another picture of the same model. The picture on this page is of the same place. It is taken from a different view, though. If you were standing above the model, looking straight down, the picture shows what you would see. Where are the trees in the picture? What do the houses in the picture look like?

This picture shows the model on page 4. How does the model look different when seen from above?

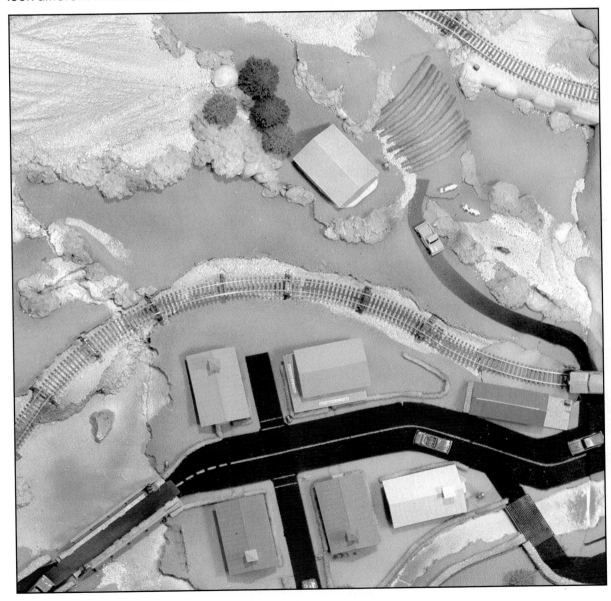

Looking at Maps

We can show this same model in another way. We can show where things are in the model by making a **map** of it. A map is a drawing of a place. Most maps show a place as it would look from above.

Here is a map of the model you saw in the pictures. How is the map different from the pictures of the model? If a map showed every tree, bush, and blade of grass, it would be too crowded. So maps use **symbols** (SIM•buhlz). A symbol is a picture that stands for something that is real on the Earth. Some symbols do not look like the things they stand for.

Look at the box to the left of the map. This box is called the **map key.** A map key tells what each of the symbols on the map stands for. Look at the map key. What symbol stands for a road? What symbol stands for a railroad?

A map key shows what symbols in a map stand for.

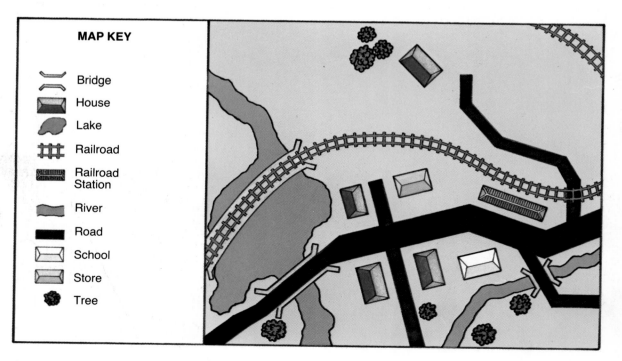

MAP KEY

Bridge

House

Lake

Railroad

Railroad Station

River

Road

School

Store

Tree

Colors in a map can be symbols, too. Usually lakes, rivers, oceans, and other things that stand for water are blue. Different colors may be used to show land.

Using a Distance Scale

Names and symbols on a map show real things and places. However, maps cannot show things in real-life sizes. The maps would have to be too big. So mapmakers made up a different way to measure. They have a small length stand for a longer, real length. For example, one inch on a map might show one mile on the real land. We call this the **distance scale** of a map.

Most maps have a distance scale. The distance scale lets you find out how far one place really is from another. To use the distance scale, you can use a ruler or a piece of paper.

The picture below shows you how to use a distance scale.

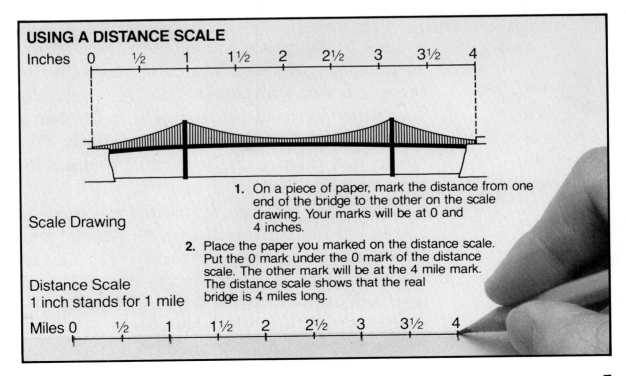

USING A DISTANCE SCALE

Inches 0   ½   1   1½   2   2½   3   3½   4

Scale Drawing

1. On a piece of paper, mark the distance from one end of the bridge to the other on the scale drawing. Your marks will be at 0 and 4 inches.

2. Place the paper you marked on the distance scale. Put the 0 mark under the 0 mark of the distance scale. The other mark will be at the 4 mile mark. The distance scale shows that the real bridge is 4 miles long.

Distance Scale
1 inch stands for 1 mile

Miles 0   ½   1   1½   2   2½   3   3½   4

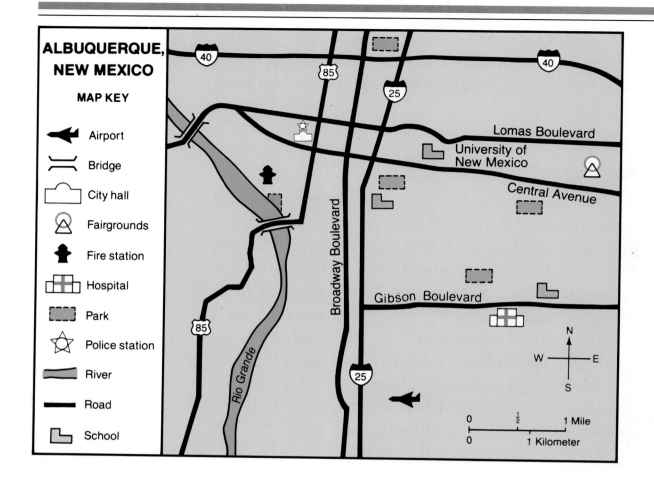

Look at the map of Albuquerque, New Mexico on this page. Mark on a piece of paper the distance from the airport to the hospital. Put your paper on the distance scale at the bottom of the map. The distance should be one inch. That means that there is really one mile between the airport and the hospital.

Look at the map again. How far is it from the hospital to the University of New Mexico? How far is it from the fire station to city hall? How far is it from the fairgrounds to the Rio Grande on this map? Could you walk that distance? How far is it from the University of New Mexico to I-25? How much of I-25 can you see on this map?

Look at this map of New Mexico. New Mexico is a big state. Only Alaska, Texas, California, and Montana are larger. Use the distance scale at the bottom of the map to learn some things about distances in New Mexico.

How far is it from Gallup to Las Cruces? How far is it from Santa Fe to Carlsbad? Albuquerque is New Mexico's biggest city. People like to come to Albuquerque. How far do they have to travel from Farmington? How far is it from Las Cruces?

Distance scales often use the metric system. You find distance in the same way. The only difference is that you use the kilometer part of the scale to measure the distance between places.

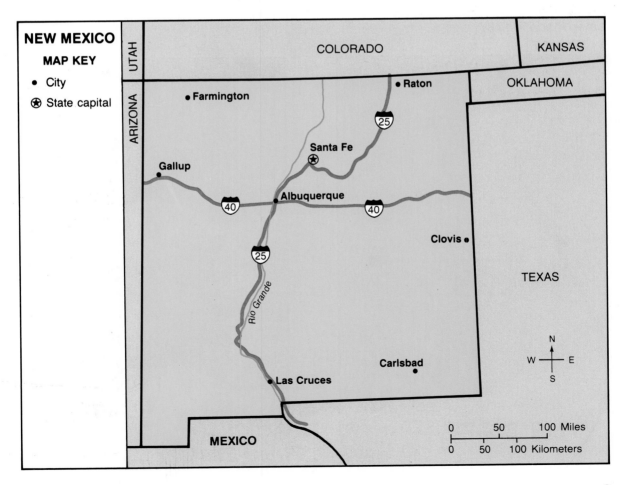

Learning About Directions

Look at the drawings below. The lines on each of the drawings look something like the petals of a rose. That is why we call each of these symbols a **compass rose.**

A compass rose tells you directions, or which way to go. Each of the arrows on the compass rose points to one of the four main directions. The main directions are north, south, east, and west. On a compass rose, **N** means north, **S** means south, **E** means east, and **W** means west.

When you face north, south is behind you. What direction is on your right? What direction is on your left?

The compass rose on the right was used on a map made in 1787.

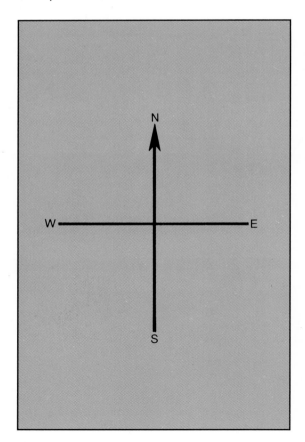

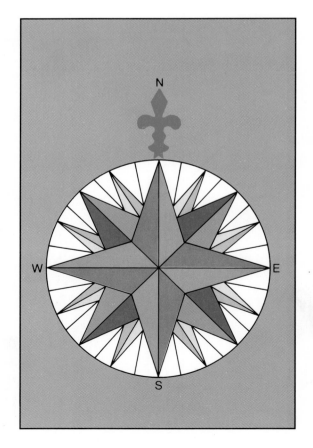

Find the compass rose on the map of Wyoming. This compass rose can help you find places in Wyoming. It could also help you show someone how to get from one place to another.

How could you show someone how to get from Saratoga to Buffalo? Find Saratoga. Now move your finger toward Buffalo. The compass rose tells you that your finger is moving north. Now move your finger from Casper to Pinedale. In what direction did your finger move?

What is the name of the state that is north of Wyoming? If you are in Wyoming facing north, what are the two states behind you? In what direction are they from Wyoming?

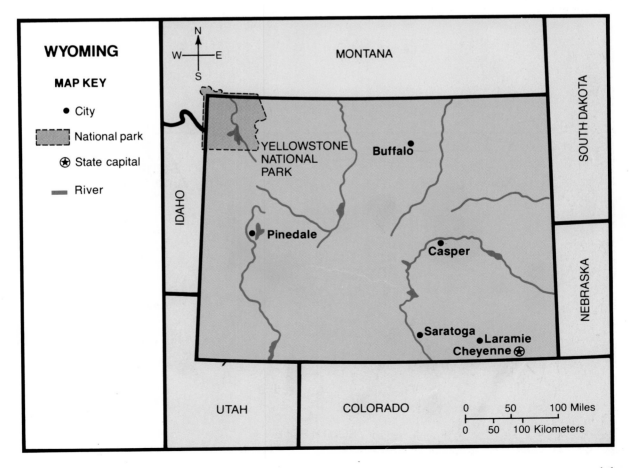

You now know the four main directions, north, south, east, and west. What do these directions really tell you? To answer that question it is helpful to look at a **globe.** A globe is a model of the Earth. Look at the picture of a globe on this page.

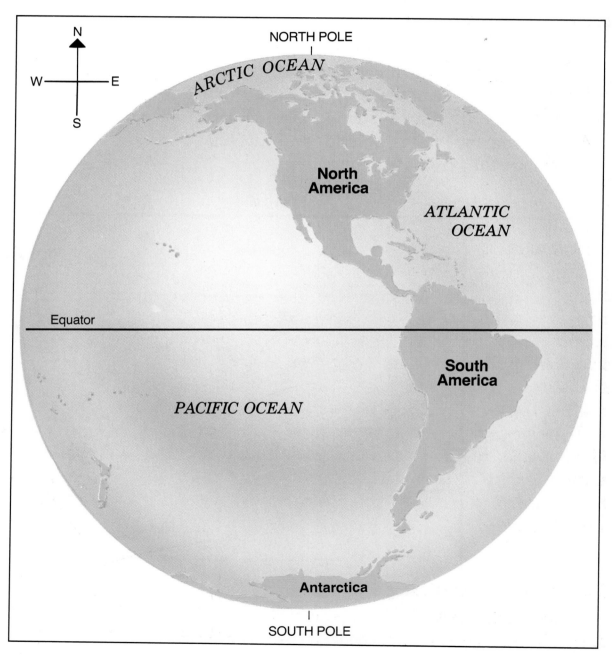

You can find directions on a globe. The North Pole is a good place to start. It is as far north as you can go on Earth. When a compass rose is pointing to **N,** it is really pointing toward the North Pole. Place your finger in the middle of the picture of the globe. Move your finger toward the North Pole. Your finger is moving toward the north. It is moving in the same direction that the compass rose is pointing.

Next move your finger toward the South Pole. The South Pole is as far south as you can go on Earth. When your finger is moving toward the South Pole it is moving in the direction south.

You can find the North Pole and the South Pole on every globe. However, maps do not always show the poles. On a map the compass rose shows you the direction of the North and South poles, even if you cannot see them.

Now look at the globe halfway between the North Pole and the South Pole. You will find a line. It is called the **equator** (ee•KWAY•tur). The equator is a make-believe line. It is not found on the real Earth. It is useful on globes because it divides the globe into a northern half and a southern half.

Place your finger on the area of land marked North America. Is it north or south of the equator? Now find South America. Is more of South America north of the equator or south of the equator?

Looking at Land and Water

Globes show you the land and water of the Earth. The large water areas are called **oceans.**

Our world has four oceans. The smallest ocean is the Arctic Ocean. The Pacific Ocean is the largest. Find the two other oceans on the globes on pages 12 and 14.

Put your finger on North America again. Move it toward the Atlantic Ocean. You are moving east.

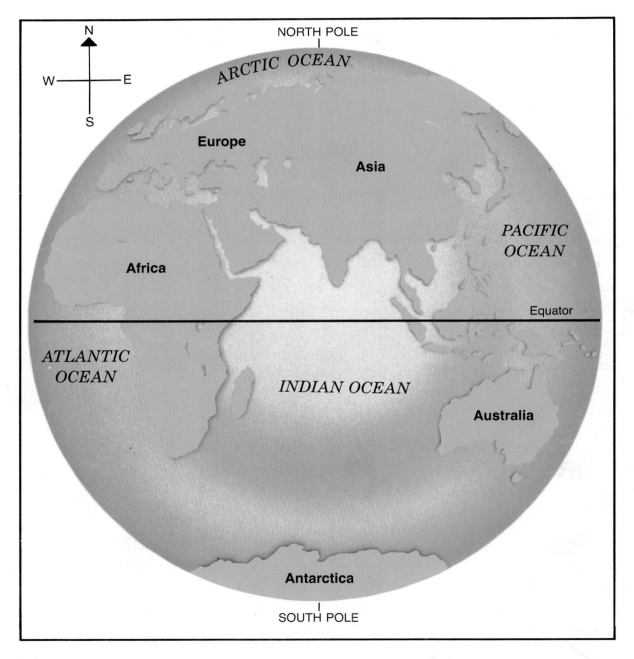

Now move your finger toward the Pacific Ocean. In what direction is your finger moving?

The large land areas on Earth are called **continents** (KAHNT•uhn•uhnts). Some continents are joined. Find North America again. It is joined to South America. The two continents separate most of the Atlantic and Pacific oceans. Can you find where these oceans meet?

Two other continents that are joined are Asia and Europe. Together they make up a huge area of land. The continent of Asia is on the eastern side. Europe is on the western side.

Africa is south of Europe. A small part of it is joined to Asia. The Atlantic Ocean is west of Africa. Which ocean is east of Africa? What direction is Asia from Africa?

Two continents, Australia and Antarctica, are not joined to other continents at all. Find these continents on the globes. Which oceans are near Australia? Which pole is in Antarctica?

The equator can help you find continents. Two of the continents are north of the equator. What are their names? Three other continents, South America, Africa, and Asia, are crossed by the equator. Find where the equator crosses Asia. Find and name the two continents which are completely south of the equator.

Questions to Answer

1. What is a map symbol?
2. What are the four main directions?
3. What is the smallest ocean? What is the largest ocean?
4. Where is North America on the globe?
5. What two continents are joined to Asia?

Community Facts and Figures

Location	New York City, New York	Cape Canaveral, Florida	Sun City, Arizona
Population (estimated)	7,164,742	5,733	40,505
Nickname/Motto	The Big Apple	Space Hub	Forerunner in American Retirement Communities
Landmark	Statue of Liberty	Kennedy Space Center	The Sundome

PEOPLE AND COMMUNITIES

Our country is made up of many communities. Every community is different. There are large communities and small communities. Communities are known for different things.

Yet all communities are made up of people. Communities everywhere are places where people can belong. Communities everywhere have places for people to see and things for them to do.

In this unit, we will look at how people live in communities across the United States. We will see how communities everywhere are alike. We will see how communities are different from one another, too.

	Spring, Texas	Boonesboro, Kentucky
Location		
Population (estimated)	3,000	100
Nickname/Motto	Old Town Spring	Kentucky's First Settlement
Landmark	The blimp	Fort Boonesboro

How Communities Are Alike

Look at the people in the picture. They are eating, shopping, and enjoying a day in their community. There are places to do these things in your community, too. Communities everywhere are alike in many ways. In this chapter, you will see how communities are alike.

Look for these important words:

Key Words
- business center
- banks

Look for answers to these questions:

1. Why do people live in communities?
2. What places are in the business center of a community?
3. What are banks?

1. WHY PEOPLE LIVE IN COMMUNITIES

If you are like most people, you live in or near a community. A community is a town, city, or other place where people live and work.

Communities are alike in many ways. For one thing, all communities have names. What is the name of your community?

Have you ever wondered why people choose to live in communities? One reason is that people like each other's company. People want to live near each other. Many people like to belong to some group. You belong to your family. You are a part of it. You do things together. In the same way, people belong to a community. They have a place in it. People do things together in a community.

All communities—large, small, or medium-sized—are places where people can belong. All communities are places where people carry on their lives.

Working in Communities

People often live in certain communities because of their work. Most communities have a downtown. We call this a **business** (BIZ•nuhs) **center.** Most of the office buildings where people work are in the business center. There are usually many stores in the business center of a community. You can also find many **banks** in a business center. Banks are places where people keep money.

People shop and go to work in business centers.

People have fun at a community parade.

Having Fun in Communities

People in a community can do many fun things together. Sports teams, Brownie Scouts, Cub Scouts, and 4-H clubs are all community activities for people your age.

Communities have many places where people can go to have fun. Most communities have parks where people can picnic, play games, and enjoy the outdoors. People can also go to places such as movie theaters and zoos. People in a community share all of these places.

Reading Check

1. Name two ways in which all communities are alike.
2. What is a business center?
3. What are some community activities for people your age?

Look for these important words:

Key Words
- shelters
- needs
- hospital

Look for answers to these questions:

1. What needs do people have?
2. What people in a community help meet our need for safety?
3. Why are schools and libraries important to people in a community?

2. COMMUNITIES HELP PEOPLE MEET NEEDS

In order to live, we need food to eat. Food makes us strong so we can play hard and do our work well. We need clothes to wear. We need sweaters and other heavy clothes to stay warm on cold days. We need light-weight clothes for very hot days. People also need **shelters** to live in. Shelters are homes, stores, and buildings where people work. Shelters protect us, or keep us safe, from the weather. Shelters keep out the rain and the snow. In very warm or hot weather, shelters protect people from the sun.

We need love and safety, too. Food, clothing, shelter, love and safety are our **needs.** Needs are things we must have to live. People working together in communities can help one another meet all these needs. That is another way communities are alike.

Think how busy you would be if you had to meet all your needs by yourself! You would have to grow your own vegetables. You would have to raise animals to get meat, eggs, and milk. You could not turn on a faucet and get water. Instead, you would have to dig a well or go to a river or lake for water.

You would have to build your own house, too. Remember, you would not be able to go to a store to buy nails or boards. You would have to make your own nails and boards.

You would have to make your own clothing, too. First, you would have to make cloth. Then you would have to sew it.

Sam must keep very busy to meet her needs. What is she doing in each of the pictures?

23

In a community, some people grow food. Others sell this food. Some people make clothes. Others sell them. Some people build houses. Others get the materials from which houses are made. Nobody has to do all these jobs. People in communities share their learning. Living in a community helps people save time.

How is this picture different from the one on page 23? How are people helping one another meet needs?

24

People Depend on One Another

People in a community depend on one another for safety. Police officers work to keep us safe. Fire fighters also protect us. Fire fighters put out fires everywhere in your community. However, fire fighters need you and others to report fires to them. By reporting fires, people help one another meet their need for safety.

People need good care when they are sick. Doctors and nurses are taught to take care of sick people. They work for the whole community.

Mr. Sanchez reported a fire that was burning in an empty building in his community. Fire fighters came quickly to put it out.

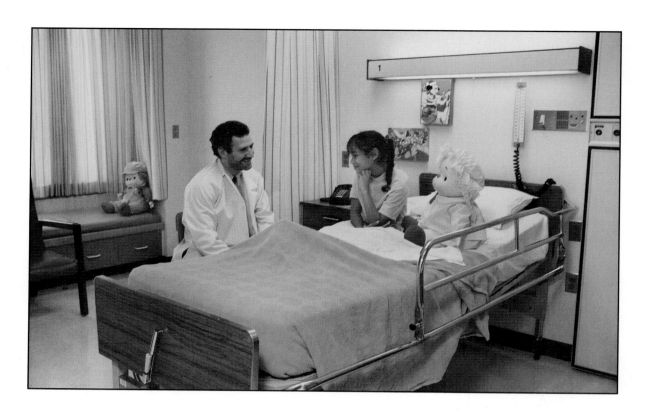

Maria went to the hospital when she became ill. With the doctor's help, she is feeling much better.

A community often has a **hospital,** too. A hospital is a place where hurt or sick people can go for special care. Doctors, nurses, and hospitals meet people's need for good health.

Schools and libraries are also important to the people of a community. Schools are places where people of all ages can learn about things. A library keeps books for the people of a community to use. Libraries are also good places where people can go to learn things.

Reading Check

1. Why do we need food?
2. What need do doctors and nurses in a community help us meet?
3. Name three ways people in a community depend on one another.

A **library** is a place where you can find books, newspapers, and magazines. Some libraries have records and films. You can learn about many things at the library.

A **librarian** is a person who works in the library. Librarians keep the books in order. They can help you find what you are looking for. Some librarians are now helped by computers. Computers can help check out books. A computer may even charge you an overdue fine!

The librarian helps children find the books they want.

Libraries Have Rules

Most books may be checked out of the library and taken home. Before you can take books out, you must know the rules of the library. Here are a few of them.

- In most libraries, you need a library card to take books home. You must show the card to the librarian.

- The librarian stamps a "due date" in each book you want to take out. You must bring the books back by that date.

- You must not mark in the books. You should take good care of them.

A due date card tells you when to return a library book.

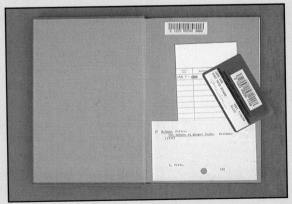

Books at the Library

You can find two kinds of books at the library. One kind is called **fiction.** Fiction books are make-believe stories. A story about a boy who meets a community of six-foot-tall talking lizards is fiction. Fiction books can also be stories that seem real but that are about made-up people and animals.

Nonfiction books are about real people, animals, places, and things. A book about lizards, where they live, what they eat, and how they grow, is nonfiction. A book about the life of a real American Indian long ago is nonfiction.

To find books in the library, you have to know the alphabet, or ABC's. Fiction books are arranged in alphabetical or ABC order by the **authors'** last names. Authors are people who write books. Most of the time you have to put more than the first letter in order. A book

by Caroline **Haywood** comes before a book by Felice **Holman,** because **Ha** comes before **Ho** in alphabetical order.

CHECKING YOUR SKILLS

Tell or write the answers to these questions.

1. You want to find a book by Pamela Rogers in the library. Does this book come before or after a book by Barbara Reynolds?

2. Is a book about a real girl who becomes a skating champion fiction or nonfiction?

3. Is a story about a boy who makes friends with a talking horse fiction or nonfiction?

4. When you borrow a book from a library, the librarian stamps a date in it. Why do you need to look at the date?

Suppose you are reading about a community in Florida. You read that **mangos** grow there. How can you find out what a mango is?

Suppose you want to read about New York City. Where can you look for information?

You can find this information in **dictionaries** (DIK•shuhn•air•eez) and **encyclopedias** (en•sy•cloh•PEE•dee•uhz). These two kinds of books can give you a whole world of information.

Using a Dictionary

Dictionaries are full of facts about words. A dictionary tells you how to say a word. It tells you what a word means. Sometimes a dictionary will show you a picture of the thing the word names. A dictionary often gives a sentence using the word, too.

Here is what a dictionary might tell you about the word "mango."

- **man•go** (mang′gō) *n.* A juicy fruit with a slightly sour taste. Many mangos grow in Florida where the weather is warm.

The letters in parentheses tell you how to say the word. The dictionary might also show a picture of a mango.

Sometimes dictionaries give more than one meaning for a word. It is important to read all the meanings listed for a word.

How can you find a word in the dictionary? It is as easy as ABC. All the words in a dictionary are listed in ABC order.

The top of a dictionary page shows two **guide words.** These words tell you the first and last words on the page. All the words that come between these two words will be on the page. For example, "mango" comes after "make" but before "map." Notice that the first two letters of these words are the same. You must look at the third letter of the words.

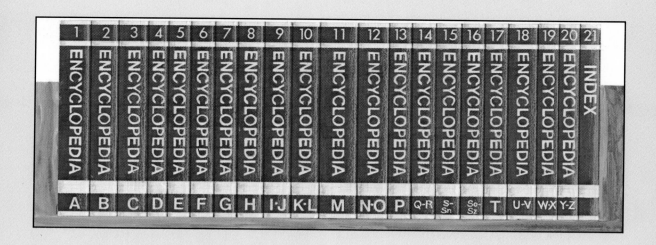

Using an Encyclopedia

An encyclopedia does not tell you about words. Instead it gives facts about a great many subjects. It tells you about people, places, things, and events. These are listed in alphabetical order, just as words are in a dictionary.

Most encyclopedias have many **volumes,** or separate books. Each book has one or two letters of the alphabet on the cover. If you want to find out about New York City, you should look in the volume that has "N" on the cover.

Here is what an encyclopedia might say about New York City.

- **New York City** (population 7,086,096) is the largest city in the United States. It is the eighth largest city in the world.

The encyclopedia tells you more about New York City. It tells you what the city looks like and what goods are made there. It tells you about the people and the ways they meet their needs. It tells you the history of the city. There might also be maps of New York City.

CHECKING YOUR SKILLS

Tell whether you would find the answers to the following questions in a dictionary or in an encyclopedia.

1. What is the meaning of the word "dependence"?
2. What is the community of Atlanta, Georgia, like?
3. How do you say the word "university"?
4. What kinds of shelter do people in South America have?

CHAPTER 1 REVIEW

USING WORDS

Use one of the words in parentheses to complete the sentence.

1. Most of the office buildings where people work are in the ____. (business center, banks)

2. People keep money in ____. (needs, banks)

3. Homes, stores, and buildings where people work are called ____. (hospitals, shelters)

4. ____ are things we must have to live. (Needs, Banks)

5. Hurt or sick people can go to a ____ for care. (hospital, bank)

REVIEWING FACTS

1. How are communities alike?

2. What happens in the business center of a community?

3. What places do people in a community share?

4. How do communities help people meet needs?

5. How do people in a community depend on police officers and fire fighters?

THINKING CRITICALLY

1. What kinds of work do people in your community do? Why is the business center in your community important?

2. Why do communities have places like parks and zoos? Who may visit them?

3. How do people depend on one another in a community? Why is it important to depend on people?

◯ PRACTICING SKILLS

1. **Using the Library** Tell whether each of these books is fiction or nonfiction.

   a. A book about food in our country

   b. A story of a talking mouse

2. **Dictionaries and Encyclopedias** Tell whether you would find the information below in a dictionary or an encyclopedia.

   a. The meaning of community

   b. How the Brownie Scouts started

Focus

How Communities Are Different

In Chapter 1 you read how communities are alike. Communities are also different from one another. In this chapter you will look at many communities across the United States. You will see how every community is a very different, very special place to live.

Look for these important words:

Key Words
- river
- lake
- ocean
- mountains
- deserts

Look for answers to these questions:

1. What are some kinds of places communities can be near?
2. What are deserts?
3. What makes communities special?

1. COMMUNITIES ARE IN DIFFERENT PLACES

Communities are different in several ways. For one thing, communities are in different places. Some are near water. They may be near a **river, lake,** or **ocean.** A river is a long, flowing body of water. A lake is a body of water with land all around. An ocean is a huge body of salt water. Remember there are four oceans on Earth. They are the Pacific, Atlantic, Indian, and Arctic oceans.

Some communities are near **mountains.** Mountains are large, raised parts of land. They rise high above the land around them. There are many mountains in our country.

Other communities are in very dry lands called **deserts.** Few kinds of plants grow there. There is not enough water. Water must sometimes be brought to deserts from somewhere else.

The top picture shows the mountain town of Silverton, Colorado. Below is Chicago, Illinois, a city on the shores of Lake Michigan.

Communities are known for different things, too. Some are known for growing food, like wheat or potatoes. Others are known for making things, like clothes or cars. Still others are known for their beauty. Many people like to visit those beautiful places.

Reading Check

1. How are communities different?
2. What kinds of water can communities be near?
3. What kinds of things can communities be known for?

Look for these important words:

Key Words
- suburb
- rural
- capital
- President
- pastures

People
- George Washington

Places
- New York City, New York
- Washington, D.C.
- Cape Canaveral, Florida
- Sun City, Arizona
- Spring, Texas
- Boonesboro, Kentucky

Look for answers to these questions:

1. What are some good things about living in a city?
2. What are some good things about living in a suburb?
3. What are some good things about living in a town?

2. COMMUNITIES ARE DIFFERENT SIZES

Communities are different sizes. A town is a small community. A city is a large community. A community that is close to a city is a **suburb** (SUB•urb). A community that is near forests or farms is a **rural** (RUR•uhl) community.

Living in Cities

A city is the largest kind of community. A city has many, many people in it. Because there are so many people, there are a lot of schools, stores, and libraries. There are also many places to have fun, like parks, museums, and movie theaters. A city offers a lot of choices of things to do.

When people are rushing to and from work, cities often have traffic problems.

There are many different jobs in a city, too. A city person might have a job fixing pianos. In a smaller community, there would not be as many pianos. So fixing pianos might not be a full-time job in a small community.

City people usually work at jobs that do not take much land. There is no room for farming in most cities. Often, there is not much room for trees, lawns, or gardens.

A city often has more problems than a smaller community. Sometimes a city is very crowded or very noisy. Sometimes there is too much traffic. The people of a city try to work together to solve these problems.

New York City, New York

New York City is very big. It has more people than any other city in the United States. New York City is in the eastern part of our country. It is right by the Atlantic Ocean.

36

Manhattan Island, a part of New York City, is an important business center. Ships travel to New York City on the Hudson River.

New York City has many tall buildings. They are very close together. Some of them are office buildings where people work. Some of the buildings are apartment houses where many people live. Other buildings are huge stores.

There is a lot to see and do in New York City. There are parks, museums, and restaurants. People can watch New York teams play football, hockey, baseball, and other sports. There are interesting and different neighborhoods. Many different groups of people live in these neighborhoods. Some of them come from different parts of our country and from other countries.

People enjoy a buggy ride in Central Park, New York City's largest park.

37

Rules for our country are made in Washington, D.C. This picture shows many of the important buildings in the city.

Washington, D.C.

There are also other large cities in our country. **Washington, D.C.,** is in the eastern part of our country. It is a very famous city. It is the **capital** of the United States. A capital is a place where rules for a state or country are made. There are fifty states in our country.

The **President,** the leader of our country, lives and works in Washington, D.C. The White House is the President's home and office. Washington, D.C., is named after **George Washington,** our country's first President. Americans are proud of this beautiful city.

Cape Canaveral, Florida

There are small cities in our country, too. One small city is **Cape Canaveral** (kuh•NAV•ruhl), **Florida.** Florida is next to the Atlantic Ocean. It is in the southern part of our country.

Cape Canaveral is famous for one thing. It has a space center. Rockets and other spaceships blast off from there. Many of the people who live in Cape Canaveral work at the space center. It is called the John F. Kennedy Space Center.

A spaceship blasts off from Cape Canaveral, Florida.

Sun City, Arizona

Sun City, Arizona, is another special kind of small city. Mostly older people live there. A lot of them worked for many years in other places. Then they decided to stop working. They moved to Sun City. They like the dry, sunny weather. They like the things they can do there.

Living in Suburbs

Many cities have suburbs. Suburbs are communities that are close to large cities. Suburbs usually have their own schools. Some have their own business centers. The stores and offices in the community are in these business centers. A suburb usually has a lot of places to shop.

People often move to suburbs because they do not want to live in big cities. They might think that cities are too crowded. They might want more open space for their families. They might like to live closer to land that has not been built upon.

People enjoy walks in the suburbs.

Spring, Texas

Spring, Texas, is a suburb of the big city of Houston, Texas. Most of the people of Spring work in Houston. Some of them lived in Houston before moving to this suburb.

A blimp is a large airship. To fly, blimps must be filled with gases lighter than air. The crew rides in a tiny cabin below the gasbag.

You may not have heard of Spring, Texas, before. You may know about something famous that comes from there, though. Spring is the home of a blimp called "America." A blimp is like a giant balloon. It looks like a huge silver football. It has a tiny engine so its crew can make it fly.

Many new houses have been built in Spring. It is a growing community. Spring used to be mostly woods. Today there are still a lot of pine and oak trees. You can still see many birds and some small animals, like raccoons.

Living in Towns

Very small communities are called towns. Most of the people in a town know one another. Everyone in the town is a neighbor. People in towns often help one another. Sometimes they all get together to have fun.

In towns, people often work at something that has to do with the land nearby. They may cut trees for boards. They may farm the land or raise animals for food.

Boonesboro, Kentucky

Boonesboro, Kentucky, is a small town. Boonesboro is in an area called "bluegrass country." Bluegrass is a special kind of grass. When breezes blow across the fields, this grass looks more blue than green.

The bluegrass country is famous for its horses. Many of the people from that area raise racing horses. The people take good care of the horses. They often keep the horses in **pastures.** A pasture is a field of grass and other kinds of plants that animals eat.

These horses eat the thick grasses that grow in Kentucky's pastures.

Reading Check

1. What city in the United States has the most people?
2. Why is Washington, D.C., important?
3. Why might people enjoy living in Spring, Texas? What city is Spring close to?
4. Why do most people in a town know each other?

USING MAPS TO SHOW YOUR ADDRESS

Joanie lives in Indianapolis (in•dee•uh•NAP•uh•luhs), Indiana. Her **address** tells where she lives. Here is her address.

> Joanie Hermann
> 5240 Michigan St.
> Indianapolis, Indiana 46219
> United States of America
> North America
> Northern Hemisphere
> Earth

Of course, we do not usually include all this when we write an address. Usually we write the person's name, the house or apartment number, street name, and the city, state, and **ZIP code.** ZIP codes are numbers that are used to make mail go places faster. If we are writing a letter to someone in a different country, we use the name of that country too.

The information that tells where Joanie lives can be seen on a map. The first map on this page shows Joanie's street.

Find the house with the number 5240. That is Joanie's house.

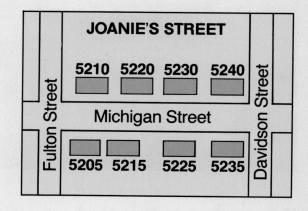

The map below shows streets in the neighborhood where Joanie lives. Her neighborhood includes the streets shown on the map. A neighborhood is usually larger than just one street.

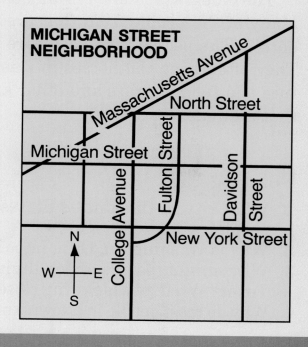

Joanie's neighborhood is in the city of Indianapolis. The map below shows the city of Indianapolis.

Now look at the map below. It shows the state of Indiana.

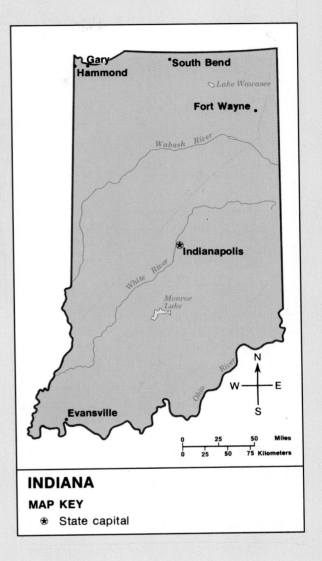

The map of Indianapolis does not show all the streets in the city. There are too many streets to show in one small map. The map shows only the main streets.

Find Michigan Street on the map. That is the street where Joanie lives. It is near the center of the city. What other streets are near Michigan Street?

Indianapolis is the capital of Indiana. Find the state **capitol** on the map. A capitol is a building where people meet to make rules for a state or country.

The symbol of the star with a circle around it tells you that Indianapolis is the capital of Indiana.

The map also shows some of the biggest cities in Indiana. What city is south of Indianapolis? What cities are to the north?

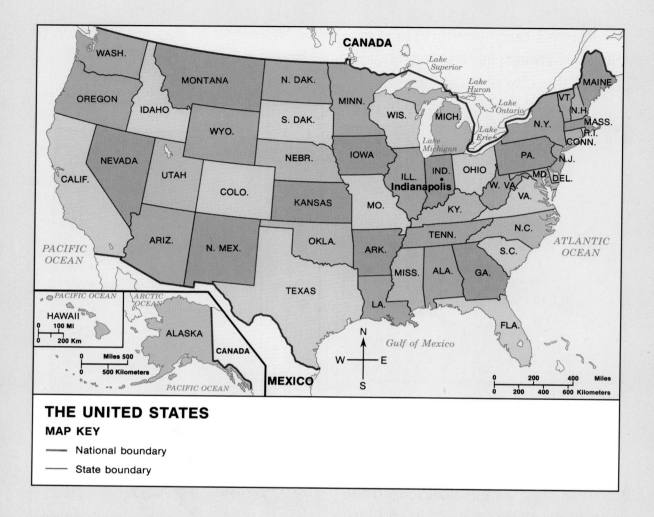

THE UNITED STATES

MAP KEY

— National boundary

— State boundary

A Map of Our Country

The map above shows the 50 states that make up the United States.

Indiana is one state in the United States. Find Indiana on the map. Point to Indianapolis.

This map shows the **borders** of Indiana. Borders are lines that are drawn on the map to show where one place ends and another begins. Borders are also called **boundaries** (BOWN•duh•reez). The

state north of Indiana is Michigan. What state is east of Indiana?

Our Country Is in North America

The map on the next page shows an even larger area. It shows the continent of **North America.** A continent is one of the main land areas in the world. The North American continent has a number of countries.

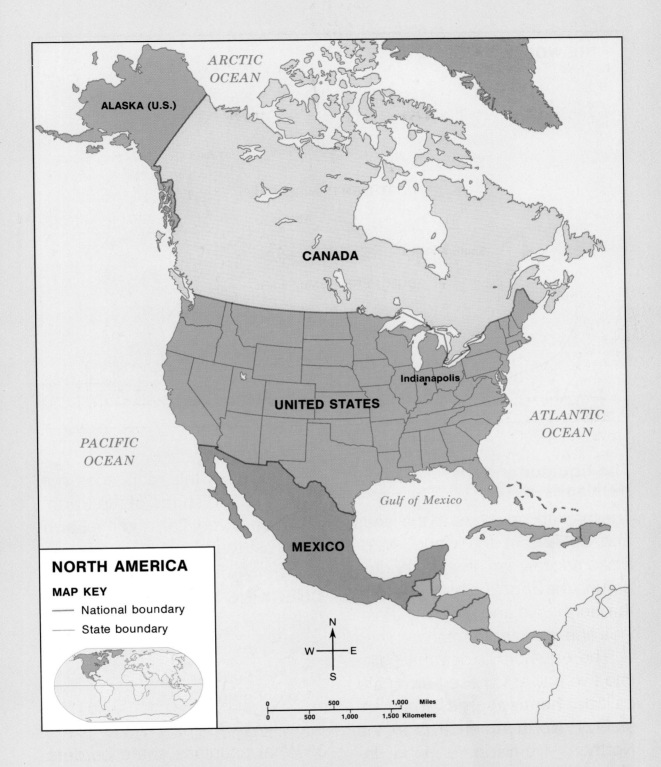

NORTH AMERICA

MAP KEY
⎯⎯ National boundary
⎯⎯ State boundary

ALASKA (U.S.)

ARCTIC OCEAN

CANADA

UNITED STATES

Indianapolis

PACIFIC OCEAN

ATLANTIC OCEAN

Gulf of Mexico

MEXICO

N
W E
S

0   500   1,000   Miles
0   500   1,000   1,500   Kilometers

The United States takes up a big part of the continent. What two other large countries do you see on the map of North America? Alaska is close to Canada. Yet it is part of the United States.

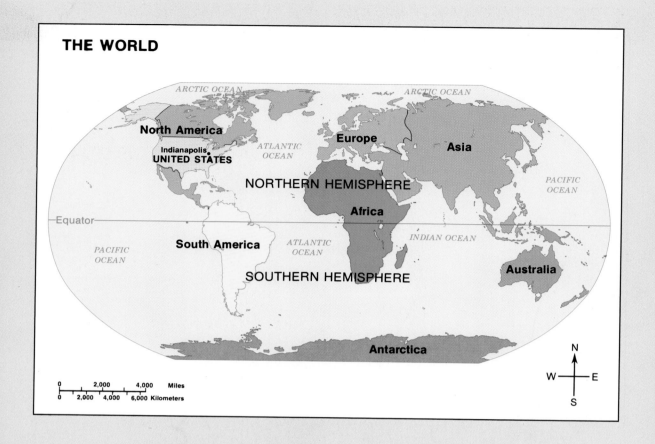

THE WORLD

ARCTIC OCEAN ARCTIC OCEAN

North America

Europe Asia

Indianapolis
UNITED STATES

ATLANTIC
OCEAN

PACIFIC
OCEAN

NORTHERN HEMISPHERE

Africa

Equator

South America

ATLANTIC
OCEAN

INDIAN OCEAN

PACIFIC
OCEAN

SOUTHERN HEMISPHERE

Australia

Antarctica

| 0 | 2,000 | 4,000 | Miles |
| 0 | 2,000 4,000 | 6,000 | Kilometers |

N
W E
S

The Equator and the Hemispheres

The map above shows all the lands and oceans in the world. Map-makers draw an imaginary line around the Earth, halfway between the North Pole and the South Pole. This line is the equator.

The equator divides the Earth into two halves. These halves are called **hemispheres** (HEM•uh•sfeerz). North America is in the Northern Hemisphere. Find Indianapolis in the Northern Hemisphere. Now find Asia. In which hemisphere is it?

Of course, this map does not show the true shape of the Earth. The map is very flat, and the Earth is almost round.

CHECKING YOUR SKILLS

Use the maps to help you answer these questions.

1. What community do you live in? What state do you live in?
2. Is Texas a state or a country?
3. What countries share borders with the United States?
4. In which hemisphere is the continent of Europe?

CLOSE-UP

NATIVE AMERICANS

European explorers came to our country hundreds of years ago. Yet long before they came, many groups of people already lived here. We call these people **Native Americans.** Native Americans include **American Indians, Eskimos,** and **Hawaiians.**

The American Indians

American Indians have lived in North and South America for thousands of years. More than half of our states today have American Indian names.

47

This Indian dress is made from deerskin. Beads decorate the dress.

Some Indian groups lived in tepees, which were made of buffalo skins stretched over poles.

Many of the first American Indians moved from place to place. They would hunt deer, buffalo, and rabbits for food. They gathered berries and plants. These groups often carried their homes with them. They had many kinds of shelters. Their shelters were often made of animal skins.

Other American Indian groups lived in larger communities. Many of these groups grew potatoes, squash, beans, and "maize." Today we call maize "corn."

These groups usually had larger shelters. They often built homes with wood or adobe (uh•DOH•bee).

Most American Indians made their clothes from animal skins. They often used bird feathers for decoration. Some groups wove beautiful cloth from cotton.

The American Indians made beautiful pottery and wove baskets. They did woodcarving, painting, and metalwork. They played games using balls. They had foot races.

Special dances help Indians celebrate the old ways of their people.

Today, many American Indians live and work across the United States. They teach school, fly planes, and run factories. Some American Indians live together in communities of their own.

The Eskimos

Eskimos live from the northeast tip of Russia across Alaska and Canada to Greenland. They have lived there for many hundreds of years. Most Eskimos live near the sea.

Far to the north, in the most western tip of Alaska, live the Eskimos of Little Diomede (DY•uh•meed) Island. The Eskimos have been there for hundreds of years. Long ago they hunted walruses, seals, whales, and polar bears. From these animals, the Eskimos got food, skins for clothing, and oil for heating and light.

Eskimos use long sticks and lines to fish in an ice hole.

49

An Eskimo builds a snow house in Alaska.

The Eskimos of Little Diomede Island made houses from snow or from wood and animal skins. Eskimos could build a snow house in a few hours. They used long knives to cut blocks of snow. Then they made a shelter from the blocks.

Sometimes the weather was so cold that the Eskimos could not hunt. They might stay inside and cut designs on walruses' teeth. Or they might gather together and sing and tell stories.

Today, Little Diomede is much the same as it has always been. The long, hard winters still cut the island off from the rest of Alaska for many months every year. However, snowmobiles are now used more often than dog sleds. There are new houses, electricity, and a modern school, too.

The Hawaiians

Some Hawaiians live in houses made from island grasses.

Hawaii, our 50th state, is in the Pacific Ocean. It is far to the west and south of California.

Hawaii is made up of many **islands.** An island is land with water all around it. Some of the Hawaiian islands are large, and others are small. The weather is usually warm in Hawaii. Rains come often to make the plants grow.

The Hawaiians lived on the islands long before people from Europe came. In those times the Hawaiians fished, hunted, and farmed the rich island soil. They made their houses from leaves and grasses. They wove their clothes from grasses and bark. They colored the clothes beautifully with dye they had made.

Hawaiians string flowers into leis.

Much later, Europeans sailed to Hawaii. Soon, the beauty of Hawaii brought many different groups of people to live there. However, many of the old Hawaiian ways are still used throughout the state.

The Hawaiian language is still spoken in some parts of the islands. Some people still make the special foods the old way, too. There are still some shelters made from leaves and grasses.

Much of our sugar comes from sugar cane grown in Hawaii. Here, sugar cane is being harvested.

51

CHAPTER 2 REVIEW

USING WORDS

Use one of the words in parentheses to complete each sentence.

1. A _____ is a long, flowing body of water. (lake, river)
2. A community that is close to a large city is a _____. (capital, suburb)
3. A community that is near forests or farms is a _____ community. (pasture, rural)
4. A _____ is where rules for a state or country are made. (capital, hospital)
5. A _____ is a field of grass and other plants that animals eat. (pasture, mountain)

REVIEWING FACTS

1. Why are communities different from one another?
2. What are four different kinds of communities?
3. What kinds of things can people do in a large city?
4. Where does the President of our country live and work?
5. For what is Cape Canaveral, Florida, famous?

THINKING CRITICALLY

1. What are some ways that life in a city is different from life in a town?
2. Would you call your community a city, a suburb, a town, or a rural community? Tell how your community is like or different from a nearby community.
3. How is the work people do in a rural community different from the work people do in a city? Which kind of work would you rather do? Why?
4. Boonesboro is special because of its horses. Spring has a blimp. What makes your community special?

PRACTICING SKILLS
Using Maps to Show Your Address

1. Write down your address. Tell which parts of the address are the house or apartment number, street, city, and state.
2. Look at the map of the United States on pages R4–R5. Find your state. Which states share borders with your state?

WORDS TO REMEMBER

Number your paper from 1 to 10. Use the words below to fill in the blanks. Use each word only once.

banks
business centers
capital
deserts
hospitals
needs
pastures
rural
shelters
suburb

1. _____ are places where people keep money.

2. Communities have stores and offices in their _____.

3. Homes, stores, and buildings where people work are called _____.

4. Food, clothing, and shelter are _____.

5. Doctors and nurses often work in _____.

6. _____ are very dry lands.

7. There are often farms near _____ communities.

8. Washington, D.C., is our country's _____.

9. Spring, Texas, is a _____ of Houston.

10. Horses eat grass and other plants in _____.

FOCUS ON MAIN IDEAS

1. Why do people live in communities?

2. How are some communities alike?

3. What groups can you belong to in a community? What can you do in these groups?

4. How do people meet needs in a community?

5. How do people in a community depend on each other?

6. What are some places that every community has?

7. What are three main things that make communities different from one another?

8. How does the community that people live in affect the work they do? What kind of work might people who live in a town do?

9. How is living in a city different from living in a town? How is a rural community different from a town?

10. Why do people live in suburbs? How is a suburb different from a city?

Find or draw pictures of your community. Write a paragraph telling how your community is like other communities. Write a paragraph telling how it is different from other communities.

ACTIVITIES

1. **Maps** Draw a map of your neighborhood. Show some parks and buildings in the area. Show some places that help people in your community meet their needs.

2. **Research/Writing** Use a telephone book to look up the address of a store. Write the name and address on a piece of paper.

SKILLS REVIEW

1. **Using the Library** Name three rules you must obey in order to use the library. Explain why they are important.

2. **Using Dictionaries and Encyclopedias** Number a piece of paper from 1 to 5. Then write these words in the order that you would find them in a dictionary or an encyclopedia.

pasture   zip code   banks
map   suburb

3. **Using Maps** Look at the map of the United States on page 44. Then answer the following questions.

a. What two countries share a border with the United States?

b. If you were in Kansas, which direction would you go to reach Utah? Which direction is Tennessee from Kansas?

c. If you traveled from Missouri to New York, in which direction would you be traveling?

d. Which states share a border with Texas?

e. What borders Montana to the north?

4. **Reviewing a World Map** Use the map on page 46 to answer the following questions.

a. What divides the northern and southern parts of the globe?

b. Which continents are in the Southern Hemisphere?

c. The equator crosses which three continents?

d. What ocean is between Africa and Australia?

e. Which continent is south of Africa?

YOUR COMMUNITY

As you read about other communities, you can compare your own community. At the end of each unit you also will find "Your Community." The activities here will help you find out more about your community.

MAKING A SCRAPBOOK

1. Make a scrapbook out of construction paper. Write "My Community" on the cover. On the first page, draw a map showing five places in your community that you like. Put a compass rose on your map. During the year, add pictures and stories about your community to your scrapbook.

DESCRIBING YOUR COMMUNITY

2. Write a paragraph describing how the land around your community looks. Tell about any hills, lakes, deserts, or rivers that may be near your community. Add your paragraph to your scrapbook.

3. On a map of your state, find the state capital, two large cities, and your community. Then trace your state on a piece of paper. Add the cities you found and your community to your map.

LEARNING ABOUT NATIVE AMERICANS

4. Many ideas for food, shelter, and art came to us from Native Americans. Find out about the Native Americans that live or used to live in your community. Do you eat any of the foods they ate? Does your community use any of the same materials for buildings? Choose one thing that the Native Americans gave to your community that is still used today. Share your choice with the class.

5. Imagine that Native Americans once lived where your school is now. Perhaps they hunted for food where your playground is or fished in a nearby stream. Draw a picture showing Native Americans and how you think your community looked.

Community Facts and Figures

Location	Merced, California	Independence, Iowa	Midland, Texas
Population (estimated)	36,000	6,392	70,525
Nickname/Motto	The Gateway to Yosemite	Proud People Promoting Progress	City of Surprises
Landmark	Courthouse Museum	Wapsipinicon Mill	Permian Basin Museum

COMMUNITIES USE NATURAL RESOURCES

Our Earth is a very special place. It gives us many things that help us meet our needs. The Earth has air and water. It has rich soil for growing things. Many different plants and animals live on the Earth. Our lives depend on these things from the Earth in many ways.

In this unit, you will see how people in many communities use our Earth. You will find out how the Earth helps us live and meet our needs. You will also see how people work together to use things from the Earth.

Location	Pikeville, Kentucky	Chicago, Illinois	Seattle, Washington
Population (estimated)	4,756	2,992,472	988,474
Nickname/Motto	Marketplace of the Mountains	The Windy City	The Emerald City
Landmark	Pikeville College	Sears Tower	Space Needle

CHAPTER 3

Farming Communities

Focus

A lot of the food you eat comes from American farms. In this chapter you will visit two of these farms. One is a vegetable farm in California. The other is a dairy farm in Iowa. You will see what life is like in farming communities. You will see how farmers use things from nature to grow food for us all.

Look for these important words:

Key Words
- natural resources
- goods
- climate

- crop
- fertilizer
- harvest

- growing season
- irrigation

Look for answers to these questions:

1. What are natural resources?
2. What can we make from natural resources?
3. How are farms alike and different?

1. NATURAL RESOURCES AND OUR FARMS

The Earth and the sun give us everything we need to meet our needs. They give us our **natural resources** (REE·sohr·suhz). Resources are things that people can use. Natural resources are resources found in nature. Natural resources are not made by people.

Clean air, soil, and fresh water are natural resources. So are trees and fish.

We use natural resources to make food and **goods.** Goods are people-made things. We use the natural resource of trees to make paper. We use the natural resource of sand to make glass.

Farmers use natural resources, too. Farmers raise plants or animals to sell. To raise things, farmers need the natural resources of good soil, enough water, and the right **climate.** Climate is the usual weather in a place. Climate means how hot or cold it is year after year. Climate is how much rain or snow falls during the year.

How Farms Are Alike and Different

There are many different kinds of farms in the United States. Some farms are large. Some farms are small. Farmers give us different things. Some raise animals, such as chickens, hogs, and cows.

Other farmers grow food. Some raise a single **crop,** or kind of plant. For example, a farmer might raise only wheat.

Joe feeds his family's chickens. These chickens are being raised for eggs and meat.

Some farmers raise vegetables. Others grow trees that produce fruits or nuts. In the United States, one farmer can grow enough food for hundreds of people.

Although farms are different from one another, they are the same in some ways. All farms must have soil, the right climate, and enough water for the animals or crops.

Above, a farmer harvests fields of wheat. Below, Susan and her friend pick apples from high in a tree.

61

From the soil, plants get a lot of what they need to grow. However, many farmers make the soil even better for growing plants by adding **fertilizer** (FUR•tuhl•eye•zur) to it. A fertilizer feeds the plants. It helps plants to grow.

Plants also need enough time to grow. Most crops will die or stop growing when the weather gets too cold. That is one reason farmers plant most crops in the spring, when the winter weather is over. Farmers **harvest,** or pick their crops, in the summer or fall, before the colder weather comes again.

These tomato plants grew well because of good, rich soil and warm weather. Here, a machine harvests the tomato crop.

Water from lakes, rivers, or wells irrigates plants. Narrow ditches carry the water between the rows.

The months in which crops can grow are called the **growing season.** Growing seasons depend on the climate of a place. In places with long, cold winters, the growing season is short. In places where the winter climate is warmer, the growing season is long.

Crops also need water. Most water comes from rain. If there is not enough rain in a farming area, water must be brought from another place. This is called **irrigation** (eer•uh•GAY•shun).

Reading Check

1. What are four natural resources?
2. How does fertilizer help plants?
3. Why are growing seasons different in different places?

SKILLS FOR SUCCESS

USING RESOURCE MAPS

Resources are things that people can use. Resources include crops and animals. They include trees and land. You can show resources on **resource maps.**

Resource maps show where you can find resources. They can also show **factories.** Factories are big buildings. People use resources to make things in factories. They use resources to make goods.

You will be looking at many resource maps in this book. Look at this resource map of Kansas.

Find Topeka on the map. That is the capital of Kansas. There are some symbols near this city. One is a building. Now look at the map key. The map key shows you that the building is a symbol for factories. There are a lot of factories near Topeka.

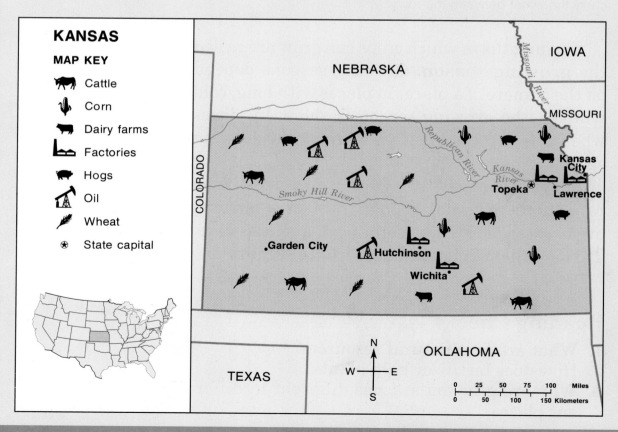

KANSAS

MAP KEY

- Cattle
- Corn
- Dairy farms
- Factories
- Hogs
- Oil
- Wheat
- State capital

People in factories make goods.
There are many factories in our country.

Ranchers often use horses to round up cattle.

There is another symbol north and to the east of Topeka. It is a picture of a cow. The map key shows you that the cow stands for the dairy farms near Topeka. Farmers get milk from cows on dairy farms.

Another symbol on the map stands for **cattle.** Cattle are cows, bulls, and steers. People raise these animals for their meat. Much of the meat that we eat comes from cattle raised in our country. Look at the map key. What other animal is raised in Kansas?

A lot of the food that we eat comes from Kansas. Look at the resource map again. Wheat and corn are two very important crops grown in Kansas. Many large farms in Kansas grow these crops.

The resource maps in this book name the states that share borders with the state you are reading about. They also show you a small map of our country with the state in color.

CHECKING YOUR SKILLS

Use the resource map to help you answer these questions.

1. What are two important crops grown in Kansas?

2. What are most factories in Kansas close to?

3. What are some resources near Garden City?

4. Oil is one resource people get from the Earth. Near what cities can oil be found?

Look for these important words:

Key Words
- factories
- valley
- farming
  community

- irrigate
- ripe

Places
- Merced, California

Look for answers to these questions:

1. How is climate important to the kinds of vegetables grown in a place?
2. Why is Merced called a farming community?
3. How do machines help farmers in Merced?

2. MERCED, CALIFORNIA

What is your favorite vegetable? Some people like sweet corn best, and others like fresh peas. Eating vegetables helps keep you healthy.

Different vegetables need different climates to grow best. Vegetables such as tomatoes and corn need lots of hot sun. Other vegetables, such as broccoli, grow best where the climate is wet. Farmers need to know what soil and climate are good for their vegetables. They must know how much water their vegetables need, too.

There are small vegetable farms near many cities. Sometimes people in the cities buy fresh vegetables from these farms. Sometimes they buy fresh vegetables at the store.

There are also large vegetable farms far from cities. Here, most farmers grow just one kind of vegetable. Then trucks, trains, or planes carry some of these vegetables to different places.

66

Many of the vegetables go to **factories.** A factory is a big building where goods are made. There are many big machines in factories. Vegetables are frozen or canned at the factories. These frozen or canned vegetables are shipped to stores all across the country.

The next pages tell you how a farmer in the state of California raises tomatoes. You will find out how tomatoes are made into special foods in factories, too.

The Garcias' Vegetable Farm

Merced (mur•SED) is a small city in the middle of **California.** Merced is in a big **valley** that is rich in natural resources. A valley is low land between hills or mountains.

The picture below shows the city of Merced. Huge fields and farms surround Merced.

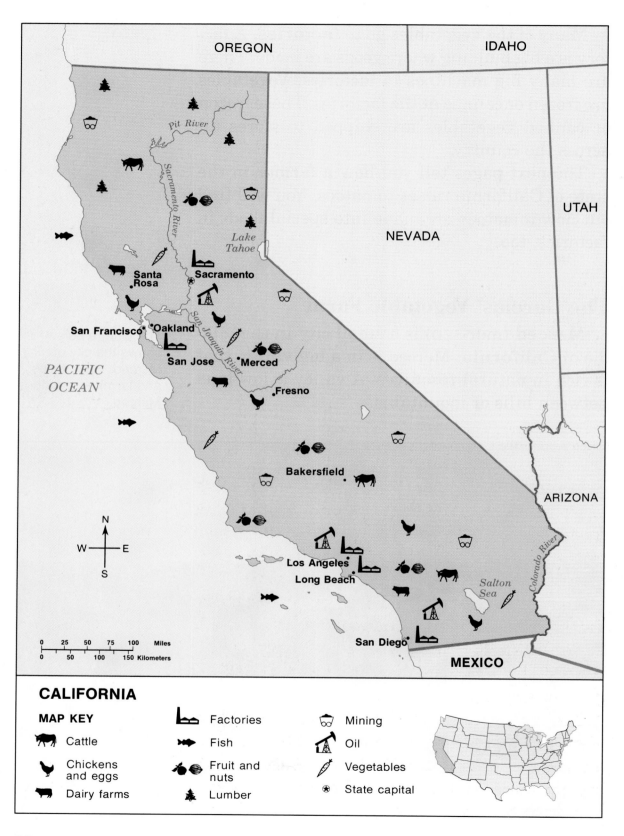

OREGON

IDAHO

UTAH

NEVADA

Pit River

Sacramento River

Lake Tahoe

ARIZONA

San Joaquin River

Santa Rosa

Sacramento

PACIFIC OCEAN

San Francisco • Oakland

San Jose

Merced

Fresno

Bakersfield

N
W — E
S

Los Angeles

Long Beach

Colorado River

Salton Sea

San Diego

| 0 | 25 | 50 | 75 | 100 | Miles |
| 0 | | 50 | 100 | | 150 Kilometers |

MEXICO

CALIFORNIA

MAP KEY

Cattle

Chickens and eggs

Dairy farms

Factories

Fish

Fruit and nuts

Lumber

Mining

Oil

Vegetables

State capital

68

The Garcia family enjoys an outdoor picnic during the long, hot California summer.

Many of the jobs in Merced have to do with farming. Because of this, Merced is called a **farming community.** Almost half of the people in Merced work on farms. Merced also has canning factories for vegetable and fruit crops.

Merced is a good place to grow tomatoes. Tomatoes need warm summers to grow well. Summers in Merced are long and very warm. Winters in Merced are mild and rainy. The soil is good for growing crops.

Mr. and Mrs. Garcia have a large farm near Merced. They raise only tomatoes. Most of their tomatoes are brought to factories. Anita Garcia is eight years old. She and her brothers and sister help with the farm work.

Planting and Harvesting Tomatoes

Raising tomatoes does not begin with planting seeds. The Garcias must first choose the kind of tomato they want to grow. The Garcias must choose tomato plants that will be strong and healthy. They must also grow a kind of tomato that fits the needs of the canning factory.

Early in the spring Anita's father gets the soil ready for planting. He uses a plow to turn over the soil. Next, he uses a special machine to plant the seeds. This machine also adds weed killer to the soil and puts fertilizer below the seeds.

As the plants grow, Mr. Garcia uses another machine. This machine kills weeds by turning them into the soil.

In Merced, little or no rain falls during the growing season. This means Mr. Garcia must **irrigate,** or water, his tomatoes. He does this about every other week.

To ready the soil for planting, a machine loosens the soil and destroys weeds. After the plants are growing, sprinkling machines irrigate the tomatoes.

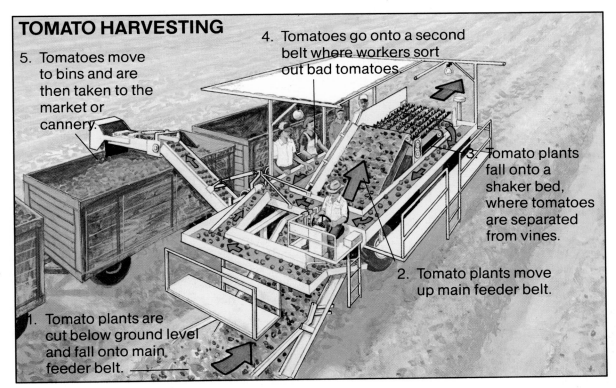

TOMATO HARVESTING

5. Tomatoes move to bins and are then taken to the market or cannery.

4. Tomatoes go onto a second belt where workers sort out bad tomatoes.

3. Tomato plants fall onto a shaker bed, where tomatoes are separated from vines.

2. Tomato plants move up main feeder belt.

1. Tomato plants are cut below ground level and fall onto main feeder belt.

The tomatoes are **ripe,** or ready to be eaten, when they are very red. This is when the Garcias harvest them for the canning factory.

A machine does the harvesting. It shakes the tomatoes off the plants. Then the machine moves the tomatoes up to the workers who are on the machine. The workers pick out rocks, dirt, and bad tomatoes. All the good tomatoes go into huge metal boxes. Then trucks take these boxes to the canning factory.

These pear-shaped tomatoes are good for canning.

Reading Check

1. Where can people get fresh vegetables? Name two places.
2. Why are factories important? Where do vegetables go from factories?
3. Why is Merced a good place to grow tomatoes?

71

SKILLS FOR SUCCESS

USING CLIMATE MAPS

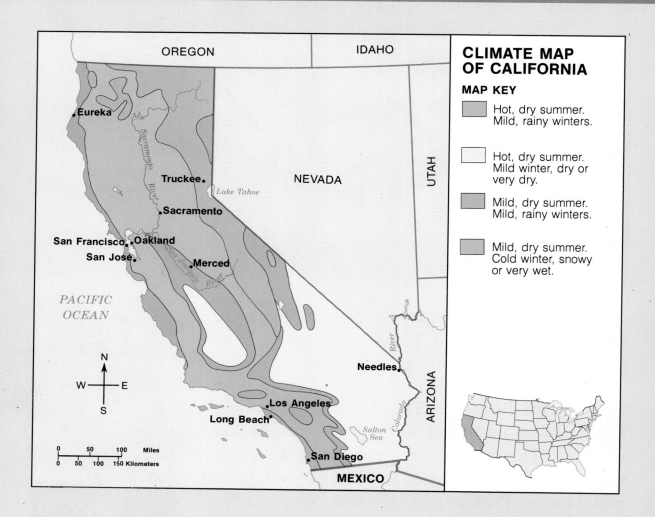

CLIMATE MAP OF CALIFORNIA

MAP KEY

Hot, dry summer. Mild, rainy winters.

Hot, dry summer. Mild winter, dry or very dry.

Mild, dry summer. Mild, rainy winters.

Mild, dry summer. Cold winter, snowy or very wet.

Climate is the usual weather in a place. Climate maps show what the weather in a place is like all year long. Climate maps show how much rain or snow falls in a place during the year. They show what the winters and summers in that place are like.

The map on this page shows climates in California. Each climate is shown by a color on the map. Look at the map key at the side of the map. How many climates does the map show? What colors are used on the map to show these different climates?

Different parts of California have different climates. In some parts of California, it snows a lot during the winter. In other parts, the winter is very dry.

Farmers Need Good Climates

Some areas in California have climates that are very good for growing crops. In other parts of California, it is hard to grow a lot of crops.

Merced is in the part of California colored green. Look at the map key. It tells you that the green area has mild, dry summers and mild, rainy winters.

The climate in the green area is very good for growing fruits and vegetables. During the dry summers, farmers irrigate the soil. Then crops can grow well. You have read about how well tomatoes grow in Merced.

Now look at the parts of California colored pink. These parts of the state are good for growing food, too. Find Sacramento in the pink area. There are many farms near Sacramento. The area around the city is famous for all the crops grown there.

Now find Needles in the southern part of the state. Needles is in the part of California colored yellow. Like the pink area, the yellow area has hot, dry summers. Winter in the yellow area, however, is dry, too. Very little rain falls in Needles. Needles is in a big desert. In a desert, few crops can be grown. There is not enough water for many plants to grow.

Find Truckee on the climate map. What color is the map there? Summers in Truckee are usually mild and dry. Winters in Truckee are very cold and snowy. It is much too cold in Truckee to grow certain kinds of crops.

CHECKING YOUR SKILLS

Use the climate map to help you answer these questions.

1. Find Los Angeles on the map. Is the area around there good for growing crops?
2. What are winters like in Eureka?
3. Most trees need a lot of rain to grow. Do you think there are more trees near Truckee or near Needles? Why?
4. Name at least two communities in areas where the climate is good for growing crops.
5. What is the climate like in San Jose?

Look for these important words:

- cannery
- tomato paste
- pulp

Look for answers to these questions:

1. What is a cannery?
2. Why are tomatoes canned and bottled?
3. How are canned tomatoes taken away from factories? Where are they taken?

3. TOMATOES AT THE CANNERY

Many goods are made from tomatoes at the canning factory, or **cannery.** Some tomatoes are boiled and then canned. Other tomatoes are used to make ketchup. Still others are used to make tomato soup and tomato juice.

Tomatoes are canned and bottled for many reasons. One important reason to can food is so that you can use it longer. Fresh vegetables and fruit are often good only for a few weeks after the harvest. People can enjoy these healthful foods all year long in cans and bottles.

The Garcias' tomatoes are perfect for making **tomato paste.** Tomato paste is a thick, rich sauce. Cooks use tomato paste on top of pizza. They use it to make spaghetti sauce, too.

In the cannery, the Garcias' tomatoes are put in a long bin. Workers go through and sort the tomatoes into the bin.

At the cannery, machines fill small cans with tomato paste.

The tomatoes that are good for tomato paste are chopped by a machine. Then the tomatoes are cooked. Cooking the tomatoes helps make sure no harmful germs enter the food. Germs can make people sick. The seeds and peels are then taken out of the tomatoes. What is left is called **pulp.**

The pulp goes to a machine that takes some water out of it. The machine cooks the pulp so that it becomes thick like paste. The pulp has now become tomato paste.

After it is cooled, the tomato paste is put in small cans. These cans are closed, cooked, and cooled. Machines close and seal the cans tightly. That way, no air gets in. Germs can grow when air is in cans. Labels are put on the cans. Later trucks bring them to our stores.

Reading Check

1. What are three goods that are made from tomatoes?
2. How is tomato paste used?
3. Why are tomatoes cooked in canneries?

SKILLS FOR SUCCESS

USING LISTS AND TABLES

A **list** is a way to order things. Lists can help you learn facts or remember things. For example, a grocery list helps you remember what you need to buy at the store.

Look at the three lists shown on this page.

The lists show some California crops, some state capitals, and some things that make up climates. As you can see, lists usually do not have sentences. When you write a list, you use only words or groups of words.

Some California Crops	Some State Capitals	Some Things That Make Up Climate
cotton	Tallahassee	amounts of rain or snow
grapes	Austin	summer weather
oranges	Boise	winter weather
vegetables	Sacramento	wind
nuts	Salem	
rice	Des Moines	
grains		

TABLE OF FACTS ABOUT THREE STATES

State	Capital	Important Crops	Climate
California	Sacramento	cotton, grapes, oranges, grapefruits, vegetables, nuts, rice, grains, hay	hot or warm summers; mild, rainy winters
Iowa	Des Moines	corn, oats, soybeans, hay	wet, hot summers; cold, snowy winters
Florida	Tallahassee	oranges, grapefruits, lemons, sugarcane, nuts, cotton, watermelons, vegetables	wet, hot summers; mild winters

Lists of facts can be put together in **tables.** You can see information quickly on a table. Tables let you compare things easily.

Now look at the table on this page. You can find out what crops are grown in California by looking at the table. Put your finger on the word "California." Then move your finger to the right across the table until you reach the column that says "Important Crops." Now read the list of crops.

If you want to find out what the climate of Florida is, find the box on the left that says "Florida." Then find the column that says "Climate." The words across from "Florida" in the "Climate" column tell about the usual weather in Florida. They tell how much rain falls in Florida and what the winters and summers are like.

CHECKING YOUR SKILLS

Use the table to help you answer these questions.

1. What is the capital of Iowa?
2. Which crops are grown in both California and Florida?
3. How is the climate of Iowa different from the climate of Florida?
4. What crop does Florida have that California and Iowa do not?
5. Which two states have wet, hot summers?

Look for these important words:

Key Words
- dairy farms
- yogurt
- dairy products

Places
- Independence, Iowa

Look for answers to these questions:

1. What is a dairy farm?
2. What kind of community is Independence, Iowa?
3. How do machines help dairy farmers?

4. INDEPENDENCE, IOWA

Farms where cows are raised for their milk are called **dairy farms.** Most dairy farms are in places where grass grows thick and green. Rain falls often enough to keep the grasses growing. Cows eat a lot of grass.

In the United States, a good dairy cow can give about 64 quarts (61 L) of milk a day. Some of this milk is used for drinking. Many things that we eat are made from milk, too. Cheese, butter, and **yogurt** are made from milk. Yogurt is thicker than milk and has a slightly sour taste. All things made from milk are called **dairy products.**

Cows graze in Iowa's pastures.

The Swansons' Dairy Farm

Independence, Iowa, is a town. Like Merced in California, Independence is a farming community. There are about 1,500 large farms in the area. Many of them are dairy farms.

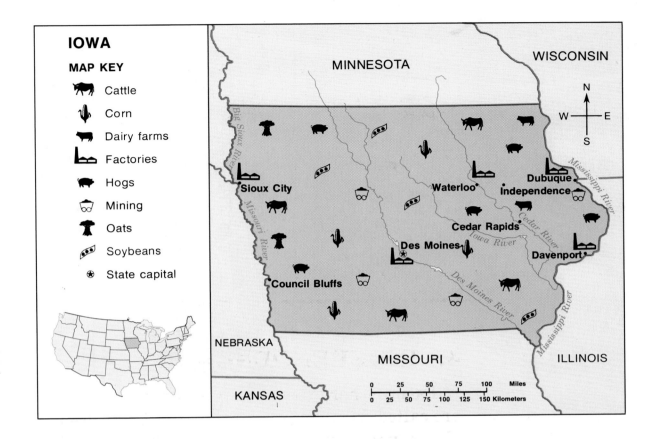

IOWA

MAP KEY

🐃 Cattle
🌽 Corn
🐄 Dairy farms
🏭 Factories
🐖 Hogs
⛏ Mining
🌾 Oats
🫘 Soybeans
✳ State capital

The dairy farm of the Swanson family is about five miles from Independence. Mr. and Mrs. Swanson live and work there. They have two children. Laura is 12, and Carl is 9. The children help milk and feed the 150 cows on the farm.

The Swansons' cows are milked very early every morning. They are milked again in the late afternoon. In the Swansons' barn, 16 cows can be milked at the same time.

The children line the cows up. Then they clean them for milking. They brush and wash the cows. Milking machines make the work go fast. A pump pulls milk from the cows into hoses. The milk goes through the hoses into a large tank. It is kept cool there.

Milking by hand used to take several hours. Now, many cows can be milked at one time using milking machines.

Getting the cows' milk is just part of the work on the dairy farm. The Swansons must check their cows to make sure they are healthy. They keep track of how much milk each cow gives. They also make sure the cows eat well in the pastures.

Reading Check

1. Why are dairy farms often in grassy places?
2. Name three dairy products.
3. How do the Swansons make sure their cows stay healthy?

Look for these important words:

Key Words
- creamery
- butterfat
- pasteurized
- homogenized
- skim milk

Look for answers to these questions:

1. How does milk get to a creamery?
2. What kinds of jobs do machines do in a creamery?
3. What products are made in a creamery?

5. MILK AT THE CREAMERY

Every day a truck picks up milk from the Swansons' farm. The truck keeps the milk cool in a special tank. Then the truck takes the milk to a **creamery.** A creamery is a factory that makes milk ready for people to buy.

At the creamery, machines do most of the work. The milk is weighed and checked for **butterfat.** Butterfat is the cream that rises when milk is left standing.

Next the milk is **pasteurized** (PAS•chuh•ryzd). This means that the milk is quickly heated and then cooled. Heating the milk kills any harmful germs that might be in it.

Some of the milk is **homogenized** (hoh•MAHJ•uh•nyzd). To make homogenized milk, a machine mixes the butterfat with the rest of the milk. The butterfat in homogenized milk stays mixed. The butterfat that is mixed in gives homogenized milk a rich taste.

Machines working at high speed fill containers with milk, and cap the containers after they are filled.

Some milk is not homogenized. Instead, the cream is taken off the top of the milk. The **skim milk** that remains is sold. Some of the rich cream is sold, too. Some of it is made into butter.

At the creamery, milk is put into cartons or containers. Then the containers are put into boxes. The creamery keeps the milk cool until trucks can take it to our stores.

Reading Check

1. What is a creamery?
2. Why is milk pasteurized?
3. How is skim milk made?

USING WORDS

Number your paper from 1 to 5. Match the words with their meanings.

1. **ripe**
2. **natural resources**
3. **dairy farms**
4. **factories**
5. **climate**

a. Things found in nature that people can use
b. The usual weather in a place
c. Big buildings where goods are made
d. Ready to be eaten
e. Places where cows are raised for their milk

REVIEWING FACTS

1. What three natural resources are important to farmers?
2. What is a "growing season"?
3. What must tomato farmers do before they plant seeds?
4. Where are most dairy farms found? Why?
5. What are three things that happen to milk in a creamery?

THINKING CRITICALLY

1. What are some ways that farms are alike? What makes farms different from each other? What are some different kinds of farms in our country?
2. How is a cannery like a creamery? How is it different?
3. You read about a tomato farm and a dairy farm. On which farm would you rather live? Why?

◯ PRACTICING SKILLS

1. **Resource Maps** Name three resources that are near your community. Go to the library if you need help. Make up and draw symbols for the three resources you choose.

2. **Climate Maps** Look again at the climate map of California on page 72. Use the map to help you answer these questions.

   a. In which town would you need to wear snow boots in the winter?
   b. What is the climate like in Needles?

CHAPTER 4

Mining Communities

Farms need sunshine, good soil, and plenty of water. These are all natural resources.

Coal and oil are two other natural resources. In this chapter you will read about communities where people work with these resources. Workers mine coal near Pikeville, Kentucky. Workers drill for oil near Midland, Texas.

Look for these important words:

Key Words
- mineral
- coal
- oil
- mines
- wells
- energy

Look for answers to these questions:

1. What is a mineral?
2. How do we use mineral resources?
3. What are some of the jobs that people in a coal mining community do?

1. MINERAL RESOURCES AND OUR COMMUNITIES

A **mineral** (MIN•uh•ruhl) is a natural resource found in the earth. **Coal** and **oil** are minerals. Coal is a dark brown or black mineral. It is like a dark rock. Oil is a dark, thick liquid found deep in the ground. Copper, gold, iron, and silver are also minerals.

We use mineral resources to meet our needs. We must dig deep into the ground to get most mineral resources. Workers dig large holes and tunnels, called **mines,** to get some mineral resources like coal. They dig narrow, deep holes, called **wells,** to get other mineral resources like oil.

We need many people to get minerals out of the earth. We need workers inside a mine or at a well for many different jobs. We need workers outside the mine or well, too. They take the minerals to factories. After that, we need workers in factories to make the minerals ready to use.

Silver (above) and coal (below) are two minerals found under the ground.

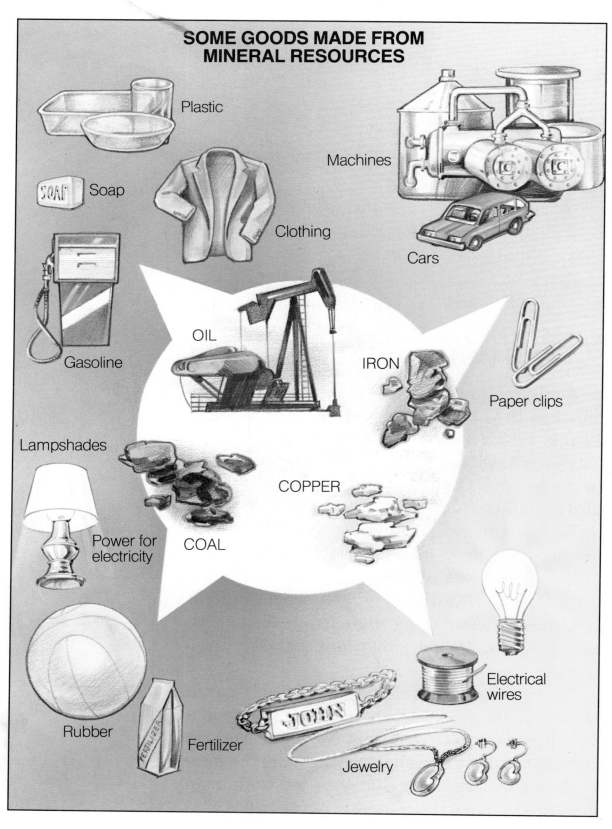

SOME GOODS MADE FROM MINERAL RESOURCES

Plastic

Machines

Soap

Clothing

Cars

Gasoline

OIL

IRON

Paper clips

Lampshades

COPPER

Power for
electricity

COAL

Electrical
wires

Rubber

Fertilizer

Jewelry

Communities near mines or wells are usually called mining communities. Many of the people in mining communities do jobs using the mineral resources nearby.

A mining community has many jobs. For example, some workers might dig coal from a mine. Others work in a factory to clean and prepare the coal. A bank might lend coal miners money to buy more machines for the mines.

People in the stores sell the coal workers clothes and food. The workers pay with the money they get from their mining jobs.

How We Use Mineral Resources

People in the United States use many mineral resources. They use them in lots of different ways. Oil is used to make plastic dishes and to pave roads. Iron is used to make big machines.

Mineral resources are used for **energy,** too. Energy is power that makes things work. Factories burn oil and coal to make energy. Energy can make our cars go and heat our homes. Energy gives us power for our lights.

Some scientists think that we may run out of some mineral resources. Most people agree that we should be very careful not to waste mineral resources. Everyone wants there to be enough coal and oil for tomorrow.

Reading Check

1. What are five minerals?
2. Why does a mining community have many jobs?
3. How do we make energy from coal and oil?

SAVING RESOURCES

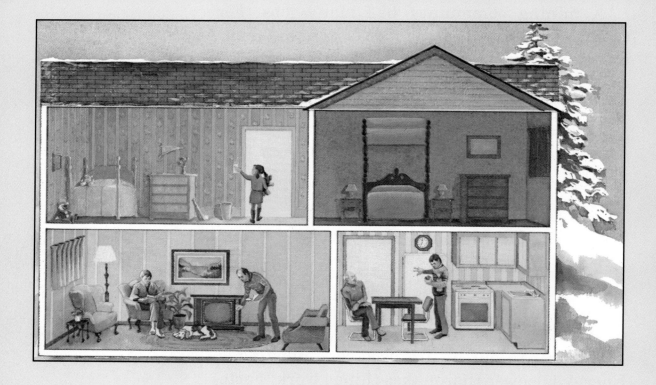

Coal and oil are natural resources that we burn to make energy. Energy makes televisions, record players, lights, and air conditioners work. We use energy when we heat our homes. It takes a lot of energy to run our cars and to heat our water.

Not every community has coal and oil nearby. Most communities use energy from coal and oil, though. We must all be careful not to waste energy.

Ways to Save Energy

There are many ways you can save energy. Here are some of them.

- Open the refrigerator door less often. Get everything you need out at once. It takes energy to keep refrigerators cold.

- If you are cold, put on a sweater. If you turn on the heat, make sure the windows and doors are closed. This will keep the warm air inside.

- Close the curtains or shades at night when the weather is cold. This will help keep the heat in the house. On cold, sunny days, open the curtains and shades. That way, the warm sun can shine through the windows.

- Air conditioners cool the air. If you turn one on, close the shades and curtains. This will keep the hot sunlight out.

- Turn off the lights when you leave a room.

- Do not leave the radio, TV, or record player on when no one is listening or watching.

- Walk, ride a bike, or take a bus instead of going in a car. You save gasoline this way.

Ways to Save Resources

You can do things to save other resources. You can save water by taking short showers and turning off dripping faucets.

People in some schools and communities save old newspapers, cans, and bottles. These are collected at **recycling** (ree•sy•kling) **centers.** To recycle something means to use it again. Companies make recycled things into new paper, cans, and bottles. Recycling things saves resources.

When you use our resources wisely, you help your community. You help make sure that there will be enough resources for the future. If you are careful about using energy and other resources, you also help your family to save money.

What are some of the things being recycled at this recycling center?

CHECKING YOUR SKILLS

Tell or write the answers to these questions.

1. What are two resources that are burned to make energy?
2. What should you turn off when you leave a room?
3. How can you save water?
4. Why do people save old newspapers, cans, and bottles?

Look for these important words:

Key Words
- electricity
- by-products
- fuel

Places
- Pikeville, Kentucky
- Appalachian Mountains
- Levisa River

Look for answers to these questions:

1. How do we use coal?
2. How do many people in Pikeville, Kentucky, make their living?
3. Where does coal go after it is mined? What happens to coal at the factory?

2. PIKEVILLE, KENTUCKY

Pikeville is a small town in **Kentucky.** The town is near the **Appalachian** (ap•uh•LAY•chuhn) **Mountains.** These mountains stretch north and south in the eastern part of our country.

This picture shows downtown Pikeville. You can see the mountains near the town.

90

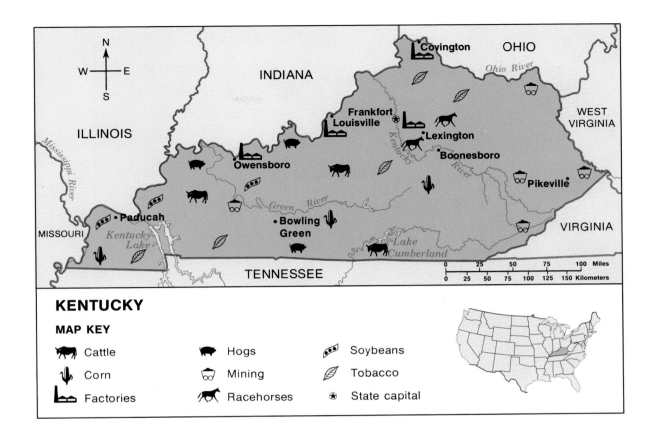

KENTUCKY

MAP KEY

🐂 Cattle   🐗 Hogs   Soybeans

🌽 Corn   Mining   Tobacco

Factories   🐎 Racehorses   ✶ State capital

The mountains near Pikeville are rich in coal. Coal makes energy when it is burned.

Many people in Pikeville work in the mines or at coal factories. Almost all other work in Pikeville has something to do with coal, too.

We Americans count on coal from communities like Pikeville, Kentucky. Coal is used to make **electricity** (i•lek•TRIS•uh•tee). Electricity gives us power for lights, heating, and machines.

Coal is used to make many other things, too. Parts of coal, called **by-products,** are used to make many goods. Coal by-products are used in plastics and medicines. Coal by-products are used to make lampshades, window screens, and airplane parts. The soles on your shoes may once have been part of a lump of coal!

Pikeville is in the mountains of eastern Kentucky. This picture shows a view of Pikeville from the air. Can you see how the path of the Levisa River has been changed?

Pikeville used to have a problem. There was not enough empty land in town to build homes for new workers. To solve this problem, people in Pikeville changed the path of a river. They made the **Levisa River** go around Pikeville instead of through it. By moving the river, the people of Pikeville gave themselves more flat land to build on.

Coal and the Miners

Now you will find out more about work in Pikeville. You will read a letter from Loretta Sommers, who lives in Pikeville. Loretta is telling her pen pal how coal is mined and used.

Dear Marty,

I will try to tell you what my community, Pikeville, is like. To do this, I must tell you about coal.

Coal is a **fuel.** Fuels give off heat when they are burned. This heat is energy. We use the energy from coal to heat buildings and for electricity. We use it to make things, too.

Some scientists think coal was made from layers of plants and mud packed together for many years. The earth's weight changed them into thick layers of coal called coal beds.

When coal is first found in a hill, workers dig two tunnels into the hill. Miners go in and out one tunnel. Machines carry coal out the other.

Miners dig tunnels that go back into the coal bed. Workers make some of the tunnels into bigger rooms. They leave some coal standing in the tunnels and rooms. The coal props up the mines. This keeps the mines safe. Then the workers mine coal from the rooms they have dug out.

Long ago, most coal mining was done with picks and shovels. Now, though, machines do most of the digging and carrying away of coal.

Loretta writes to her friend, Marty.

Miners working underground must be careful. Roof-bolts on the ceiling of the mine protect the workers from falling rock.

Machines dig the coal from the walls of the rooms. The coal is loaded onto small trains. These trains carry the coal out of the mines. The trains run on railroad tracks that workers have built.

My father drives one of the trucks that take coal away from the mines. The coal goes to a factory nearby that makes it ready for people to buy.

I hope you liked my letter about coal mining, Marty. Please write soon and tell me about your community.

Your pen pal,
Loretta

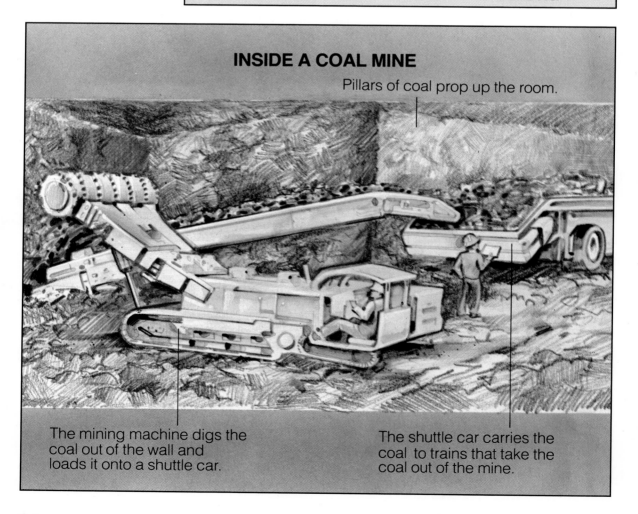

INSIDE A COAL MINE

Pillars of coal prop up the room.

The mining machine digs the coal out of the wall and loads it onto a shuttle car.

The shuttle car carries the coal to trains that take the coal out of the mine.

Coal at the Factory

When coal first gets to the factory, it is put on moving screens. These screens have holes of different sizes. They separate the coal by sizes. Then the coal is washed in water.

After all the coal is washed and sorted, it is dried. A machine dries the coal so it can be used. All this work is done for the different people who buy coal.

Trucks, trains, and boats move the coal from Pikeville. Trains do most of the work. They take the coal to other factories. In these factories, coal is used to make heat, electricity, and goods.

The picture on the left shows a computer being used at a coal processing factory. On the right, loaded trains take the coal from the factory.

Reading Check

1. How do we use the electricity that coal makes?
2. Name three things made with coal by-products.
3. How are trucks, trains, and boats important to the coal business?

SKILLS FOR SUCCESS

READING LANDFORM MAPS

A **landform map** tells you about the shape of the land. It tells you where the mountains and hills are. It tells you where the **plains** and **plateaus** (pla•TOHZ) are. Plains are low, flat lands. Plateaus are usually high, flat lands. Different colors and markings on the map show you where these landforms are.

Look at the landform map of Kentucky.

Find the brown box in the map key. The color brown is used to show mountains. Now find the brown area on the map. What are these mountains called?

Much of the coal in Kentucky is found in the mountains. You have seen how much coal there is in the mountains near Pikeville. People in many Kentucky communities mine coal for a living.

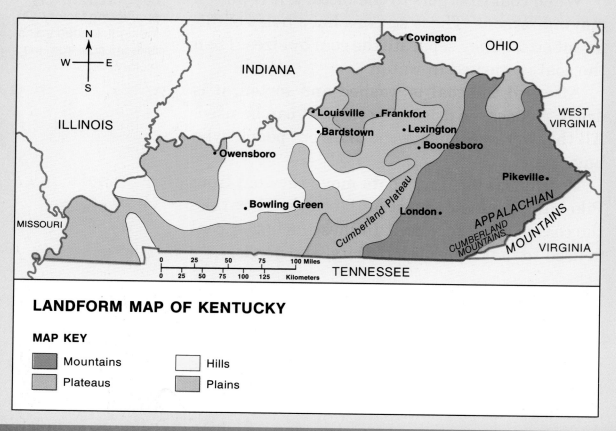

LANDFORM MAP OF KENTUCKY

MAP KEY

- Mountains
- Plateaus
- Hills
- Plains

Plains

Plateaus

Hills

Mountains

Hills are not as high as mountains. Look at the map key. What color is used to show hills?

Look at the map key again. It tells you that plateaus are colored orange. Plateaus often have steep sides. Their tops are flat. Find the orange area on the map. Which cities are on plateaus?

Look at the map key once more. What color is used for plains? Now find the plains on the map. Plains are lower than plateaus. Their land is flat, or gently rolling.

CHECKING YOUR SKILLS

Tell or write the answers to these questions.

1. Is Pikeville in the mountains or in the hills?

2. On what kind of land is Lexington?

3. What is the name of a plateau in Kentucky?

4. Which city is on higher land, Lexington or Boonesboro?

5. Which cities are in the plains?

Look for these important words:

Key Words
- petroleum
- derrick
- drill

- valves
- refinery

Places
- Midland, Texas

Look for answers to these questions:

1. What are some of the jobs that people in an oil-drilling community do?
2. How do we use oil?
3. What happens in an oil refinery?

3. MIDLAND, TEXAS

Midland is a medium-sized city in **Texas.** The people in Midland enjoy the things they can do in their community. They like to use the many parks in Midland. People can swim, eat a picnic lunch, and play games at these parks. Small buses make it easy to get around Midland.

Young people rehearse for a play at the Midland Community Theatre.

98

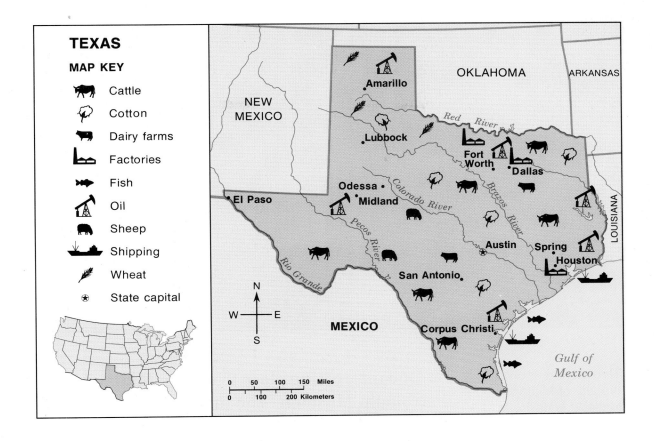

TEXAS

MAP KEY

- Cattle
- Cotton
- Dairy farms
- Factories
- Fish
- Oil
- Sheep
- Shipping
- Wheat
- State capital

The oil wells around Midland show you that this is an oil-drilling community. Oil was first found in Midland about 60 years ago. You know that oil is a mineral. Oil is also called **petroleum** (puh•TROH•lee•uhm).

Before oil was discovered, very few people lived in Midland. More people moved to Midland after oil was found. Many of these people went to work in the oil business. Some helped to drill for oil. Some found jobs at factories that make oil ready to use.

Many jobs in Midland depend on how much oil our country needs. If very little oil is needed, people in Midland may lose jobs. If a lot of oil is needed, new jobs will open up. Oil is important to Midland's future.

This picture shows the city of Midland. Midland is part of a large oil-producing area called the Permian Basin.

One interesting place to visit in Midland is the Petroleum Museum. The museum shows how oil was probably formed. It has some of the machines used to get oil long ago.

On the next pages you will meet a boy who lives in Midland, Texas. He knows a lot about oil and oil drilling. His mother works in the oil fields.

In front of the Permian Basin Petroleum Museum is an outdoor exhibit showing some of the machines used in oil drilling.

At the Oil Museum

"Hi, my name is Al Kimball. I live in Midland. I want to tell you what I learned about oil at our museum.

Al talks about oil.

"People at the museum said that oil, like coal, is a fuel. It makes energy when it is burned. In fact, petroleum gives us almost half the energy used in the world! We use oil to heat our homes. Oil is used to make gasoline for our cars. Oil is used to make the roads we drive on, too! We use oil to make many goods. Fertilizer, clothing, and plastic are just a few goods made with oil.

"One part of Midland's oil museum shows how scientists think oil began. Long ago, plants and animals lived in seas that covered much of the Earth. As they died, they fell to the bottom. Mud fell on them. Many years passed. More mud fell on them. Then the seas began to dry up. The heat and weight of the earth slowly changed the dead animals. Over a long time, they were changed into oil."

A guide shows Al and his class a museum exhibit. The exhibit shows layers of rock and sand from oil zones in the earth.

101

Drilling for Oil

"My mother drills for oil near Midland. I can tell you about her work.

"Mom works on a **derrick** in the oil fields. A derrick looks like a tall tower. It fits over an oil well. The derrick holds machines for drilling, lifting, and pumping oil.

"Once I went to see Mom at work. I saw her start the **drill.** A drill is made up of pieces of pipe. The drill makes a deep hole going down into the earth. The tip of the drill is called a drill bit.

"The bit turned as it went into the ground. The bit went down about 30 feet (9 m) each time. Then it stopped. I saw the workers pull the bit out. They added more pipe to make the drill longer. Then they started the drill again.

The machines and controls at an oil site must be checked often to make sure they are running smoothly.

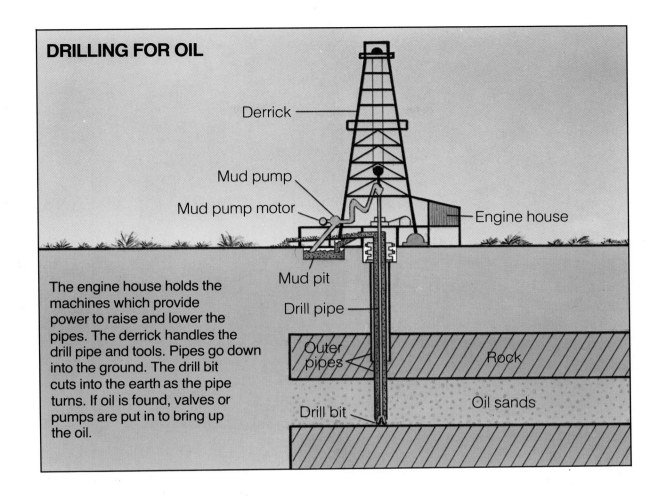

DRILLING FOR OIL

Derrick

Mud pump

Mud pump motor

Engine house

Mud pit

The engine house holds the machines which provide power to raise and lower the pipes. The derrick handles the drill pipe and tools. Pipes go down into the ground. The drill bit cuts into the earth as the pipe turns. If oil is found, valves or pumps are put in to bring up the oil.

Drill pipe

Outer pipes

Rock

Oil sands

Drill bit

"As the bit drilled down through rock, it got very hot. To cool the bit, the drillers pumped mud down the pipes and back up.

"No oil was found when I was there. Mom said the bit had to break through hard rock first. Then the drillers would have a good chance of finding some oil.

"Oil sometimes has water or gas mixed with it. Water or gas can make the oil come up too fast. Drillers put **valves** on the well to slow down the oil. A valve controls how fast a liquid flows.

"Oil sometimes does not come up fast enough. Then drillers use a pump. The pump pulls the oil up out of the well."

103

There are many towers, tanks, and pipes at an oil refinery. Work at a refinery goes on day and night.

Oil at the Refinery

"I asked Mom what happens to oil after it is found. She said the oil goes through pipes or by trucks to a **refinery.** A refinery is a special kind of factory. Oil is made ready for different uses in a refinery. The refinery makes gasoline and motor oil for our cars. It makes heating oil for homes.

"Someday maybe I will drill for oil, too. It is not easy work, but I think it's exciting. It's like a science lesson and a treasure hunt, all in one."

Reading Check

1. Why did a lot of people move to Midland?
2. How is a derrick used?
3. Why does oil go to a refinery?

104

USING BAR GRAPHS

Sometimes you need to compare things quickly. Look at the shapes below.

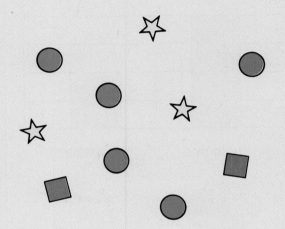

Are there more circles than squares? How many stars are there? It is hard to answer these questions fast just by looking at the drawing.

One easy way to compare numbers of things is to look at a **bar graph.** A bar graph uses bars of different heights to show amounts of things. Look at the bar graph on the right.

The bar graph shows how many stars, squares, and circles are in the drawing. The numbers are shown along the left side of the

graph. The different shapes are shown across the bottom. The bars show how many of each shape there are.

Find the bar for the circles. Move your finger to the top of the bar. Then move your finger across to the number at the left. The bar comes up to the number 5. This tells you that there are five circles in the group.

Find the bar for the stars. How many stars are in the drawing?

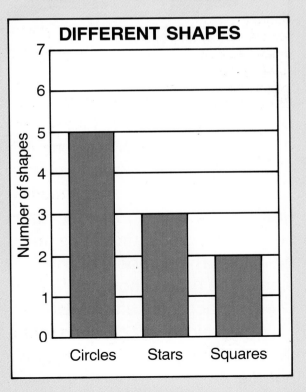

DIFFERENT SHAPES

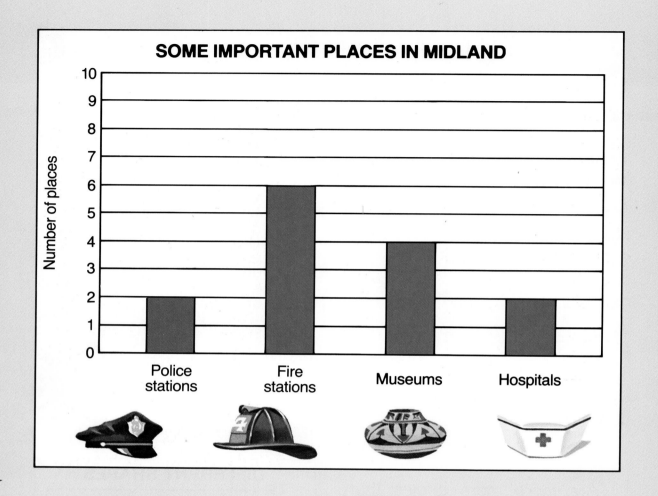

SOME IMPORTANT PLACES IN MIDLAND

A Bar Graph of Midland

Now look at another bar graph. This bar graph shows some important places in Midland. Most communities have these places.

Look at the bottom of the bar graph. It shows you police stations, fire stations, museums, and hospitals. The numbers on the left side of the graph show how many of each place there are in Midland.

What kind of place shown on the bar graph has the highest number?

CHECKING YOUR SKILLS

Use the bar graph to answer these questions.

1. Are there more fire stations or police stations in Midland?

2. How many hospitals are there in Midland?

3. How many museums are there in Midland?

4. How many fire stations are in Midland?

5. Are there more hospitals or museums in Midland?

USING WORDS

Look at the five words below. Two tell about work in Pikeville. The other three tell about work in Midland. Write the five words on a piece of paper. Write **P** beside each word that tells about Pikeville. Write **M** beside each word that tells about Midland.

1. **mines**
2. **wells**
3. **derrick**
4. **coal**
5. **petroleum**

REVIEWING FACTS

1. Where do we find most of our mineral resources?

2. Why did the people in Pikeville change the path of the Levisa River?

3. How do coal miners make sure that tunnels and underground rooms are safe?

4. Why are valves important in oil drilling?

5. Name four goods that are made from oil.

THINKING CRITICALLY

1. How are coal and oil important in your life? Think of three ways they help you meet your needs.

2. Pretend you are a store owner, a doctor, or a restaurant owner. You live in an oil drilling town. How do you depend on the oil workers in your community?

3. Machines are very important in mining. How do machines help make miners' jobs easier?

◯ PRACTICING SKILLS

1. **Saving Resources** Make a list telling three things you did today that used energy. Now make a list of three ways you could have saved energy today.

2. **Using Bar Graphs** Make a bar graph. Use it to show these things.

   a. the number of chalkboard erasers in your classroom
   b. the number of pencils you have in your desk
   c. the number of books you have in your desk

Port Communities

Water is one of our most important natural resources. People must have clean water to drink and to wash with.

Water is very important for communities, too. Many communities were started because of the water nearby. This chapter tells about Chicago, Illinois, and Seattle, Washington. These two communities are built near water.

Look for these important words:

Key Words
- salt water
- fresh water
- dam
- transportation
- harbor
- port

Look for answers to these questions:

1. Why do our water resources need to be protected?
2. How do people use water to make a living?
3. Why do people build communities near bodies of water?

1. WATER AND OUR COMMUNITIES

There are two kinds of water, **salt water** and **fresh water.** The water in oceans is salt water. People cannot drink salt water.

The water in most lakes and rivers is fresh. Rain water is also fresh. People must have fresh water to drink. The water people need in homes and businesses is fresh, too.

Often, people build cities and towns near bodies of water. Then they can use the water to meet their needs.

Using Water

How many ways do people use water at home? We use water for drinking and cooking. We use it to keep plants and gardens healthy. We wash clothes and dishes with water. We wash ourselves with water, too.

This water was ruined because people did not care for it.

People have cared for this water. It has stayed beautiful.

How much water do you think you use in a day? You may use more than you think. In the United States, each person uses about 70 gallons (260 L) a day. That much water would almost fill two bathtubs!

Water is a natural resource that we need to save. We need to use it wisely. We need to save water because some areas do not have enough. In other places the water has become dirty and cannot be used.

Our water resources also need to be protected. In the past, people have spoiled rivers and lakes. They threw things into them and did not care for them. In the last few years, government and citizens groups have formed. The groups work to protect our nation's rivers and lakes.

There are many important reasons to save and protect our water supply. One reason is that many people use water to make a living. In some areas farmers do not get enough rain to grow crops. In these areas farmers must irrigate. This water for irrigation comes from rivers, lakes, and wells. It is important that there is enough water for our crops. It is also important that the water used to grow our crops is clean. People might become sick if the water used for crops is unclean.

Factories need water, too. Factories in the United States use water more than any other resource. To make just one car, a factory uses 15,000 gallons (57,000 L) of water. That much water would fill about 400 bathtubs.

Water also gives us energy for our homes. Water from a **dam** can be used to make electricity. A dam is a wall built across a river or a lake. The wall lets water rush through it. The rushing water turns machines. These machines make electricity.

The High Gorge Dam goes across the Skagit River, in the Cascade Mountains of Washington.

People go river rafting on the Ocoee River in Tennessee. They wear helmets to protect themselves if the raft tips over.

It is also important to care about water because we use it to have fun. Some of our favorite times are on water. We can swim and fish in water. We can ice-skate on a frozen lake. We may enjoy going to an ocean beach.

Communities Near Water

For thousands of years people have chosen to live near water. Some communities have been built near the ocean so people could catch fish for food. Cities are often built near lakes or rivers so that factories can have fresh water to use.

Many towns and cities built near water have become **transportation** centers. Transportation means moving people or things from one place to another. Transportation centers are communities that depend on transportation for many jobs.

Why are cities near water transportation centers? The answer is that water makes it easy to move heavy loads. It takes many railroad cars to move a huge load of coal over land. It also takes a lot of fuel. Yet the same amount of coal can be moved on one ship, using less fuel.

A **harbor** is a protected place where ships or boats can stay. Ships are safe from high waves and strong winds in harbors.

A **port** is a community where ships dock. You will read more about some important port cities in the next pages.

Boats traveling along Alaska's coast often stop at the harbor of Petersburg, Alaska.

Reading Check

1. What are two kinds of water?
2. How can water give us energy for our homes?
3. Why are cities near water transportation centers?

113

Look for these important words:

Key Words
- cargo
- containers
- canal

Places
- Chicago, Illinois

- Lake Michigan
- Great Lakes
- Mississippi River
- St. Lawrence Seaway

Look for answers to these questions:

1. What are some groups of people who live in Chicago?
2. What made Chicago grow?
3. What is the St. Lawrence Seaway?

2. CHICAGO, ILLINOIS

People swim and sun on Lake Michigan's shores.

Chicago, Illinois, is a big, busy city. It is in the middle of a large farming area. Many of the crops grown nearby are moved through Chicago. Chicago is an important transportation center.

Chicago is a port city. Chicago is on the shore of **Lake Michigan.** Lake Michigan is one of the five large lakes called the **Great Lakes.** There are also several rivers in and near Chicago.

Goods can be shipped out of Chicago on many waterways. From Chicago, goods are shipped from the Great Lakes to the **Mississippi River.** They are shipped on the **St. Lawrence Seaway** to the Atlantic Ocean.

Chicago has almost 30 miles (48 km) of land along the shore of Lake Michigan. Much of the land next to the lake is parkland. People like to use the beaches and playing fields there.

Like other big cities, Chicago has many kinds of jobs for people. Many of them have to do with the water resources nearby. Some people work in shipping. Others work in different kinds of transportation. There are many other businesses in Chicago, too.

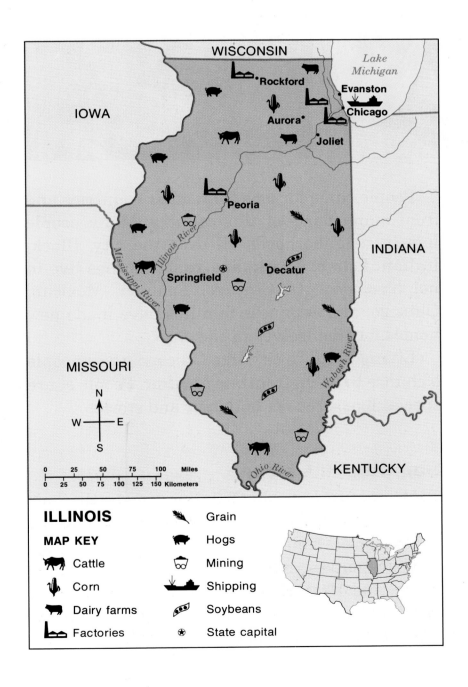

ILLINOIS

MAP KEY

🐂 Cattle

🌽 Corn

🐄 Dairy farms

🏭 Factories

🌾 Grain

🐖 Hogs

⛏ Mining

⛵ Shipping

🫘 Soybeans

✪ State capital

On the left, Polish Americans in Chicago dance in a parade. On the right, black American students carry flags in a Columbus Day Parade.

People came for jobs from other countries and from many parts of this country. Many people live in neighborhoods all over the city. Black, Italian, Polish, Greek, and Irish families live in neighborhoods in Chicago. Spanish, Mexican, Chinese, and Japanese families have made new homes for themselves in the city.

Living in a big city like Chicago gives people a chance to learn from one another. People share special foods, music, holidays, and stories.

Shipping in Chicago

Mary and Patrick O'Malley live with their parents in Chicago. Mary and Patrick's parents were born in Ireland. They came to the United States about 15 years ago.

Mr. and Mrs. O'Malley work. Today, they took time off from work to show Chicago to their nephew Mike. Mike is visiting from Ohio.

"How did Chicago get to be so big?" asked Mike.

"Shipping and other kinds of transportation made it grow," said Mr. O'Malley. "We want to show you Lake Calumet. It is our biggest harbor."

Mrs. O'Malley told Mike about shipping today. "**Cargo** ships are important in Chicago. Cargo is goods carried on ships or planes. There has been a big change in cargo shipping. Instead of loading goods one at a time, shippers can now pack things into large steel boxes. These boxes are called **containers.** Containers are easily moved from a ship to a train or a truck."

"What is shipped from Chicago?" asked Mike.

"Crops are shipped from here. Steel is shipped from here. So are many goods made in our factories. Much of the cargo goes through Canada on the St. Lawrence Seaway."

At Lake Calumet, the O'Malley family saw containers being loaded onto cargo ships.

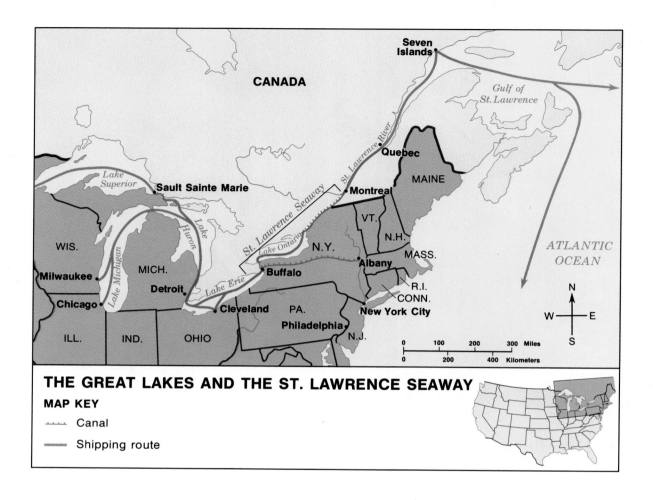

THE GREAT LAKES AND THE ST. LAWRENCE SEAWAY

MAP KEY

⊥⊥⊥⊥ Canal

⸻ Shipping route

The St. Lawrence Seaway

"Is the St. Lawrence Seaway a **canal**?" asked Mike. "I know that canals are people-made waterways. They are used by ships and boats."

"No, the St. Lawrence Seaway is not just a canal. The seaway is made up of the St. Lawrence River and lakes, canals, and dams. It helps join the Atlantic Ocean and the Great Lakes."

Reading Check

1. Name some waterways near Chicago.
2. Why are containers used in cargo shipping?
3. How is the St. Lawrence Seaway used?

Look for these important words:

- location

- O'Hare International Airport

Look for answers to these questions:

1. What does "location" mean?
2. How do crops get from farms to Chicago?
3. What kinds of transportation make Chicago the busiest transportation center in our country?

3. TRUCKS, TRAINS, AND PLANES

"Shipping is important in Chicago. Yet that is only part of Chicago's story," Patrick O'Malley said to Mike. "Chicago is a center for other kinds of transportation, too. That is because of Chicago's **location** (loh•KAY•shuhn). Location means where something is. Chicago is located near the middle of our country.

"Goods go from the East through Chicago to the West. Goods also go from the West to the East through Chicago. Steel for building, foods, and goods made in factories are just a few of the things carried into and out of Chicago. These goods are carried by trucks, trains, and planes."

"How do crops get from the farms to Chicago?" Mike asked.

At the railroad station, the O'Malleys saw containers being taken off trucks and loaded onto railroad cars.

"Railroads are one way to carry food from the farms to Chicago. Railroads are an important kind of transportation," said Mr. O'Malley.

"Chicago is the biggest railroad center in the United States," said Mrs. O'Malley. "Trains carry all kinds of goods into and out of Chicago."

Trucking in Chicago

"I see a lot of trucks on the road here," said Mike as the O'Malleys drove along.

"That is because Chicago is the busiest trucking center in America. Many goods are sent by truck into and out of Chicago," said Mrs. O'Malley.

Planes in Chicago

Mike pointed to the sky. "Where are all the planes going?" he asked.

"They are landing at O'Hare," said Patrick. "Our **O'Hare International Airport** in Chicago is the busiest airport in the world. More people and goods go through O'Hare than any other airport."

Containers are taken off trucks and loaded onto planes at O'Hare International Airport.

Reading Check

1. Where is Chicago located?
2. How did Chicago's location help Chicago become a transportation center?
3. Why is Chicago's O'Hare International Airport the busiest airport in the world?

121

SKILLS FOR SUCCESS

FINDING ROUTES

A **route** is a way to get from one place to another. A route can be a river, a road, a railroad, or even a bicycle path.

Look at the route map below. It shows routes between cities. The map key tells you what the symbols stand for. Find the symbol for railroads. It is ┼┼┼┼. Find the railroad on the map. It connects Brownsville and Blue City.

Find the Snail River. Brownsville and Greenville are near this river. You could travel between these two cities by boat. What other route connects Brownsville and Greenville?

Find Red Rock. The only way to get to Red Rock is to take Highland Road north from Brownsville. How could you get from Greenville to Red Rock?

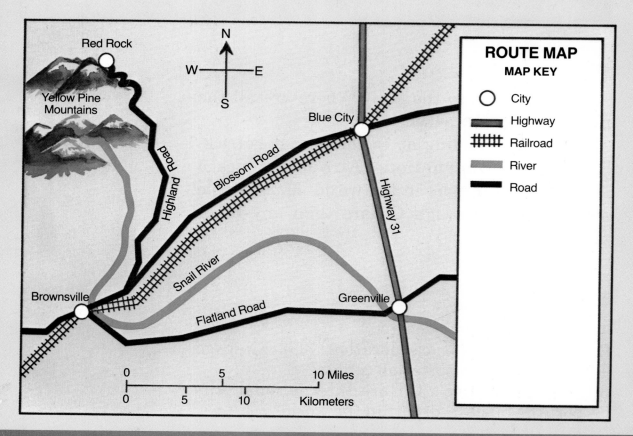

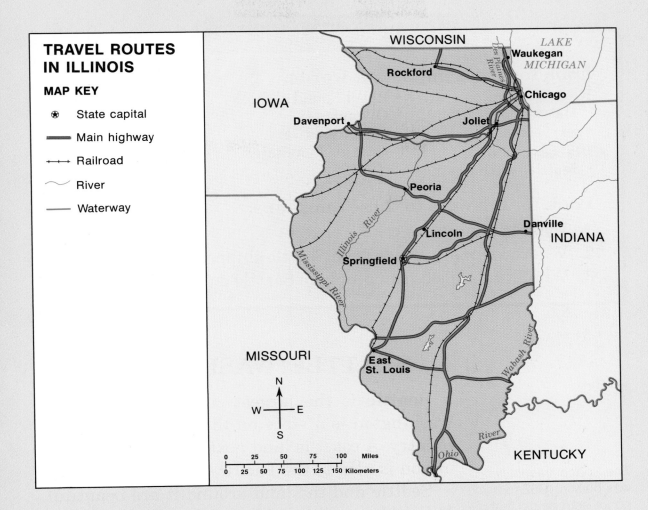

TRAVEL ROUTES
IN ILLINOIS

MAP KEY

⊛   State capital
━━━ Main highway
╅┼┼ Railroad
∿∿∿ River
──── Waterway

Travel Routes in Illinois

The map above shows some travel routes in Illinois. Find Chicago on the map. Railroads, highways, and waterways go to and from Chicago. Waterways are made up of rivers and canals.

Find Joliet on the map. The map shows ways to go from Chicago to Joliet. You could take a train, or you could take a boat on the Des Plaines River. You could also go by car.

CHECKING YOUR SKILLS

Use the route map to help you answer these questions.

1. What kinds of routes run between Chicago and Rockford?

2. What are two ways to get from Chicago to Springfield?

3. If you took the railroad north from Springfield, what city would you reach?

4. How could you ship goods from East Saint Louis to Peoria?

Look for these important words:

Key Words
- coast
- ferryboats

Places
- Seattle, Washington

- Puget Sound
- Olympic Mountains
- Cascade Mountains

Look for answers to these questions:

1. What is a coast?
2. Where are many goods from Seattle shipped?
3. What kinds of jobs can people in Seattle do?

4. SEATTLE, WASHINGTON

Seattle is the largest city in **Washington.** Washington is a state on the west **coast** of our country. A coast is land next to an ocean. Washington is next to the Pacific Ocean.

Seattle and the land around it are beautiful. The mild, wet climate keeps trees and fields green most of the year.

Seattle is a port city. Seattle is located on a natural harbor in **Puget Sound** (PYOO•juht SOWND). Puget Sound is a part of the Pacific Ocean. Seattle also sits between the **Olympic Mountains** and the **Cascade Mountains.**

There are many places to have fun in Seattle. People like to go to the Space Needle. The top of this tall tower turns slowly, like a wheel. People can eat lunch there and watch the changing view. Later they can go to the Pike Place Market. There they find outdoor sidewalk shops. They can buy fresh things like flowers, fish, and fruit.

The Space Needle was built in 1962 to honor astronauts' first trip in space around the Earth.

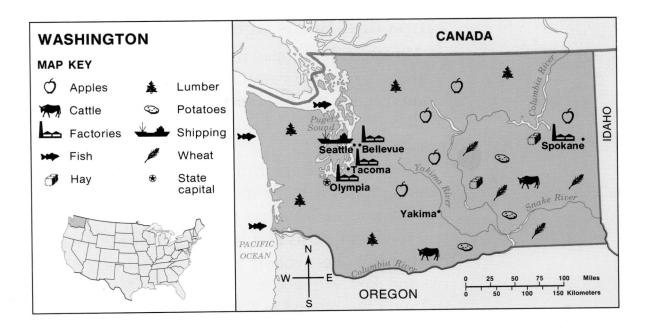

WASHINGTON

MAP KEY

🍎	Apples	🌲	Lumber
🐄	Cattle	🥔	Potatoes
🏭	Factories	⛴	Shipping
🐟	Fish	🌾	Wheat
Hay		✪	State capital

CANADA

Columbia River

Puget Sound

Seattle • Bellevue

• Tacoma

✪ Olympia

Yakima River

Spokane •

IDAHO

Snake River

Yakima •

PACIFIC OCEAN

Columbia River

N
W — E
S

OREGON

| 0 | 25 | 50 | 75 | 100 | Miles |
| 0 | | 50 | 100 | 150 | Kilometers |

Many people who live in Seattle love the water. On a nice weekend thousands of boats are out on Lake Washington, to the east of Seattle. Every August there is a big celebration called Seafair. People come from all over to join in the fun.

At Seafair in Seattle, Lake Washington is crowded with people playing on rafts and watching a water show.

Ships and Boats in Seattle

Many goods shipped in and out of Seattle come from or go to the country of Japan. Goods also come from or go to the state of Alaska. Seattle's location near the Pacific Ocean makes this possible.

Most of the ships that come to Seattle carry cargo in containers. Seattle is one of this country's four busiest container ports.

Passenger ships and huge **ferryboats** dock in Seattle, too. Ferryboats are boats that carry people and cars. Ferryboats from Seattle go to islands in Puget Sound and to ports in British Columbia, Canada.

A ferryboat loaded with passengers from Seattle is on its way to Vancouver, Canada.

Making airplanes is one of the most important businesses in Seattle. Workers put the airplanes together in huge buildings.

There are many different jobs for people living in Seattle. The biggest company in Seattle makes very large airplanes.

Other people in Seattle work for companies that make railroad cars or ships. Still others work to make fish or wood ready to use.

Reading Check

1. What mountains are near Seattle?
2. Why do many goods from Seattle go to Japan?
3. Why are ferryboats needed in a city like Seattle?

Look for these important words:

Key Words
- industries
- lumber
- sawmill

Look for answers to these questions:

1. How do machines help people in the lumber industry?
2. What happens to lumber in a sawmill?
3. What are some kinds of fish caught near Seattle?

5. LUMBER AND FISHING IN SEATTLE

In the next pages, you will read more about work in Seattle. You will visit a classroom in Seattle. Students in Mr. Drake's class will talk about two **industries** (IN•duhs•treez) in Seattle. Industries are big businesses.

Mr. Drake's class talks about important industries in Seattle.

The Lumber Industry in Seattle

"The **lumber** industry is very important in Seattle," said Mr. Drake. "Lumber is wood that is sawed and used to make goods. Sam, can you tell us about Seattle's lumber industry?"

"The first industry in Seattle was cutting and shipping logs," said Sam. "Trees were cut down with handsaws. The logs were rolled or dragged to a river. They were then chained together in a big raft. The raft was floated to the **sawmill.**

A sawmill is a factory at the edge of the river in a logging area. At the sawmill big saws cut the logs into boards."

"How are trees cut down today?" asked Mr. Drake.

"People use chain saws to cut them. Chain saws have motors. Chain saws cut down trees much faster than handsaws. Tractors pull the logs out of the forest. Then most of the logs are put on trucks. The trucks take them to sawmills near Seattle.

"Trucks and tractors have made a big difference in the lumber industry. Yet some of the logs are still chained together and floated down to the sawmill.

Sam talks about lumber.

Wood chips fly as a worker saws a tree. On the right, logs are pushed down the river to the sawmill.

At the sawmill, huge saws cut through logs. The picture on the right shows the cut lumber.

"At the sawmill, very strong sprays of water wash the logs and take off the bark. Huge electric saws cut the logs into lumber. The lumber is used for things like fences, houses, and other buildings.

"Sawdust and wood chips come from sawing the wood. These are used to make things like paper and cloth."

"Where does the lumber go from the sawmill?" asked one student.

"Much of it is shipped in containers to other countries," answered Sam. "Some of it is used for houses and other buildings in the United States."

The Fishing Industry in Seattle

Mr. Drake asked Lynn to tell the class what she knew about Seattle's fishing industry.

"There are hundreds of big fishing boats that work from Seattle," Lynn began. "Many of these boats bring back salmon (SAM•uhn). Salmon live most of their lives in the ocean. Then they swim back up rivers to the place they were born.

"Many of the boats from Seattle go all the way to Alaska," Lynn continued. "Some bring back crabs. Others catch halibut, a large fish."

Lynn talks about the fishing industry in Seattle.

This fishing boat carries a huge net. The net is drawn in a circle around groups of salmon or tuna.

At Seattle's Pike Place Market, shopkeepers offer crab and other seafood fresh from the Pacific Ocean.

"How are fish caught?" a student asked.

"Each kind of fish may be caught in a different way," Lynn replied. "Sometimes huge nets are used. Long lines with bait and hooks are also used."

"What happens to the fish after they are caught?" asked another student.

"Some of the fish are sold fresh in our stores. Many of the salmon are frozen in Seattle. Some are put in cans here, too. The fish are sent to all parts of our country. Many frozen or canned fish are shipped to other countries, like Japan."

Reading Check

1. Name four ways we use wood.
2. Why does Seattle have many sawmills?
3. Why is the fishing industry in Seattle important to other parts of our country?

SKILLS FOR SUCCESS

USING FLOW CHARTS

Suppose you are going to give your dog a bath. You must do some things before you do others.

First, brush the dog to get rid of extra hair. Next, get a tub and fill it with water. Then, put the dog in the tub and get the dog wet. Scrub the dog with soap. Now rinse the dog. Last, take the dog out of the tub and dry the dog off.

These steps need to be done in order. If you dry the dog before rinsing the soap off, you will have a soapy, itchy dog.

Many things have steps that must be done in order. The right order can be shown in a **flow chart.** A flow chart has arrows to show the order of steps. To read this chart, just follow the arrows.

WASHING A DOG

Brush dog.

Fill tub with water.

Get dog wet in tub.

Rinse dog.

Soap and scrub dog.

Take dog out of tub and dry dog off.

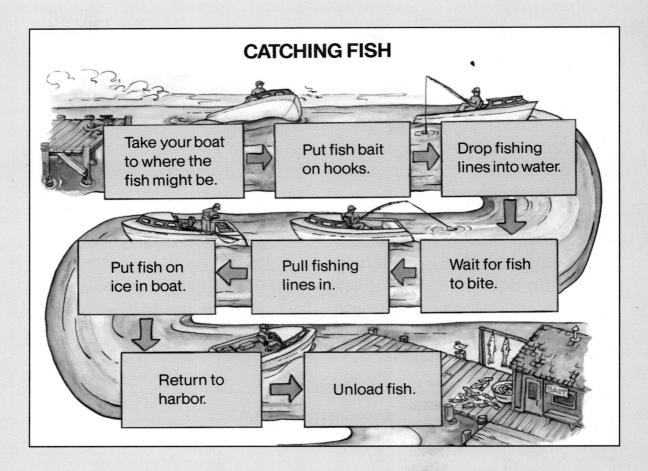

CATCHING FISH

Take your boat to where the fish might be. → Put fish bait on hooks. → Drop fishing lines into water.

Put fish on ice in boat. ← Pull fishing lines in. ← Wait for fish to bite.

Return to harbor. → Unload fish.

A Flow Chart for Fishing

The second flow chart shows the steps to take to catch fish. In Seattle's fishing industry, many workers take these steps. Follow the arrows and read the chart.

Find the box that says "Drop fishing lines." Follow the arrow from this box to the box below it. What does it say? The arrows in the second row go in the opposite direction from the first line of the chart. Reading this flow chart is a little like following a path that goes back and forth.

CHECKING YOUR SKILLS

Use the flow chart "Catching Fish" to answer these questions.

1. What is the first step in catching fish?
2. What is the second step in catching fish?
3. What must you do before you wait for the fish to bite?
4. Which comes first, putting the fish on ice in the boat or pulling in the fishing lines?
5. What must be done after all the fish have been put on ice?

CLOSE-UP

WHY PEOPLE WORK

Pretend that you have a huge piggy bank at home. It is filled with wonderful coins. What could you buy with them? Would that shiny penny buy a bicycle? Would that brand new quarter buy a pair of boots? Of course not! You know that because you know the **value** (VAL•yoo) of the coins. Value means how much something is worth.

135

Suppose you buy something for ten dollars. You are trading your ten dollars for something having the same value as ten dollars.

Some of the things people buy are **goods.** Goods are things like food, clothing, roller skates, and washing machines. Goods are things that you can see and touch. Sometimes people buy **services.** Services include piano lessons, car repairs, haircuts, or a checkup with the doctor. Services are jobs you pay someone else to do for you.

How People Use Money

People work to earn money that they can use to buy goods and services. The money people get is called **income.** We use our income to meet our needs and wants.

136

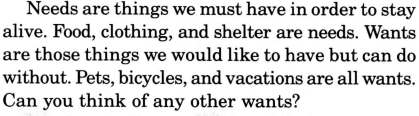

Needs are things we must have in order to stay alive. Food, clothing, and shelter are needs. Wants are those things we would like to have but can do without. Pets, bicycles, and vacations are all wants. Can you think of any other wants?

People usually spend a lot of their income on their needs. Then they try to put aside, or save, a little money. People often keep their money in banks.

The money people set aside is called **savings.** Savings are "just in case" money. Sometimes a person needs money because something unexpected happens. Savings can also be used to go to college or to buy a house.

The money that people do not save or spend on needs is used for wants. People decide what they want to buy with this money.

Tinker, An Auto Mechanic

Tinker is an auto mechanic. An auto mechanic fixes cars and makes sure they run well. Tinker gives the service of fixing cars. She makes an income from this service. Tinker likes her work. It is a way for her to be active and useful. It also makes her feel that she is helping her community. These are good things that she gets from her job in addition to the money.

Tinker is a **producer** (pruh•DOO•sur) when she is working at the garage. Producers make goods or give services. The service Tinker gives is fixing other people's cars.

Tinker spends much of her income on her needs. She needs to eat, so she buys good food. For clothing, she buys coveralls for work and nice clothes for parties and other special times. She uses a big part of her income to pay for her apartment.

Once Tinker's needs are met, she can buy other things. She might buy flowers for her apartment. She also likes to see movies. When Tinker spends money, she is a **consumer** (kuhn•SOO•mur). This means she is buying goods or services.

The money Tinker has not spent at the end of the month goes into her savings. It will be there for her to use if she needs it.

The money that consumers pay for goods or services goes to the producers. When producers spend the money they have made, they become consumers. It is all a big circle, with money going from consumer to producer and back again.

PRODUCERS AND CONSUMERS

The ticket seller is a consumer when he pays to have his car fixed. Tinker is a producer when she fixes the car.

Tinker is a consumer when she buys a ticket. The ticket seller is a producer when he sells tickets.

The ticket seller takes his car to the auto repair shop.

The ticket seller receives an income for his services.

How Economics Works

We can show this information in a flow chart. The flow chart shows how **economics** (ek•uh•NAHM•iks) works in our country. Economics means how our goods, services, and money are traded back and forth.

Look at the flow chart. Tinker is a producer when she fixes the ticket seller's car. When is Tinker a consumer? What is she buying?

The ticket seller is a producer when he sells Tinker a ticket to the movie. When is the ticket seller a consumer?

CHAPTER 5 REVIEW

USING WORDS

Number your paper from 1 to 5. Match the words with their meanings.

1. **industries**
2. **transportation**
3. **canal**
4. **cargo**
5. **port**

a. Moving people or things from one place to another
b. A community where ships dock
c. Goods carried on ships or planes
d. People-made waterway used by ships and boats
e. Big businesses

REVIEWING FACTS

1. How is water used in people's homes?
2. Name four things that different groups of people can share in a city.
3. What are Chicago's important kinds of transportation?
4. What are three important industries in Seattle?
5. How has the lumber industry in Seattle changed over the years?

THINKING CRITICALLY

1. Big loads are moved more easily and cheaply by boats than by trains or trucks. Why do you think all big loads are not moved by boats?
2. How does being near water help Seattle's industries? How does it help Chicago's industries?
3. Does your community have lakes or an ocean nearby? How do you think they help the community?

PRACTICING SKILLS

1. **Finding Routes**   Draw a map that shows your home and a building you know on a nearby street. Show a route for walking from your home to this building. Use the symbol • • • • •. Then show a route for driving from your home to this building. Use the symbol — — — —.
2. **Using Flow Charts**   Look at the flow chart on page 133. Think about something you do every day. Make a flow chart that shows how you do it.

WORDS TO REMEMBER

Number your paper from 1 to 10. Use the words below to fill in the blanks. Use each word only once.

containers	industries
dairy farms	fuels
energy	natural resources
goods	refinery
harbor	transportation

1. Air, soil, and water are _____.

2. _____ are people-made things like paper and glass.

3. Cows are raised for their milk on _____.

4. _____ give off heat when they are burned.

5. _____ is power that makes things work.

6. Oil goes through pipes or by trucks to a _____.

7. Shipping and railroads are important kinds of _____ in Chicago.

8. Ships and boats are safe in a _____.

9. Goods are often packed into large steel boxes called _____.

10. Fishing and lumber are important _____ in Seattle.

FOCUS ON MAIN IDEAS

1. How do we use natural resources?

2. How are all farms alike?

3. What is a farming community?

4. Name some things that happen to milk at a creamery.

5. How do workers in a mining community depend on one another to meet their needs?

6. How do we use mineral resources?

7. How do we get oil?

8. Name some reasons that it is important for us to have clean, fresh water.

9. What are some important industries in Chicago? Why are these industries important to other communities in our country?

10. Name two big industries in Seattle. Why are they important? Why are they important to other parts of our country?

Interdependence means how people depend upon each other. Choose a miner or a farmer and write a paragraph on how you depend upon these workers. How do they depend on other workers?

ACTIVITIES

1. **Art** What new kind of transportation might be invented someday? Draw a picture of how it might look. Show how this new transportation would move people and goods.

2. **Making a List** Think of all the ways you use water every day. Then make a list of everything you would not be able to do without water.

3. **Remembering the Close-Up** In the Close-Up, you read that Tinker was a producer when she fixed cars. Name a time when you were a producer or a consumer.

SKILLS REVIEW

1. **Landform Maps** Look at the landform map, pages R6–R7 Answer these questions.

    a. Are most of the plateaus in the eastern or in the western part of our country?

    b. Name three states on the west coast of our country that have mountains.

    c. What mountains stretch across West Virginia?

    d. What are two landforms in Wisconsin?

2. **Finding Routes**

    a. If you took I-45 south from Dallas, what city would you reach?

    b. Could you reach Austin from Fort Worth by boat?

    c. Which highway would you take from El Paso to San Antonio?

3. **Flow Charts** Choose something you read about in this unit, such as coal mining or tomato growing. Make a flow chart showing the steps that happen.

YOUR COMMUNITY

In this unit you read about a farm community, an oil community, and a coal mining community. You found out that communities have many different kinds of natural resources. Use the following activities to learn more about your community's natural resources.

MAKING A NATURAL RESOURCE MURAL

1. Work with other students to find out about natural resources near your community. Make a class mural showing people working with resources.

TAKING A FIELD TRIP

2. Write to or visit a farm, factory, or other business in your community. Find out how natural resources are used there. Write a report telling what you learned.

MAKING A POSTER

3. Find out if there is a recycling center near you. Make a poster telling people why they should recycle cans, bottles, and newspapers.

MAKING A TABLE

4. On a separate piece of paper, complete the table below.

	STATE	RESOURCES
Your Community		
Midland		
Seattle	Washington	Lumber

MAKING A RESOURCE MAP

5. Draw a map of your state. Then make up symbols for crops and animals raised near your community. Place the symbols on your map.

LEARNING ABOUT WATER

6. Think of all the ways water is used for fun in your community. Draw pictures of people having fun in or near the water.

LEARNING ABOUT TRANSPORTATION

7. Look at a transportation map of your state. Make a list of the railroads, airports, or major highways connect your community to other places.

Community Facts and Figures

Location	Santa Rosa, California	Newfane, Vermont	Washington, D.C.
Population (estimated)	83,000	119	622,823
Nickname/Motto	The City Designed for Living		The Capital City
Landmark	Fountaingrove Round Barn	The Newfane Commons	Lincoln Memorial

COMMUNITY GOVERNMENTS AND SERVICES

Look at the courthouse on page 144. This courthouse is a place where rules for the community are made. Many people work in the courthouse. Some help make sure that the rules of the community are obeyed. Others work to see that the people in the community have the services they need. Some community leaders also work in the courthouse.

In this unit, you will read about rules in communities. You will see how communities make rules. You will also read about the services that communities provide. You will see how people work together to make communities run smoothly.

Location	Orlando, Florida	Durham, North Carolina
Population (estimated)	99,006	95,438
Nickname/Motto	The City Beautiful	City of Medicine
Landmark	Lake Eola Fountain	Duke Chapel

CHAPTER 6

Communities Have Rules and Governments

Focus

We grow up with rules. There are rules at home and at school. Communities have rules, too. They are usually very important rules.

In a community, some people make the rules. Other people make sure that the rules are obeyed. This chapter shows how communities make and carry out rules. Members of the community have a say in the kinds of rules they want.

Look for these important words:

Key Words
- responsible
- detour
- laws
- citizens

Places
- Santa Rosa, California

Look for answers to these questions:

1. How do rules help people?
2. Why are many rules the same around the country?
3. What do we call the rules that communities make?

1. RULES IN COMMUNITIES

Rules help people know what to do. When you are riding a bicycle, you know you should stop at a red light. If you do not stop, you might run into a car or a person. Someone could get hurt. Other people count on you to be **responsible** (rih• SPON•suh•bil). Responsible means following rules.

People in communities everywhere obey rules. Many rules are the same around the country. Because many rules are the same, people know what they should do in different places. If you went to a community in another state, you would know to stop at a red light. You would also know that you should cross the street when the light turns green.

When people obey rules, it helps everyone in the community. Now let's look at how people obey rules in a medium-sized city in California.

147

Santa Rosa, California

Mary Pang and her mother live in **Santa Rosa, California.** Santa Rosa is a city in northern California. There are many new businesses in Santa Rosa. There are redwood forests nearby. People grow fields of grapes in the area around the city.

Mary and her mother have just been shopping in downtown Santa Rosa. Now they are driving home from the store. Suddenly, Mrs. Pang stops the car. Mary sees that the road is blocked. A sign says that there is a **detour** (DEE•toor).

"What does 'detour' mean?" Mary asks.

"It means we will have to go around," her mother says. "We will have to go a different way."

"Why?"

"Well, maybe there has been an accident. Or maybe the city is repairing the street. For some reason, it is not safe to drive on this road," says Mrs. Pang.

When Mary Pang and her mother saw the detour sign, they knew to go a different way.

148

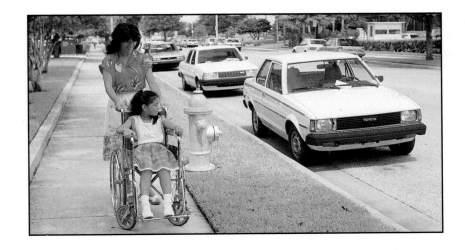

Look at the car on the right. There is a ticket on it because there is a law against parking in front of fire hydrants.

"Do people always do what the sign says?".

"Usually they do," Mrs. Pang answers. "You see, most people understand that rules make our community safer."

Laws in Communities

"The rules that our community makes are called **laws.** Laws are rules for everyone. If people break laws, they may be punished," says Mrs. Pang. "Sometimes they have to pay money. Or, if a very serious law has been broken, they may have to go to jail.

"It is better for everyone to obey laws," says Mrs. Pang. "When we obey laws, we are being good **citizens.** A citizen is a member of a community, state, or country. We are all citizens of the United States."

Reading Check

1. What does "detour" mean?
2. Why should people obey laws? Give two reasons.
3. What is a citizen?

Look for these important words:

Key Words
- government
- lawmakers
- mayor
- judges

- city council
- city manager
- elect
- courts

Look for answers to these questions:

1. Who are the lawmakers in Santa Rosa?
2. Who helps the mayor in Santa Rosa?
3. What do judges in Santa Rosa do?

2.   HOW GOVERNMENTS WORK

Every community has a **government.** A government is a group of people who make laws, and make sure laws are obeyed. The government of a community does the things needed to keep the community safe and pleasant.

People in Governments

Governments usually have three parts. In one part, people make laws. These people are called **lawmakers.** In another part, there is a leader who makes sure things get done. In many communities, this leader is called the **mayor.**

The third part of government is made up of **judges.** Judges are people who decide if laws have been broken. If laws have been broken, judges decide what punishments should be given out.

Together, lawmakers, leaders, and judges make up the government.

Lawmakers and leaders work together at a city council meeting in Santa Rosa. People in the community often listen and add ideas.

Government in Santa Rosa

Santa Rosa has a mayor and a **city council**. The people on the city council are the lawmakers. The mayor is the leader. In Santa Rosa, there is a vice mayor to help the mayor. There is also a **city manager** in Santa Rosa. The city manager also helps make sure things get done.

Many people work for the mayor and city manager. Police officers and fire fighters work for Santa Rosa, and so do highway and parks people.

Together, the mayor and the city council make plans for Santa Rosa. They try to do what the people of Santa Rosa want and need.

151

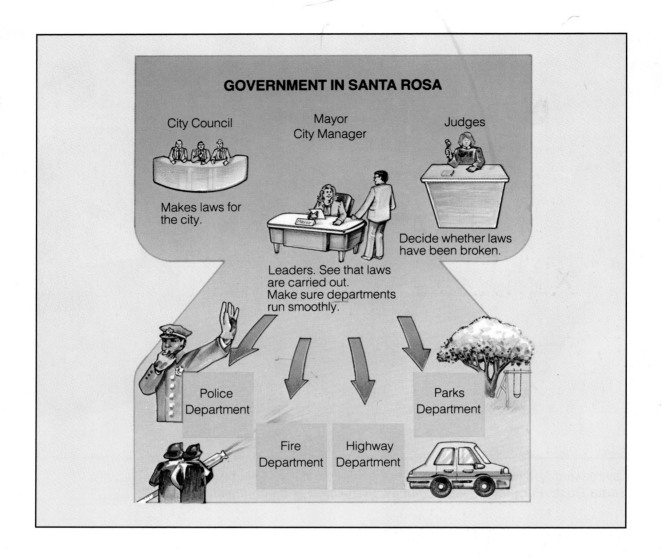

GOVERNMENT IN SANTA ROSA

City Council

Makes laws for the city.

Mayor
City Manager

Leaders. See that laws are carried out. Make sure departments run smoothly.

Judges

Decide whether laws have been broken.

Police Department

Fire Department

Highway Department

Parks Department

The people in Santa Rosa **elect,** or choose, judges. The judges decide whether people are obeying Santa Rosa's laws. The judges also decide how people who break laws should be punished. Judges work in places called **courts.**

Reading Check

1. What is a government?
2. Why is a city council important in Santa Rosa, California?
3. How are the judges chosen for Santa Rosa?

Look for these important words:

Key Words

• town meeting
• Board of Selectmen

Places

• Newfane, Vermont

Look for answers to these questions:

1. What kind of community is Newfane, Vermont?
2. How do the people in Newfane, Vermont, take part in their community's government?
3. What do people do at a town meeting?

3. NEWFANE, VERMONT

Newfane, Vermont, is a small town. It is located in the rolling hills of southern Vermont. About 1,100 people live in and around Newfane. Many of the people who live near Newfane are farmers. Others have jobs in one of the larger towns many miles away.

Town buildings surround the central green in Newfane, Vermont.

153

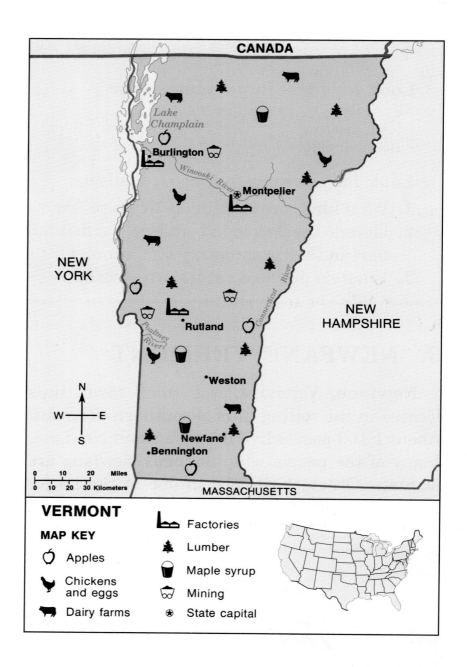

VERMONT

MAP KEY

- 🍎 Apples
- 🐓 Chickens and eggs
- 🐄 Dairy farms
- 🏭 Factories
- 🌲 Lumber
- 🪣 Maple syrup
- ⛏ Mining
- ✳ State capital

Government in Newfane

On the first Tuesday in March each year, the people of Newfane gather together. They meet in Grange Hall or in a big hall called the Union Hall. There all of the people have a **town meeting.** A town meeting is a way for everyone to take part in Newfane's government.

In Newfane, there is no city council or mayor. Instead, the government is a group of five people. This group is called the **Board of Selectmen.** The Board helps run the town. One of the jobs of the Board of Selectmen is to choose the heads of town departments, like the Police Department.

People on the Board of Selectmen are elected each year at the town meeting. Both men and women can be Selectmen.

The citizens of Newfane help choose what to talk about at the town meeting. If enough people want to talk about something or make a new law, it is put on a special list. The list lets everyone know what will be talked about at the meeting.

Newfane has a lot of snow in the winter. That makes travel difficult. So this problem is talked about at the town meeting. Should the town buy a new snow plow? Should town workers put more salt on the roads to make them less icy? Anyone who wants to has a chance to talk.

The town meeting in Newfane is held every other year in Union Hall.

This picture shows the Board of Selectmen in Newfane.

The legal voters of the Town of Newfane, Vermont, are hereby notified and warned to meet at the Williamsville Grange Hall on Tuesday, March 4, 1986, at 10:00 a.m. to act upon the following articles:

Article 1   To elect a Moderator and Town Clerk.

Article 2   To act on the Auditors' Report.

Article 3   To see how the Town will vote to collect taxes for the ensuing year.

Article 4   To see how much the Town will vote to pay its officers for the ensuing year.

Article 5   To see if the Town will authorize the Selectmen to appoint one or two Road Commissioners for the ensuing year, or elect them by ballot.

Above is a list of some articles that were discussed at a town meeting in Newfane.

People often have different views. Sometimes the talk gets very lively. Then a vote is taken. The people in Newfane are the lawmakers.

If more people vote yes, the plan or law "passes." This means that the plan will be carried out, or that the law must be followed. If more people vote no, the plan or law "fails." This means that the government does not do anything about it. After people vote on all the plans and laws, the town meeting is over. The town's business has been settled for another year.

Reading Check

1. Why is it important for the citizens of Newfane to attend the town meeting?
2. What group helps run the government in Newfane?
3. How do people make laws in Newfane?

SKILLS FOR SUCCESS

MAKING CHOICES

Personal Choices

Making a choice means picking one thing instead of another. If you choose to watch one television show, you are choosing not to watch other shows. You cannot watch two shows at the same time.

You make many choices every day. Did you ever think about the reasons for making the choices you make?

Here are some reasons you might have for making choices.

- **You like one thing more than another.** Maybe some of your friends are going to play baseball after school. Some of your other friends want to go roller skating. You like roller skating better, so you decide to go roller skating.

- **One thing is more important than the other thing.** Maybe you have time to either clean your fish tank or play soccer with your friends. It may be more important to clean the fish tank. The fish could get sick if you do not.

- **Your choice depends on a rule.** Suppose you want to ride your bike on the playground. However, there is a rule against this. You would get into trouble for breaking the rule if you rode on the playground. You might also run into someone on the playground. If you put your bike in the bike rack instead, you will not hurt anyone. You will also be following the rules.

Some choices are harder to make than others. We must always think carefully before choosing.

These children are following a rule by walking their bikes to the bike rack.

Community Choices

People in communities also have to make choices. These may be very hard choices to make. Suppose a new highway is being built. It can be built through the town, or it could pass by the town.

Some people in the community want the highway to go through the town. Then people passing through can stop at the town restaurants and stores. The town will get more business that way.

Not everyone agrees. Other people don't want the highway to go through town. They say all the cars going through could cause big traffic problems. People don't want their children having to cross a busy highway to get to school.

In our country, people can meet together to talk about choices. The more information we have about choices, the better choices we can make. People can talk about the good and bad points of each choice. Then they can **vote.**

When people vote, they say what their choices are. People vote for leaders and lawmakers. They also vote for or against things.

In an **election,** people go to special voting places. They write their choices down or use a machine to vote. Then all the votes are counted. The choice with the most votes wins the election. This is called **majority rule.** Majority rule means that more than half of the people voted in the same way.

On voting day, people in the community make important decisions. They put their votes on machines in voting booths.

Government Leaders and Choices

Government leaders make many choices for the community. People who want to be leaders tell what kinds of choices they might make. Voters usually elect someone they agree with.

Here are some things that a government leader might have to make choices about.

- Should a piece of land be used for a new park or for a parking lot?

- Should the city spend money to repair some streets with holes in them? Or should it put up stoplights at a busy corner?

- Should the city build a new city hall or fix up the old one?

- Should the city pay police officers more, or hire more police officers with the money?

These choices may sound simple, but each choice means spending thousands of dollars. Also, each choice might change how people live. Government leaders must think long and hard before they make important choices like these.

The people standing want to be on the city council. They are telling some voters their views about government.

CHECKING YOUR SKILLS

Tell or write the answers to these questions.

1. What does making a choice mean?

2. What are two reasons people choose one thing instead of another?

3. How do communities in the United States make choices?

4. Look at the list on this page of choices that government leaders have to make. Choose one pair of choices. Then think of some reasons that a leader might have for making each choice. Tell these reasons.

Look for these important words:

Key Words
• governor
• Congress
• Supreme Court

Places
• Washington, D.C.

Look for answers to these questions:

1. Where do state governments meet? Where does the government for our country meet?
2. Who leads state government?
3. What is the Supreme Court?

4. GOVERNMENTS FOR OUR STATES AND COUNTRY

You have read about community governments. We also have state governments. Our country has a government, too, which meets in **Washington, D.C.**

State Governments

A state government makes laws for the whole state. It also takes care of state parks, state forests, and public schools.

Each state government has lawmakers. Each state also has a leader called a **governor.** The lawmakers and the governor are both elected by the people. There are also state judges. Many judges are not elected. They are chosen by the governor. Each state government meets in the state capital.

Our Country's Government

The United States government also has lawmakers, a leader, and judges. The people of each state elect lawmakers from their state. These lawmakers from all the states together meet in Washington, D.C. to form the **Congress.** The Congress makes laws for the whole country.

The leader of our nation is the President of the United States. The President is elected, too. The citizens in our country help elect the President.

The President chooses the judges who are part of our country's government. Nine judges make up the **Supreme Court.** The Supreme Court is our most important court.

This picture shows President Ronald Reagan speaking to the Congress. Members of the Supreme Court are in the front row of the picture.

It is important for leaders to know how citizens feel about their government. Here, California lawmaker Barbara Boxer meets with citizens.

You have read how lawmakers, leaders, and judges run our government. Citizens help run our government, too. They choose the people to be our leaders. They tell our government how they feel about what the government is doing. The people in our government have to listen if they want to be elected again.

Reading Check

1. What is the leader of a state called?
2. How is a state capital like Washington, D.C.?
3. What is the Congress of the United States? How is the Congress different from the Supreme Court?

FINDING THE INFORMATION YOU NEED

How do you find out information about things? There are a number of places you can look to find news and information.

Television and Radio News

News programs on television and radio can tell you what is going on in your community, your country, and the world. They bring you news very quickly. The news they bring you can be important.

For example, imagine that a big storm has hit your community. Your telephone does not work. You want to know whether your school has been closed because of the storm.

You can get a lot of information by watching television news programs.

To find out, you might listen to news on the radio. You may watch news on television. Perhaps the reporter tells you your school is closed for the day. Then you know that you should stay home.

Radio and television give news of our country and the world, too. These news reports are often very short. So when you need to know more about a news story, you must look somewhere else.

News in Newspapers

Newspapers are another place to find information. Newspapers cannot bring you news as fast as the television and radio stations can. However, stories in a newspaper are usually more complete.

A newspaper tells you more about community happenings than a television or a radio program does. A newspaper has news about community and world events. A newspaper also has sports stories. A newspaper tells about movies, television programs, and special radio programs.

Newspapers also have ads, or **advertisements,** in them. Stores and businesses pay to have the newspaper print their ads. Advertisements might give readers information such as where and when a sale is being held.

Information on Signs

Another way people get information about their community is by reading signs. For example, a ROAD CLOSED sign may tell you that a road is not safe to drive on. Signs tell people what the rules of a community are.

Information in Your Telephone Book

A telephone book can give you information. **Emergency** phone numbers are usually on the inside front cover of the phone book. These numbers tell you where to call if you see a fire or need police help quickly.

If you need help quickly, you can dial an emergency number on your phone.

Pages that tell about **first aid** are near the beginning of many telephone books. These pages tell you how to help someone who is hurt in an accident. These pages may also tell what to do in weather emergencies.

CHECKING YOUR SKILLS

Read the sentences below. Tell or write where you could find information in each of the cases.

1. You want to know whether you are allowed to ride your bicycle in the park.

2. It has been raining hard all day. Is the river that runs through your town going to flood?

3. Hurricanes sometimes happen where you live. You want to know what you should do in case of this weather emergency.

USING WORDS

Number your paper from 1 to 5. Use the words below to fill in the blanks. Use each word only once.

citizens
city council
laws
judges
elect

We are all ____(1) of the United States. People here can ____(2) people for the government. In many communities, we vote for our ____(3) and our ____(4). These people help make and carry out the ____(5) of our government.

REVIEWING FACTS

1. What are laws?
2. What are three parts of most governments?
3. What are some groups of people that work for the mayor of Santa Rosa?
4. What does the Board of Selectmen do in Newfane, Vermont?
5. How do citizens help run our government?

THINKING CRITICALLY

1. What are two important laws you know? Why are these laws important?
2. What would you want to talk about if your community had a town meeting?
3. A mayor is the leader of a community. The President is the leader of our country. How are their jobs the same? How are their jobs different?

PRACTICING SKILLS

1. **Making Choices**   A group of your friends wants to do something together on Saturday. List some of the things you all could choose to do. Tell how you think you should make your choice.
2. **Finding Information**   Decide where you could find out about each of these things.

   a. Whether there are any traffic problems on nearby roads
   b. What to do if someone is hurt
   c. What movie is showing at a nearby theater

CHAPTER 7

Communities Provide Services

Focus

One important job of government is to make laws. Another important job of government is to provide services for the people of a community. Services are things one person or group does for another.

The picture on this page shows people and places that provide services. Can you tell what some of these services are?

166

Look for these important words:

Key Words
- property
- crime
- detectives
- public property
- private property

Look for answers to these questions:

1. How did people meet their needs before there were community services?
2. Who chooses people to run community services?
3. How does a police department protect people and property?

1. COMMUNITY SERVICES PROTECT US

Long ago, many people lived on farms or in houses far from one another. They had to do many things for themselves. They made most of their own clothes. They had to build their own houses. Sometimes neighbors would come and help with big jobs. There were no community workers to do things for people.

Today we live together in communities. It does not make sense to do everything by ourselves. That is why communities provide services. Communities can provide more services than people working by themselves could.

Every community has services for its people. The people in community governments make sure these services run smoothly. They choose people to run the services. For example, they choose the heads of the police and fire departments.

Police Protection

The police department protects **property.** Property is land, buildings, and other things people own. One kind of property is **public property.** Public means open to all. Zoos, parks, libraries, and museums are kinds of public property. Anyone may visit them. They belong to everyone.

Another kind of property is **private property.** Homes and businesses are kinds of private property. It is part of the job of the police to see that private property is not entered without permission.

Public property belongs to everyone. You must be careful not to damage it.

You must respect private property. You may not enter private property without permission.

The police department also helps us in many other ways. Police officers direct traffic when the signals are broken. They help people when their cars have trouble on the roads. Sometimes they give us directions when we are lost. They help keep our community a safe place to live and play.

You can find police officers easily. Most communities have police stations. These are places where police officers are on duty 24 hours a day, every day. There they work at many different jobs.

Directing traffic is one important job police officers have. Here, an officer directs people and cars on a busy street.

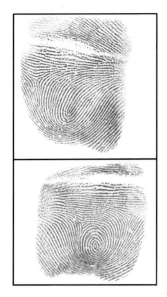

After this store was robbed, Detective Lewis brushed the cash register for fingerprints. This may help the police find the person who did the crime.

The police do not stay just in the station. Sometimes they walk in the community to make sure everything is safe. They drive around the community in police cars, too. Then they can move quickly if there is a call for help or a **crime.** A crime is something that is against the law.

Sometimes when there is a crime, the police do not know who did it. So, specially trained **detectives** try to find out. They ask questions and look for clues. The tiniest bit of cloth or a fingerprint might lead to the person who did the crime.

Reading Check

1. Who makes sure community services run smoothly?
2. What are some services police officers provide?
3. How do detectives help us?

Look for these important words:

Key Words
- hazards
- crew

Places
- Orlando, Florida

Look for answers to these questions:

1. What do fire fighters do when they first get to the fire station?
2. Why do fire fighters study the streets in their part of the city?
3. Why do fire fighters visit different homes and businesses?

2. A FIRE DEPARTMENT IN ORLANDO, FLORIDA

Orlando is a city in the middle of **Florida.** Plains cover much of Florida. The climate in Florida is warm and rainy.

There are many beautiful lakes and parks in Orlando, Florida. Across this lake, you can see some buildings in the city.

171

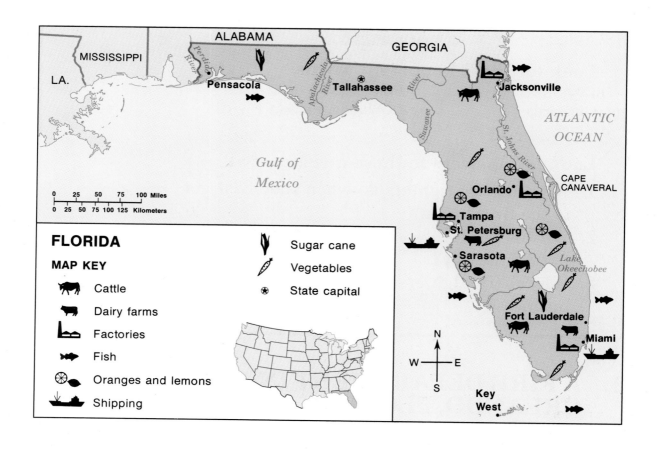

FLORIDA

MAP KEY

- 🐄 Cattle
- 🐄 Dairy farms
- 🏭 Factories
- 🐟 Fish
- 🍊 Oranges and lemons
- ⛴ Shipping
- 🌿 Sugar cane
- 🥕 Vegetables
- ✪ State capital

Baby Shamu and Kandu are stars in the whale show at Sea World in Orlando.

Visitors are the most important industry in Florida. Orlando is a very important visitor center. There are many places to see, such as Walt Disney World and Sea World. Cape Canaveral, where space ships blast off, is near Orlando.

Orlando has many community services. One of these services is the fire department.

Fire fighters in Orlando go to the fire stations at 8:00 A.M. The first thing they do is put their work things on the trucks. They also check all the equipment on the trucks. They make sure the hoses and ladders are ready to go.

The fire fighters go to a special school in the morning, too. They have classes in the newest ways to fight fires and save lives.

172

A Visit to a Fire Station

In the afternoon, a class from the neighborhood school may visit the fire station. The children get to see how the fire fighters live and work. A fire fighter shows them the equipment on the truck. He or she tells them how it works.

The fire fighter also tells the children how to spot fire **hazards** in their homes. A hazard is a danger. A fire hazard is something that could cause a fire. The children are told to make sure plugs and wires are not worn out. They are told not to put things that can catch fire near a flame or heater. The fire fighter tells the children to practice getting out of their homes quickly. That way, they will be ready if a fire happens.

Fire fighters sometimes visit schools. Below, the class listens as a fire fighter explains how to use a fire extinguisher.

Fire fighters in Orlando make sure their fire engines are clean and ready to be used.

The fire fighters may spend part of the afternoon studying the streets in their part of Orlando. They have to know if a street is closed for repairs. They need to know which streets are usually blocked with traffic.

Fire fighters also visit homes and businesses. They look for fire hazards and tell people how to get rid of them. Keeping fires from happening is a big part of a fire fighter's job.

At 8:00 A.M. the next morning, a new **crew,** or group, takes over at each fire station. The first crew gets three days off. Still, if there is a big fire and help is needed, they will be there to protect the people of Orlando.

Reading Check

1. Why do many people visit Orlando, Florida?
2. Why do fire fighters go to a special school?
3. Why is it important to know about fire hazards? Name two fire hazards.

SKILLS FOR SUCCESS

USING MAPS AND GRIDS

A **grid** shows lines that cross one another. Grids use letters and numbers to help you find things. Look at the grid below.

The pictures in this grid are symbols you might find on the map of a community. Put your finger on the number 1. Now move it down until your finger is even with the letter D. Your finger should be on the box with the symbol for "river" in it. This square is called box D-1. Now find the tree on the grid. Look at the top of the column. The number 4 is there. Look across to the letters. The letter C is across from the tree. What box is the tree in? Find box B-3. What is in it?

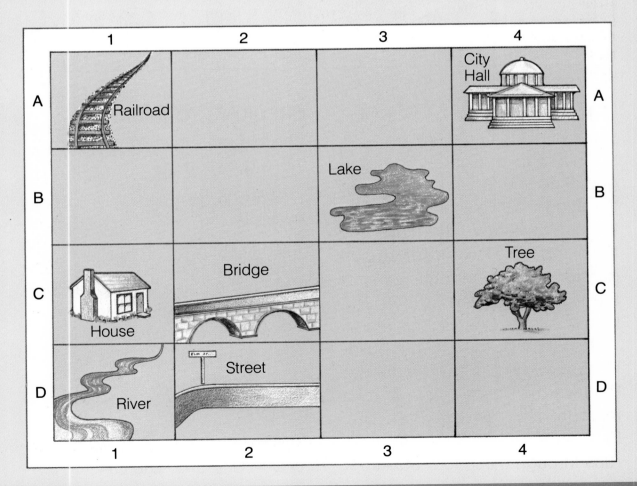

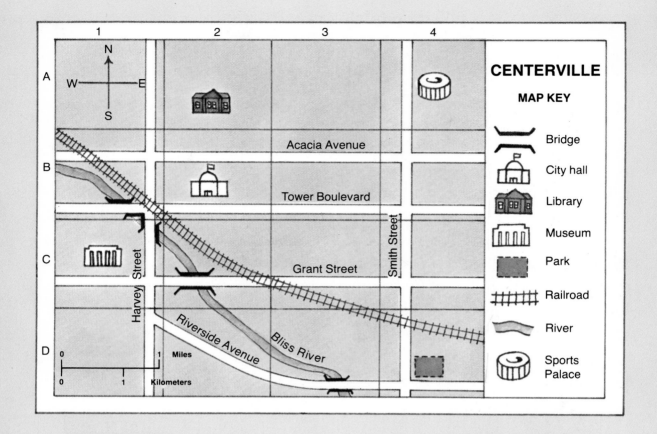

Maps often have grids to help you find places on them.

This map of Centerville has a grid. Find the library and put your finger on it. Move your finger up to the number above the map. It is the number 2. Now move your finger from the library to the letter at the side of the map. It is A. The library is in box A-2 on this map.

Now find box C-1. What building is shown in that box? Find Tower Boulevard. Notice that it runs through four boxes—B-1, B-2, B-3, and B-4. What other road runs through these four boxes?

CHECKING YOUR SKILLS

Use the map to help you answer these questions.

1. What large building is in box A-4?

2. In which box is City Hall?

3. Find the place where the Bliss River goes under the bridge at Grant Street. What box is the bridge in?

4. What things do you see in box D-4?

5. What road runs through boxes D-1, D-2, D-3, and D-4?

Look for these important words:

Key Words
- public works
- reservoirs
- sewage
- sewage treatment plants
- public transportation
- clinics
- board of education

Look for answers to these questions:

1. What does the public works department do?
2. What are two kinds of public transportation?
3. What does a board of education do?

3. MORE COMMUNITY SERVICES

The **public works** department provides services to meet our day-to-day needs. We depend on it for many things. Public works crews see that the streets are kept clean and in good repair.

City workers in New York are laying down bricks for a new crosswalk.

177

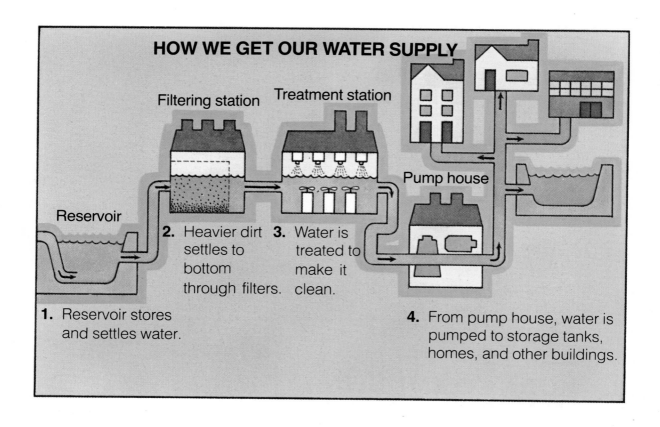

HOW WE GET OUR WATER SUPPLY

Filtering station

Treatment station

Pump house

Reservoir

1. Reservoir stores and settles water.

2. Heavier dirt settles to bottom through filters.

3. Water is treated to make it clean.

4. From pump house, water is pumped to storage tanks, homes, and other buildings.

Water is cleaned at a sewage treatment plant.

Whenever you turn on the faucet in your house, you expect clean, fresh water to come out. Public works crews make sure this happens. They put in pipes to pump water from rivers or **reservoirs** (REZ•urv•wahrz). A reservoir is a lake used for collecting and storing water. The crews treat the water to make it clean.

Public works departments take care of the waste water from homes, businesses, and streets. This waste water is called **sewage**. It is carried in pipes to buildings called **sewage treatment plants.** Sewage treatment plants clean the water before returning it to the rivers. That way, the sewage does not hurt fish, plants, or animals.

In some communities, the public works department collects garbage. If garbage is not removed, it can be a health hazard.

Transportation Services

Do you take a city bus to school? If so, you are using **public transportation.** Buses and trains are two kinds of public transportation. They are another kind of service many communities provide to people. Buses and trains can carry many people. People pay money when they ride public transportation.

Health Services

Many communities have hospitals to care for people who are very hurt or sick. Most hospitals have emergency rooms. People can get help right away at a hospital emergency room.

Community **clinics** are also places that treat people who are hurt or ill. At many clinics there are doctors and dentists who can take care of the whole family.

Public transportation (left) and medical clinics (right) are two services that communities provide.

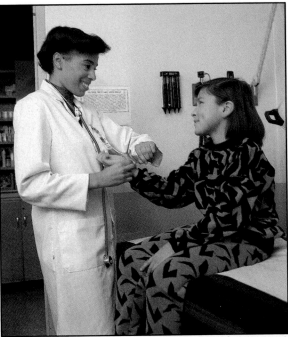

At a board of education meeting, people meet together to make decisions about how the schools should be run.

Public Schools

One community service you know about is the public school system. Most communities have a **board of education.** Its members are elected by the people of the community.

In many communities, it is up to the board of education to help choose teachers. The board decides how the schools should be run. The board does an important job. A good education gives people a good start in life.

Reading Check

1. Which department is in charge of a community's water supply?
2. Where can people go when they are very sick or hurt?
3. Why is the board of education important?

Look for these important words:

Key Words
- recreation

Places
- Durham, North Carolina

Look for answers to these questions:

1. What can you find out about at a library? What, besides books, do libraries often have?
2. What services are provided by the parks and recreation department?
3. Where, besides libraries, can people go to learn about many things?

4. LIBRARIES, PARKS, AND MUSEUMS

Do frogs have toes? How long would it take to get to Mars? Whatever you want to know, you can usually find out about at your public library.

Librarians are there to help you. They can help you find books on just about anything that interests you. Some libraries also have records, films, and pictures you can borrow.

A librarian can help you answer questions and find information.

181

Parks and Recreation

Many communities have parks and public gardens. People can go to these places to enjoy nature and open space. This is especially important to city people. They often live in apartments or houses without gardens.

Parks give people a place to play, too. A community's parks and **recreation** (rek•ree•AY•shuhn) department provides many services. Recreation is something you do for enjoyment. Reading, playing games, and listening to music are all kinds of recreation.

Parks and recreation departments take care of community swimming pools. They also take care of baseball diamonds, basketball and tennis courts, and golf courses. In the summer, the parks and recreation department offers special programs for children.

The children below are keeping cool and learning how to swim at their community pool.

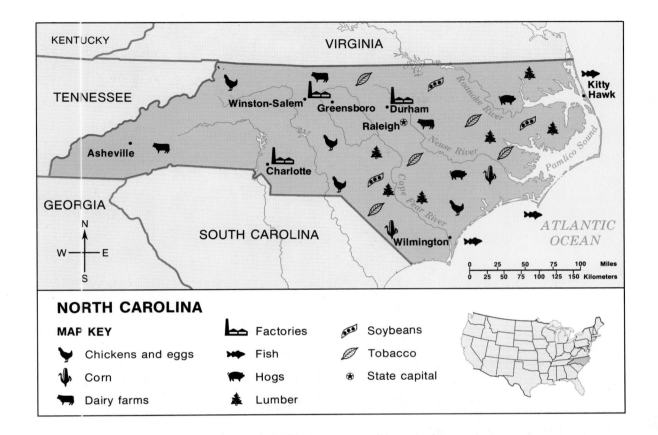

A Museum in North Carolina

Durham, North Carolina, is a medium-sized city. North Carolina is in the eastern part of our country. Durham is famous for its very fine museum. The museum is the North Carolina Museum of Life and Science.

Many school classes come to visit the North Carolina Museum of Life and Science. Let us join one class on its visit.

First, the students are greeted in the main building by a museum guide. The guide tells the visitors about things in the museum.

The students go to a room to hear a talk about the space program. After the talk, the students see many things from our space program. The Durham museum has a large space exhibit.

Children with hearing problems use sign language to discuss airplanes at the Durham museum.

So much is going on at the Durham museum. The students cannot see it all in one day. There is a wildflower trail, a wildlife area, and a small railroad. Computer classes are given. There are classes on protecting animal and plant life—and much, much more.

Reading Check

1. Why are parks important?
2. What is recreation?
3. Name two reasons why classes visit the North Carolina Museum of Life and Science.

Look for these important words:

Key Words
- taxes
- property tax
- sales tax
- volunteer

Look for answers to these questions:

1. How is tax money used?
2. Do large communities or small communities usually get more tax money? Why?
3. What is a volunteer? How do volunteers give community services?

5. TAXES PAY FOR COMMUNITY SERVICES

Community services cost money. The people who work to give people these services must be paid. Equipment must be bought, too.

Where does money that pays for community services come from? Most of it comes from the people in a community. People in communities pay **taxes.** A tax is money people pay to support their government and its services.

One kind of tax that brings money to communities is the **property tax.** This is a tax on the land and buildings a person owns.

Another kind of tax is a **sales tax.** Many states have this kind of tax. People in these states pay a sales tax every time they buy something. The amount they pay as sales tax may be something like five cents for every dollar. So, when a person

Look at the sales slip. How much is the tax?

185

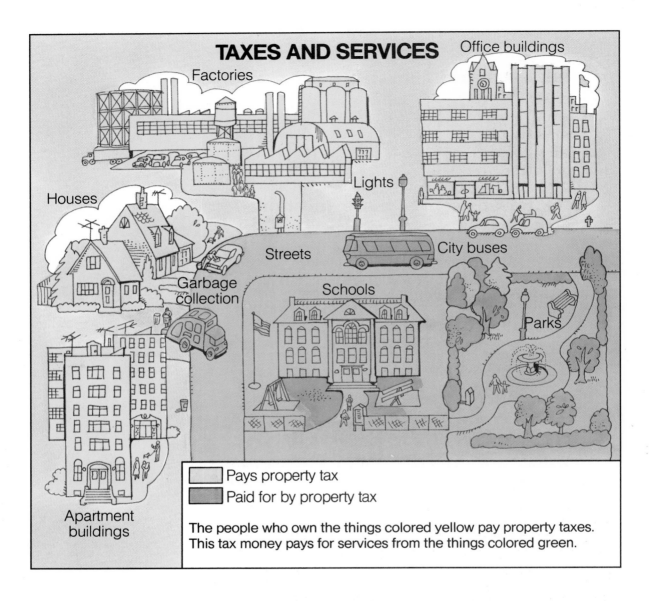

TAXES AND SERVICES

Office buildings

Factories

Lights

Houses

Streets

City buses

Garbage collection

Schools

Parks

Apartment buildings

Pays property tax

Paid for by property tax

The people who own the things colored yellow pay property taxes. This tax money pays for services from the things colored green.

buys goods for $10.00, the tax would be fifty cents. The total cost is then $10.50.

Large communities usually get more tax money because there are more people, stores, and other property. So large communities can often provide more services than small communities.

Each community must decide how to spend its money. Community governments must make choices based on the needs and interests of the people.

186

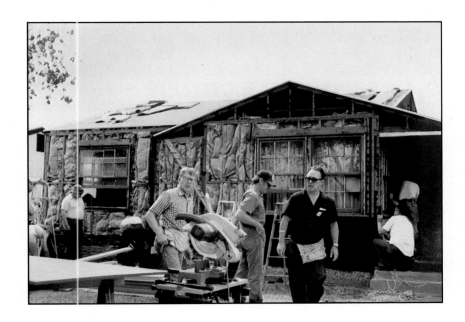

People in Midland, Texas, are helping fix a house during "Christmas in April."

Volunteer Community Services

Most community services are paid for by taxes. However, many communities also have another kind of community service—**volunteer** services. A volunteer is a person who offers to do something for free.

Do you remember the oil-drilling community of Midland, Texas? Every April, people in Midland volunteer their own time and money to a project called "Christmas in April." For one weekend, hundreds of volunteers work together to help people in need. During one "Christmas in April," volunteers repaired more than 120 homes for needy people.

Reading Check

1. What are taxes?
2. How are people who work in community services paid?
3. How do volunteers help communities?

SKILLS FOR SUCCESS

BEING A RESPONSIBLE CITIZEN

Communities provide many kinds of services. They give people police and fire protection. They build roads and bridges. They run libraries, schools, and hospitals. Communities provide parks.

You have a right to use these services because you are a member of your community. But you also must obey the rules and laws that go along with using community services.

When you follow rules and laws, you are being a responsible, or good, citizen. You are making it easier for people to do their jobs.

Following Rules

Each community has its own set of rules and laws about using its services. Many of the rules are like the ones you will read about here.

Here are some rules that many schools have.

- Take care of school books and other equipment.

- Do not run in the halls.

- Talk only when you are asked to in the classroom.

- Keep the cafeteria or eating area neat.

The students in Mrs. Colbert's class are following a rule. Before they speak in class, they raise their hands and wait to be called upon.

Community parks and swimming pools have rules. Read the following ones and think about why each is important.

- Keep the park clean. Put your litter in the special baskets provided.

- Play sports only in places where signs say you can.

- Share tennis courts and playground equipment.

- Do not run in the pool area.

Rules like these are made for reasons. For example, it would be dangerous to play baseball in a place where small children play. Someone could get in the way and be hurt.

Here are some rules for fire safety at home or school. Think about why you should follow each of them.

- Do not put matches on hot stoves or pipes.

- Keep a screen in front of the fireplace.

- Do not let papers or rags pile up anywhere.

- Keep gasoline, paints, and paint thinner away from heat. These liquids catch fire easily.

How are the children in this picture being responsible citizens?

What fire safety rule is being followed in this picture?

A guard is helping these children cross a busy street safely. Drivers follow safety rules by stopping when they see her sign.

Following Laws

There are many rules and laws for safety. Here are a few of them.

- Never play in streets.

- Cross streets only at corners. Look both ways before crossing.

- Never try to cross a street when you hear a police car or fire engine coming.

- Always do what a police officer tells you.

- Always do what a fire fighter tells you.

- Never call an emergency fire or police number unless there is a real emergency.

CHECKING YOUR SKILLS

Tell or write the answers to these questions.

1. What are two rules schools have?

2. Why should you not run at swimming pools?

3. Why should you do what a fire fighter tells you?

4. Why should you look both ways before crossing a street?

CLOSE-UP

THE SAN DIEGO ZOO

The big yellow school buses pull into the parking lot and the children jump out. Already they can hear the peacocks and other animals. The children follow the sounds into the world-famous San Diego Zoo.

This zoo is in a park owned by the City of San Diego, California. The zoo is a service that the community provides to everybody. The zoo was started in 1916 with just a few animals. Today it has one of the biggest collections of animals and plants in the world.

ANIMALS IN THE ZOO		
Animal	Foods Needed	Natural Home
aardvark	ants, termites	Africa
flamingo	shellfish, algae, small water plants	many places such as South America, Africa, West Indies
giraffe	leaves, twigs, fruit from high trees	Africa
kangaroo	plants	Australia, New Guinea
orangutan	fruit, leaves	Indonesia

191

Animals from many parts of the world live at the San Diego Zoo. The elephant in this picture first lived in Africa.

Most of the animals in the zoo live in big areas. The zoo makes these areas as much like the animals' natural homes as it can. This gives visitors a chance to learn how the animals behave in nature. The animals are happier and healthier this way, too.

Animals and Escapes

Keeping animals in their areas is not always easy. The orangutans (uh·RANG·uh·tanz) are a good example. They are very good at getting out of places they are supposed to stay in.

192

This is one of the orangutans at the zoo.

In 1975, a group of five orangutans was moved into a new area of the zoo. Within a few months, they escaped from their area. Swinging on a net from their jungle gym, an orangutan grabbed a bamboo branch. The bamboo branch was growing outside the orangutan area. The orangutans used this branch as a ladder. Two of them climbed up and out. They did not seem interested in going too far—just out.

The giraffes are much easier to keep in their area. Giraffes are very heavy on top. Their legs are very long and thin. Giraffes do not like to step down into things. So workers dug a ditch that is only 5 feet (about 1.5 m) deep around the giraffe area. The giraffes do not try to get away.

At about 18 feet tall, giraffes are the tallest animals alive.

The pictures above show the huge birdcage at the San Diego Zoo.

The Biggest Birdcage

Birds are a different case. The question is how to keep them inside the zoo and still give them flying room. The zookeeper's answer was to build one of the biggest birdcages in the world.

The cage holds the zoo's collection of South American birds. Walking inside the cage is like entering a jungle. The cage is thick with trees and flowering plants. The cries of the colorful birds fill the air.

Animals in the Nursery

Animals living in zoos do not always act as they would outside the zoo. In the wild, most animal mothers care for their young. In the zoo, though, sometimes they cannot or will not. Then the babies are taken to the zoo nursery. They are raised by people.

194

At the left, a zoo worker feeds a baby aardvark. At the right, a baby spider monkey peeks out from its blankets.

"NO ONE IS ALLOWED IN," says the sign on the nursery door. This sign is very important. Many times the baby animals brought to the nursery are sick or weak. Baby animals can catch colds or flu from humans. So only nursery workers are allowed inside.

Visitors can watch what is going on through big windows. At first, the zoo nursery looks like a regular nursery. There are cribs with blankets, toys, and bottles. But tucked neatly under a special heat lamp is a tiny aardvark. A baby chimp is getting its last bottle of the day.

The big yellow buses roll out of the parking lot at the end of the day. The last visitors leave. In the nursery the light stays on. A baby spider monkey is being rocked to sleep.

195

USING WORDS

Number your paper from 1 to 5. Match the words with their meanings.

1. **reservoir**
2. **hazard**
3. **taxes**
4. **recreation**
5. **property**

a. A danger
b. A lake used for collecting and storing water
c. Things you do for enjoyment
d. The land, buildings, and other things people own
e. Money that people pay to support their government and its services

REVIEWING FACTS

1. Why do communities provide services?
2. What community departments help protect people?
3. What department provides mostofourday-to-dayservices?
4. How are community services paid for?

5. What happens at "Christmas in April" in Midland, Texas?

THINKING CRITICALLY

1. What two community services do you think are most important? Explain your answers.
2. Pretend that your community has enough money to build either a public library or a new park. Which do you think should be built? Why?
3. Have you ever been to a museum? Why are museums important?
4. What kind of community service worker would you like to be? Why?

⬤ PRACTICING SKILLS

Being a Responsible Citizen
Here are three rules. Find out and tell why you should obey each rule.

a. Be quiet in a library
b. Never put your hand or arm out the window of a bus
c. Do not swim where signs tell you not to swim

UNIT 3 REVIEW

WORDS TO REMEMBER

Number your paper from 1 to 10. Use the words below to fill in the blanks. Use each word only once.

citizens   **public works**
courts   **sales tax**
crime   **town meeting**
government
hazards
laws
public transportation

1. Lawmakers, leaders, and judges are part of our ____.

2. Some people in government make our ____.

3. When we obey laws, we are being good ____.

4. People in Newfane, Vermont have a ____ once a year.

5. The places where judges work are called ____.

6. Police move quickly when they hear about a ____.

7. Plugs and wires that are worn out are fire ____.

8. The ____ department sees that streets are clean and in good repair.

9. You are using ____ when you take a train somewhere.

10. When you buy something at a store, you usually pay a ____.

FOCUS ON MAIN IDEAS

1. Why is it important to obey laws in a community?

2. How is the government of a city different from the government of a small town?

3. How do we choose our government?

4. Who makes the laws for our country?

5. What is the most important court in our country?

6. How does the police department help your community?

7. Name two services of the public works department.

8. What kinds of recreation do communities provide?

9. How do taxes help communities?

10. How and why are community services in a big city different from those in a town?

Make a list of the branches of government in your state and country. Then write a paragraph telling how your state's government is like our country's government.

ACTIVITIES

1. **Research** Find out more about your community's government. Who are its leaders? Who makes the laws?

2. **Art/Bulletin Board** Cut out or draw pictures of parks, libraries, zoos, houses, and businesses. Display them on the bulletin board. Under each picture, write whether it is public property or private property.

SKILLS REVIEW

1. **Finding Information** Suppose your community is having a fair. Name two places where you might find out when the fair is being held and what kinds of things will happen there.

2. **Using Maps and Grids** The following grid map shows part of a town called Green Hill. Answer these questions.

    a. In what square is City Hall?

    b. What is in square C-3?

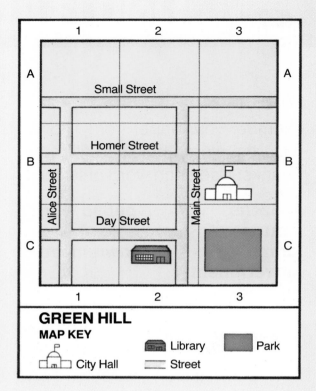

GREEN HILL
MAP KEY
City Hall   Library   Park   Street

3. **Making a Choice** Pretend that some students in your class would like to have a fish tank in your classroom. Other students do not think it is a good idea. Make a choice about the fish tank. Tell how and why you made your choice.

4. **Being a Responsible Citizen** Divide a piece of paper in half by drawing a line down the middle. On one side, make a list of ten rules or laws. Label this side "Being a Responsible Citizen." On the other side, list the reasons these laws and rules are important. Label this side "Why being a responsible citizen is important."

YOUR COMMUNITY

In Unit 3 you read about local, state, and our country's government. You also studied about community services, such as police and fire departments. Now find out more about these services in your community.

LEARNING ABOUT SERVICES

1. Visit a museum, library, or park in your community. Report to your class about your visit.

LEARNING ABOUT GOVERNMENT

2. You want to be elected mayor of your community. Make an election poster for yourself. Tell what you want to do for your community.

3. Find out more about your community's government. Look through your community newspaper to find stories about your local government. Cut out any pictures or stories. With other students in your class, make a scrapbook showing your community government in action. Title your scrapbook "My Government At Work."

LEARNING ABOUT MAPS AND GRIDS

4. Find a grid map of your community. Use the map to tell where a police station, a fire station, and a school are.

LEARNING ABOUT VOLUNTEER SERVICES

5. Make a list of three volunteer services groups in your community. Find out what each group does. Choose one group that you would someday like to belong to. Explain what the group does and why you would like to belong to it.

TAKING A FIELD TRIP

6. With your class or parents, visit a fire station in your community. Ask the fire fighter what you can do to help keep your home and school safe from fire. Ask what you should do in case a fire does start. Draw a map showing the route you take when you have a fire drill in your school.

Community Facts and Figures

Location	Denver, Colorado	Plymouth, Massachusetts	Philadelphia, Pennsylvania
Population (estimated)	492,365	37,092	1,688,210
Nickname/Motto	Mile High City	Land of the Pilgrims	City of Brotherly Love
Landmark	Colorado Capitol Building	Plymouth Rock	Independence Hall

COMMUNITIES OF YESTERDAY, TODAY, AND TOMORROW

Look at the picture on page 200. Are there any old homes like these in your community? If the houses and buildings could talk, they might tell some interesting stories.

Of course, buildings cannot talk. However, we can learn about the past in other ways. We can learn by visiting places. We can talk to people who remember things that happened long ago.

In this unit, we will find out about the pasts of communities in the United States. We will see how communities change. We will think about how communities may be different in the future.

Location	Jamestown (historic Virginia)
Population (estimated)	100 men
Nickname/Motto	First Permanent English Settlement
Landmark	Old Church Tower

CHAPTER 8

Communities Grow and Change

Focus

In this chapter you will see how communities begin, grow, and change. You will look closely at the community of Denver, Colorado. You will look at how Denver began. You will see how it grew and changed over the years.

Look for these important words:

Key Words
- history
- trade centers
- crossroads

Look for answers to these questions:

1. What is history?
2. Why did many communities begin near water?
3. Why are communities still starting up now?

1. HOW COMMUNITIES BEGIN

History is the story of the past. Everything that has already happened is history.

All communities have histories. Many communities began long ago. Different communities began for different reasons.

Places Where Communities Began

Many communities began near water. Long ago, one of the main ways to travel was by boat. Goods were shipped by boat, too. A community near water was easy to reach. People could catch food from rivers, lakes, and oceans. They could water their crops with fresh water from rivers and lakes.

Later, railroads were built. Railroads made new places easy to reach. Many new communities started up where the railroads were built. Some became **trade centers**. Trade centers are places where people buy and sell many goods. The railroads carried many of these goods.

Communities also began at **crossroads.** Crossroads are places where main roads meet. Crossroads can also be places where railroads and roads meet. Perhaps a store was built at a crossroad. Soon people stayed at the crossroads instead of going on.

Many communities grew up near natural resources like coal and other minerals. Towns sprang up quickly in places where gold or oil was found. People came to earn money from mining these resources. They built communities.

New Communities Today

Today new communities are still starting. They often begin for the same reasons that communities began long ago. In Alaska, new communities are growing where oil has been found. Some new communities start near new businesses or industries. Some start up along new highways.

This small oil-drilling community in Alaska was built with many underground tunnels. People can travel within the community while being protected from the icy cold.

204

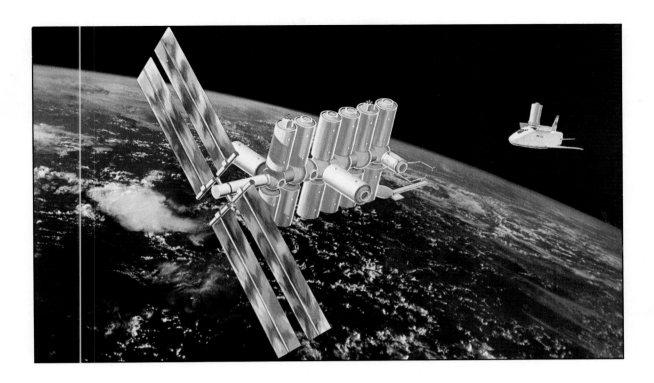

Other new communities are starting near big cities. This is because some cities have become too crowded or cost too much to live in. So people move outside the cities.

This picture shows an idea for a space station where people could live. The spaceship on the right would travel to and from Earth.

Communities of the Future

Communities will continue to start up. Someday there may be communities in space, high above the Earth. A space station is already planned. There would be places there for people to live, work, and grow food.

Reading Check

1. How did railroads help our country grow?
2. Why did communities begin near places that had gold and coal?
3. Where might there be communities someday?

Look for these important words:

Key Words
- ghost towns
- tepees
- Arapaho Indians
- Plains Indians

- buffalo

Places
- Denver, Colorado
- Rocky Mountains

Look for answers to these questions:

1. Who first lived where Denver is now?
2. What animal did the Plains Indians use to meet their needs?
3. What important jobs did Arapaho women have?

2. DENVER, COLORADO— THE EARLY YEARS

Communities begin in different ways. They also grow in different ways. Some communities start small and grow into large cities. Others do not grow much at all. Still other communities grow fast but then become **ghost towns.** Ghost towns are places where no one lives anymore.

Many ghost towns began as mining communities. When the mines were empty, people left the towns and moved to new places.

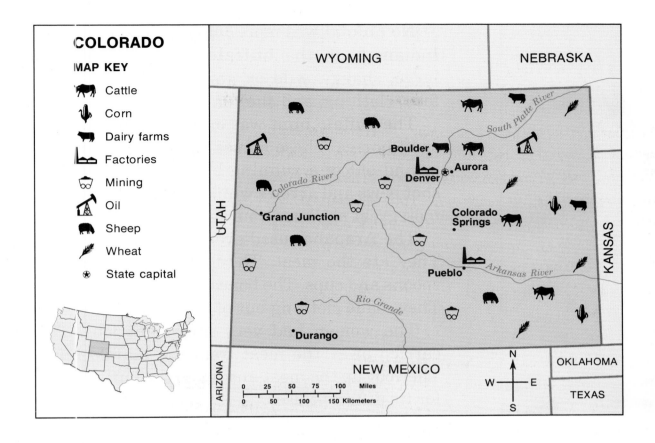

COLORADO

MAP KEY

🐂	Cattle
🌽	Corn
🐄	Dairy farms
🏭	Factories
🛒	Mining
🛢	Oil
🐑	Sheep
🌾	Wheat
✪	State capital

WYOMING

NEBRASKA

South Platte River

Colorado River

Boulder

Denver ✪ Aurora

UTAH

Grand Junction

Colorado Springs

KANSAS

Pueblo

Arkansas River

Rio Grande

Durango

ARIZONA

NEW MEXICO

0	25	50	75	100	Miles
0	50	100	150	Kilometers	

N
W ✛ E
S

OKLAHOMA

TEXAS

We will now look at how one city has grown and changed. This city is **Denver, Colorado.** Denver is a city near the **Rocky Mountains.**

The Buffalo Hunters

American Indians were the first people to live where Denver is now. They were there long before others came to settle.

The **Arapaho** (uh•RAP•uh•hoh) **Indians** lived in **tepees,** or cone-shaped tents. The Arapahos were **Plains Indians.** Plains Indians lived on the Great Plains east of the Rocky Mountains. The Arapahos moved from place to place and followed the animals they hunted. In the winter, they settled in camps or villages.

The Indians made pottery from clay which they dug from the ground.

207

No animal was more important to the Plains Indians than the **buffalo** (BUHF•uh•loh). This large, shaggy, wild ox gave the Plains Indians food, clothing, and shelter.

The buffalo hunt was exciting. The men rode swift horses. These horses were trained to move in and out of a running buffalo herd. The men shot bows and arrows while riding fast. The hunt took great skill and courage.

The Arapahos used every part of the buffalo. They ate the meat. They made the horns into spoons and cups. The bones were made into tools. They made clothing out of the skins.

The women had very important jobs. They carried away the meat from the buffalo hunts. They cut up the meat and made the buffalo ready for its different uses.

The Plains Indians hunted buffalo for food, and for the hides which they made into shelter and clothing.

208

This picture shows Indians working on the hide of a buffalo. The tepees in the picture are also made of buffalo skins.

The women used the buffalo skins to make the tepees, too. First, they sewed several skins together. Then they stretched the skins over poles set up in the shape of a cone. The tepees could be moved easily. When the Arapahos moved to where the buffaloes were, they took their tepees along with them.

Reading Check

1. What kind of American Indians were the Arapahos?
2. How did the Arapaho way of life depend on the buffalo?
3. How did Arapaho women make tepees?

Look for these important words:

Key Words
- gold pan
- gold dust

Look for answers to these questions:

1. Why was gold important to Denver?
2. Why did Denver become a trading center?
3. How did miners get gold dust from rivers?

3. MINING IN DENVER

"Gold!" That was the cry that started the city of Denver. Gold was found in the sands of Cherry Creek in 1858. Many people came from other states to mine the gold.

A New Community

Soon a community of 25 cabins lined the banks of the creek. The community was not too far from the Arapaho village you just read about.

A store was opened right away. There was not much food, though. There were no farms close by, so food had to be brought from far away in wagons. This made food cost a lot. In fact, food was sometimes harder to find than gold.

The little mining community of Denver began growing fast. A lucky miner found more gold in nearby mountains. Then thousands of people came to the mountains in search of gold. Mining camps sprang up all around.

Because of its location, Denver became the trading center for all the mining camps. The miners came to buy food and tools. Denver soon had many stores, a hotel, and a bank. Denver's first newspaper was started. The people built a log cabin school for children.

Children learned to read and write at Denver's first schoolhouse.

Gold and Silver Mining

Many Mexicans were good at gold mining. They had been finding gold in Mexico for years. From them, gold miners in the West learned ways to mine gold. The Mexicans invented the **gold pan.** It had a wide, flat bottom and sloping sides. Miners used it to get loose grains of gold, called **gold dust,** from the rivers. Water was swished around in the pan. The sand went over the sides of the pan. The heavy grains of gold stayed in the bottom of the pan.

Miners looked for gold in the rivers of the West. Some found gold and became rich, but many found nothing.

211

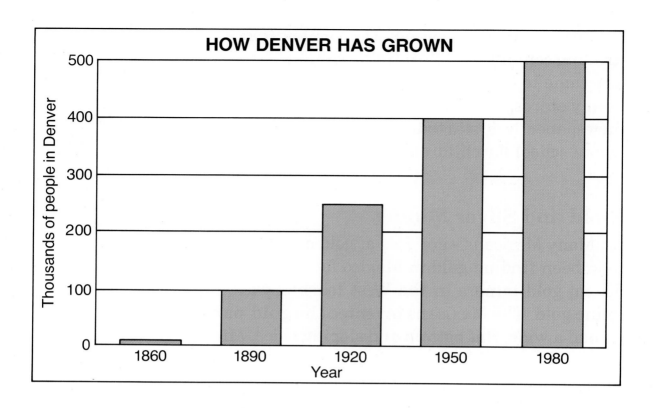

HOW DENVER HAS GROWN

Thousands of people in Denver

500 — 400 — 300 — 200 — 100 — 0

1860   1890   1920   1950   1980

Year

The Mexicans also had special ways to mine gold and silver from rock. They taught the Americans these mining skills, too.

In 1859, when gold and silver mining began, Denver had 5,000 people. Twenty years later, about 35,000 people lived there. Ten years after that, there were about 100,000 people!

By 1889, most of the gold and silver around Denver had been mined. By then, however, the people of Denver had other ways to make a living.

Reading Check

1. Why were stores, banks, and hotels first built in Denver?
2. Why did food in early Denver cost so much?
3. Who taught the miners ways to mine gold and silver?

Look for these important words:

Key Words

• spur
• aerospace
• manufactured

Look for answers to these questions:

1. When did the railroad come to Denver?
2. Why has Denver grown in the last thirty years?
3. What problems are people in Denver trying to solve?

4. MODERN DENVER

In 1870, the first train steamed into Denver. The people of Denver were proud. They had raised the money themselves to build the **spur,** or branch of the railroad.

The railroad linked Denver to the rest of the country. Goods could be brought in and out easily. People could travel to Denver more easily, too.

After the railroad was built, people watched for the trains that brought visitors and trade to Denver.

213

The railroad also made Denver into a market for cattle and farm crops. The ranchers of the Great Plains could now use the railroad. Trains carried their cattle and sheep to Denver. The farmers of the Plains could use the railroad, too. The railroad carried their wheat, corn, and sugar beets to Denver.

Denver Today

For the last 30 years Denver has been growing faster. One reason for Denver's new growth is the **aerospace** (AIR•oh•spays) industry. Aerospace means having to do with air and space. The aerospace industry makes planes and spacecraft.

In Denver today, many different kinds of goods are **manufactured,** or made in factories. These goods include foods, sporting goods, computers, and machines for transportation. There are a lot of different, new jobs for the people of Denver.

Denver, Colorado's capital, is an important transportation and manufacturing center for the whole Rocky Mountain area.

Denver is also well known for its location. Thousands of people come every year to ski and hike in the Rocky Mountains.

Much of Denver's new growth happened because oil, coal, and other resources were found in the Rocky Mountain area. Some people in Denver worry that their city might be growing too fast. They worry about the air that people breathe and the water that they drink. They are looking for ways to keep their air and water clean. People in Denver are used to solving problems, though. Several years ago, downtown Denver was full of old, run-down buildings. Today most of these buildings have been fixed up.

Skiing is a popular sport in the Rocky Mountains near Denver.

Reading Check

1. How did the railroad help Denver's people?
2. What goods does the aerospace industry make?
3. Why do Denver's citizens worry about the city growing too fast?

SKILLS FOR SUCCESS

USING PICTURES TO TELL A STORY

The first photograph was made about 150 years ago. Before that time the only way to make a picture was to paint or draw one.

The picture at the bottom of this page was painted before cameras were widely used.

Look at this picture carefully. The picture shows how the Plains Indians lived long ago. You can tell that the picture shows a scene from long ago. There are no modern houses or clothing. There are no television antennas or wires for electricity or telephones.

People still paint pictures today. But you can usually tell whether a painting is very old or new. For example, if a painting shows people in modern clothes, you know the picture cannot be very old.

Photographs

Early photographs did not have color. They could only show things in black, white, and gray. The top picture on the next page is a photograph of Denver, Colorado. It was taken in 1860.

This picture was taken when people used horses and wagons. The streets were made of dirt. The buildings do not look much like the ones we see today.

This picture was painted in 1850. It shows Indian groups on the Great Plains, near where Denver is now.

The photograph at the bottom of this page was taken 40 years later in Denver.

You can tell that this photograph is newer than the top one. You can see cars, street lamps, and wires and tracks for electric streetcars. The buildings in the bottom picture look different from the ones in the 1860 picture, too.

You can tell that the picture at the bottom is not a modern scene, though. The people are wearing old-fashioned clothes. How else can you tell that it is not a modern picture?

This picture of Denver was taken in 1860.

This picture of Denver was taken in 1900.

This picture shows Denver as it looks today. What are some things that tell you it is a new picture?

Now look at this photograph of Denver. The photograph was taken just a few years ago. You can see modern buildings in the background. Modern cars drive down a wide street. The photograph is in color. It shows what Denver looks like today.

CHECKING YOUR SKILLS

Use the pictures to help you answer these questions.

1. Look at the painting on page 216. What clues tell you that it is an old picture?

2. Look at the photograph on this page. What clues tell you that it is a new picture?

3. What are some ways that you can tell whether a photograph is old or new?

4. Has Denver gotten bigger or smaller since 1860? What in the pictures makes you think the way you do?

5. Look at the date of the painting in the first picture. Why didn't the painter use a camera instead of a paintbrush to make this picture?

USING WORDS

Number your paper from 1 to 5. Match the words with their meanings.

1. **aerospace**
2. **history**
3. **spur**
4. **tepees**
5. **trade centers**

a. The story of the past
b. Places where people buy and sell many goods
c. Cone-shaped tents
d. Branch of a railroad
e. Having to do with air and space

REVIEWING FACTS

1. Where do communities often begin? Name three places.
2. How did Arapahos meet their needs for food, clothing, and shelter?
3. Why did people from other parts of the country first come to Denver?
4. How did a gold pan work?
5. Why is Denver a big city today? What do people do there?

THINKING CRITICALLY

1. What was life like for the Arapaho Indians? How were the jobs the women did different from the jobs the men did?
2. A lot of communities near Denver became ghost towns when the gold ran out. Why didn't Denver become a ghost town? How did Denver change after the gold-mining days?
3. Why was the railroad important to Denver?
4. What might it be like to live in a community that is growing very fast? What would be some good things about having many new people there? What problems might be caused when the community grows? How might these problems be prevented?

⬤ PRACTICING SKILLS

Using Pictures Choose a photograph or a painting from this chapter. Do not use a picture from the skills lesson. Tell whether the picture is from long ago or now. Tell how you know.

CHAPTER 9

Our Country Has a History

Focus

Like communities, countries have histories. Our country has a long and proud history. In this chapter we will look at the history of the United States. We will also read about some of our holidays. We will see how our country became strong and free.

Look for these important words:

Key Words
- Navajo Indians
- Columbus Day
- explorers
- claimed

People
- Christopher Columbus
- Amerigo Vespucci
- John Cabot

Look for answers to these questions:

1. How did American Indians live long ago? Why were there differences in the ways they lived?
2. Why did Christopher Columbus cross the Atlantic Ocean?
3. Why did explorers come to America?
4. What countries claimed land in America?

1. EARLY YEARS IN AMERICA

Long ago, American Indian groups lived in almost every part of our country. The way a group lived depended on where it was and what resources were nearby.

For example, **Navajo** (NA•vuh•hoh) **Indians** lived in Arizona and New Mexico. There it is often warm and sunny. The Navajo Indians raised crops for food. Corn was one important food they grew. The Navajos also hunted for food.

Some Indian groups lived near the ocean in the state of Washington. Their land had thick forests and many rivers. These Indian groups built large houses of wood. They built big wooden boats. They sailed these boats on the rivers and on the ocean. They caught fish for food and they hunted whales.

Navajo shelters are called hogans (HOH•gunz). Hogans are made of earth and wood.

221

The Indians in this painting lived near the Great Lakes. They are picking wild strawberries for food.

There were many more Indian groups in America. These groups were different from each other in many ways. Their names were different. Their languages were different. Their ways of getting food were different. They built different kinds of shelters. Yet each group was able to meet the needs of its people.

Columbus Sails to America

In 1492, almost 500 years ago, **Christopher Columbus** sailed from Spain, in Europe. Christopher Columbus wanted to find a new way to get to China from Europe. He decided to try to cross the Atlantic Ocean.

Columbus and his crew did not reach China. Instead, they found a land that people in Europe did not know about. They found the land that we call America.

After two long months at sea, Columbus was glad to find land. Taking a flag ashore, he said the land belonged to Spain.

The day that Columbus first landed in America was October 12, 1492. Today we have a holiday in October to celebrate the landing. It is called **Columbus Day.** On that day we remember when Columbus landed in America.

Explorers in America

News of Columbus's discovery spread through Europe. Many other sailors from Europe set out across the Atlantic Ocean. They hoped to find gold and other treasures. They were **explorers.** Explorers traveled to new lands. They brought back stories of what they had found.

One of these explorers was an Italian named **Amerigo Vespucci** (ahm•uh•REE•goh veh•SPOO•chee). Later, America was named after him.

This painting shows Amerigo Vespucci as a young man.

223

The picture on the left shows John Cabot, an explorer for England. The picture on the right shows Robert La Salle, who claimed land in America for France.

John Cabot sailed from England five years after Columbus found America. Cabot sailed along the northern coast of America. He told the king of England about the lands he had discovered. The king of England then **claimed** these lands for England. This means that he said that these lands belonged to England.

French explorers also came to America. They sailed up and down the Mississippi, St. Lawrence, and Missouri rivers. They sailed the Great Lakes. They claimed much land for France.

Meanwhile, Spanish explorers were finding gold in the southern parts of America. They claimed much land for Spain.

Reading Check

1. How did American Indians in the state of Washington get their food?
2. When did Columbus land in America?
3. How did America get its name?

Look for these important words:

Key Words | People | Places
- settlers
- Mayflower
- Pilgrims
- Thanksgiving
- slaves

People
- John Smith
- Squanto

Places
- Jamestown
- Plymouth

Look for answers to these questions:

1. What are two communities that settlers started in America?
2. How did the Pilgrims meet their needs?
3. What were slaves? How were they not free?

2. SETTLERS COME TO AMERICA

In 1607 a group of people sailed to America from England. They were **settlers,** not explorers. Settlers are people who go somewhere to live. These people decided to start a community in what is now the state of Virginia.

Jamestown

The new community was called **Jamestown.** The community did not do well at first. People built shelters that did not keep out the rain or cold. They did not spend enough time planting crops and meeting their needs.

Then a person named **John Smith** became the leader of the community. He made people build better shelters. He sent them to plant crops. Soon the community was doing much better.

The picture below shows John Smith, the leader of Jamestown.

The Pilgrims

Another group of settlers came to America in 1620. They sailed from England on a ship called the **Mayflower.** The Mayflower landed at a place called **Plymouth,** in what is now Massachusetts.

These settlers were called **Pilgrims.** Pilgrims wanted to be free to have their own beliefs. They wanted to build their own church.

The Pilgrims worked hard to build their new community. They had chosen a good place for their community. There was clear, fresh water for drinking. They were near a good harbor. They knew how to build good shelters. An American Indian named **Squanto** helped them grow food.

One year after they landed, the Pilgrims picked their first crops. Plymouth was doing well. The Pilgrims had a great celebration that November. They wanted to show how thankful they were for their new way of life. We celebrate this same holiday, **Thanksgiving,** every November.

At the first Thanksgiving, the Pilgrims shared food with the Indians who had helped them. The Indians brought gifts of food to the celebration.

Settlers cleared the land's thick forests and built their houses from wood. To get water, they dug wells.

Soon more and more people came to America. They came from England and France and the Netherlands and Sweden. In America they could own their own land and farm it. Soon people began building towns.

Slaves in America

One group of people in America was not free. People in this group were taken from their homes in Africa. They were brought by ship to America to work for other people. They did not get paid. They were **slaves.** Slaves were people who were owned by other people. Many slaves in America were put to work on large farms. They were often kept apart from their families.

Many Americans believed that slavery was wrong. Years later, a war was fought about this.

Reading Check

1. Who became the leader of Jamestown?
2. Why did the Pilgrims come to America?
3. Why did many think slavery was wrong?

Look for these important words:

Key Words
- colonies
- nation
- freedom
- Declaration of Independence
- American Revolution
- Fourth of July
- Constitution

People
- Thomas Jefferson
- George Washington

Look for answers to these questions:

1. In what part of America were the English colonies?
2. Why did Americans want to have freedom from England?
3. What was the Declaration of Independence?

3. A NEW COUNTRY IS BORN

By 1763 there were many communities in America. England now claimed much of the eastern part of North America. That is where most of the communities were. The land in America ruled by England was called the English **colonies.**

Laws in the Colonies

For a long time Americans did not mind being ruled by England. Then lawmakers in England began passing new laws for the colonies. Many of the colonists did not like these new laws. They did not like the taxes that England was making them pay. They also did not like being told what to do by people who lived so far away.

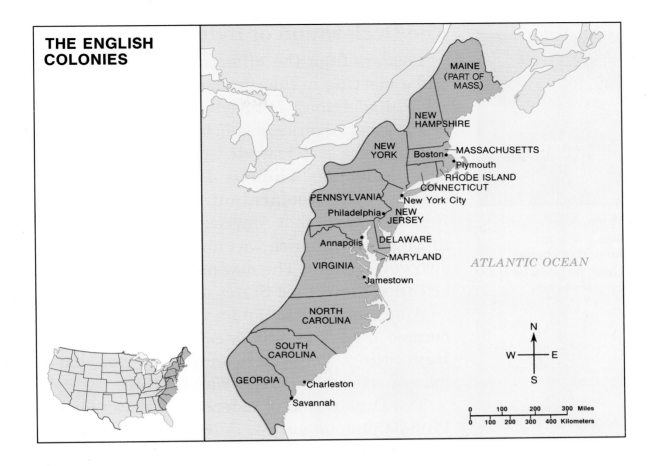

THE ENGLISH COLONIES

Many Americans felt that they could not obey the new laws or pay the new taxes that England wanted. People began talking about starting a new country, or **nation.** A nation is a land with a government of its own.

The Fighting Begins

In 1775 some American farmers fought against the soldiers from England. The farmers had decided that they needed to be free. They and other Americans decided to fight for **freedom.** Freedom to them meant having their own government in America. Freedom meant that they would be able to make their own laws.

The Declaration of Independence

Leaders from the different parts of America had a meeting in the summer of 1776. They met in Philadelphia, Pennsylvania. The leaders decided that America should become a new nation.

One of the leaders wrote a message to the world. This leader was **Thomas Jefferson.** His message was the **Declaration of Independence.** It told everyone that America no longer belonged to England. America was now a nation with its own government. The new nation would come to be called the United States of America.

Americans had to fight a war with England to become free. This war is called the **American Revolution.** The American soldiers were led in many battles by **George Washington.**

The Declaration of Independence was read in Philadelphia on July 4, 1776. Today the **Fourth of July** is one of our most important holidays. It is the birthday of our country.

Thomas Jefferson was a strong American leader. Later, he became our third President.

Leaders met in Philadelphia to vote for the Declaration of Independence.

A New Government

Americans wanted a government that would make fair rules. So our country's leaders got together again. They planned how the new government would work.

The leaders wrote laws for the government. These laws were called the **Constitution.** We still use the Constitution today.

Then Americans voted to elect their first President. They chose George Washington. We have a holiday in February to celebrate George Washington's birthday.

The picture above shows George Washington after he was elected President for the second time.

The famous picture below was painted by Gilbert Stuart in 1796.

Reading Check

1. Why didn't people in the colonies like being ruled by England?
2. What important message did Thomas Jefferson write?
3. Why was the Constitution written?

SKILLS FOR SUCCESS

READING CALENDARS AND TIMELINES

Look at this **calendar.** It shows days and months of the year. The months are arranged in three rows. You read each row from left to right.

January, February, March, and April are in the first row. May, the month that follows April, begins the second row. June follows May, July follows June, and August follows July. What month follows August?

Look at the month of January. It ends on Thursday. February starts on Friday. Each month starts on the day after the last day of the month before. March ends on a Sunday. On what day does April begin? On what day does May begin?

JANUARY	FEBRUARY	MARCH	APRIL
Su M Tu W Th F Sa	Su M Tu W Th F Sa	Su M Tu W Th F Sa	Su M Tu W Th F Sa
1 2 3 4 5	1 2,	1 2	1 2 3 4 5 6
6 7 8 9 10 11 12	3 4 5 6 7 8 9	3 4 5 6 7 8 9	7 8 9 10 11 12 13
13 14 15 16 17 18 19	10 11 12 13 14 15 16	10 11 12 13 14 15 16	14 15 16 17 18 19 20
20 21 22 23 24 25 26	17 18 19 20 21 22 23	17 18 19 20 21 22 23	21 22 23 24 25 26 27
27 28 29 30 31	24 25 26 27 28	24 25 26 27 28 29 30	28 29 30
		31	

MAY	JUNE	JULY	AUGUST
Su M Tu W Th F Sa	Su M Tu W Th F Sa	Su M Tu W Th F Sa	Su M Tu W Th F Sa
1 2 3 4	1	1 2 3 4 5 6	1 2 3
5 6 7 8 9 10 11	2 3 4 5 6 7 8	7 8 9 10 11 12 13	4 5 6 7 8 9 10
12 13 14 15 16 17 18	9 10 11 12 13 14 15	14 15 16 17 18 19 20	11 12 13 14 15 16 17
19 20 21 22 23 24 25	16 17 18 19 20 21 22	21 22 23 24 25 26 27	18 19 20 21 22 23 24
26 27 28 29 30 31	23 24 25 26 27 28 29	28 29 30 31	25 26 27 28 29 30 31
	30		

SEPTEMBER	OCTOBER	NOVEMBER	DECEMBER
Su M Tu W Th F Sa	Su M Tu W Th F Sa	Su M Tu W Th F Sa	Su M Tu W Th F Sa
1 2 3 4 5 6 7	1 2 3 4 5	1 2	1 2 3 4 5 6 7
8 9 10 11 12 13 14	6 7 8 9 10 11 12	3 4 5 6 7 8 9	8 9 10 11 12 13 14
15 16 17 18 19 20 21	13 14 15 16 17 18 19	10 11 12 13 14 15 16	15 16 17 18 19 20 21
22 23 24 25 26 27 28	20 21 22 23 24 25 26	17 18 19 20 21 22 23	22 23 24 25 26 27 28
29 30	27 28 29 30 31	24 25 26 27 28 29 30	29 30 31

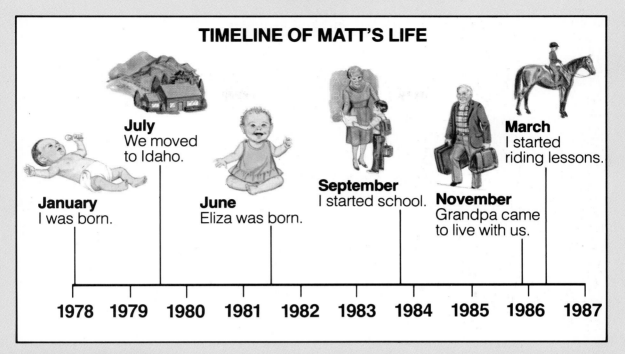

TIMELINE OF MATT'S LIFE

January
I was born.

July
We moved to Idaho.

June
Eliza was born.

September
I started school.

November
Grandpa came to live with us.

March
I started riding lessons.

1978   1979   1980   1981   1982   1983   1984   1985   1986   1987

Reading Timelines

In the study of history, we need to keep track of more than one year. So we use a **timeline.** A timeline can show a number of years at once. It can show when things happened.

The timeline above was made by a boy named Matt. It lists some important things that have happened in his life.

You read a timeline from left to right, just like a sentence. The events on the left happened the earliest. The events on the right happened later. The first thing on this timeline happened in 1978. Matt was born in that year. In 1981, Matt's sister was born. In 1983, Matt started school. The last thing on the timeline was that Matt started his riding lessons. In what year did that happen?

CHECKING YOUR SKILLS

Tell or write the answers to these questions.

1. Look at the calendar in this lesson. On what day of the week is the Fourth of July?

2. On what day of the week does October begin?

3. Look at the timeline on this page. Which happened first for Matt, getting a baby sister or starting school?

4. Did Matt move to Idaho before or after he started riding lessons?

Look for these important words:

Key Words
- reservations
- Civil War
- Memorial Day

People
- Abraham Lincoln

Look for answers to these questions:

1. Why did people move west after the American Revolution?
2. What happened to American Indians when settlers moved to their lands?
3. Why was Abraham Lincoln an important President?

4.   THE NEW NATION GROWS

The American Revolution took place in the eastern part of our country. Most Americans lived there at the time. However, some people had already moved west. After the American Revolution, more and more Americans moved west.

Many American settlers packed what they owned and headed west in wagons.

Colorful, wood-burning steamboats carried passengers and goods along the nation's large rivers.

Moving West

There was plenty of open land for farms in the West. People had to work hard to clear the land and to plant crops. They started new communities.

Some people moved west in wagons pulled by horses or oxen. In time, railroads were built. Railroads made it easier for people to move west. Big steamboats began sailing up and down rivers in the center of the United States. These boats helped move people west.

New settlers often fought terrible battles with the Indians. The settlers were taking land that the Indians had called their own. Many Indians tried to stop the settlers. Finally the Indians lost. There were too many settlers and too few Indians.

Indians were forced to move to reservations. This painting shows one Indian group's move along the "Trail of Tears."

In time, the United States government made most of the American Indians give up their lands. Some were given new lands on which to live. These places were called **reservations** (rez•ur•VAY•shuhnz). Reservations were not always on lands the Indians knew. Indians often could not live in the ways they were used to.

Many people went west to California in 1849. Gold had been found there. New cities were built as more people came west to try to get rich. People were also coming west to farm in Oregon and Washington. Now there were communities in the United States from the Atlantic Ocean to the Pacific Ocean.

The Civil War

In 1861 Americans fought a terrible war. One half of the country fought against the other half. This war between the North and the South is known as the **Civil** (SIV•uhl) **War.**

Many people in the North thought that having slaves was wrong. They wanted a law saying that no one in our country could own slaves.

The problem of slaves was not the only reason for the war. The North and the South did not agree about many other things. People in the South wanted to start their own country. They wanted to have their own government and laws.

Abraham Lincoln was the President of the United States when the Civil War began. He felt very strongly that the country should stay together. He also felt that owning slaves was wrong. In 1863 he said that all slaves in the United States should be set free. We celebrate Abraham Lincoln's birthday on a holiday in February.

Below, Abraham Lincoln meets with soldiers from the North during the Civil War.

This picture of Memorial Day was drawn in 1887. It shows people remembering those who died in the Civil War.

The North finally won the war in 1865. It was a sad time for our country, though. Thousands of brave Americans died fighting for the North or for the South. We remember these soldiers on the holiday in May called **Memorial Day.** On this day we also remember other soldiers who have died fighting for our country.

Reading Check

1. What were some kinds of transportation Americans used to move west?
2. Why did American Indians try to keep settlers from moving west?
3. How did President Abraham Lincoln make a difference in our country?

Look for these important words:

Key Words
- Labor Day
- labor

Places
- Ellis Island

Look for answers to these questions:

1. In what ways did the United States grow after the Civil War?
2. How did labor make our country strong?
3. How are we trying to make the United States even better today?

5. MODERN AMERICA

After the Civil War, the United States grew faster. Farmers and ranchers settled throughout our country. Mineral resources were discovered. New machines, such as cars, were invented. Big factories were built.

This picture shows automobiles being built in a huge factory in the early 1900s.

More People Come to Our Country

America is a mix of many people. This is because people from many different nations have come to live in America. They have joined together to form one nation.

New Americans came from countries such as Ireland, Germany, England, Italy, Russia, and Mexico. They often chose places to live in America that reminded them of their homeland. For example, many Scotch-Irish people settled in the mountains of Tennessee, Kentucky, and

People who came to America brought different languages. They brought different foods and clothing. They also brought their celebrations and holidays.

Ellis Island is now being restored. Here is a picture of how it will look when the work is completed.

Virginia. The mountains made them think of the land they had left behind. People from Norway and Sweden chose to live in Wisconsin and Minnesota. The weather there was much like the weather in their homeland.

People came to America for different reasons. Some came for land. Some came to find a better way of life. Some came for freedom. However, many were alike in one way. Millions of new Americans took their first step in America at Ellis Island in New York Harbor. It was called "The Gateway to the New World."

Most of these people went right to work. They became farmers and fishers. Some went to work in factories. All helped America to grow by working hard.

We have a holiday in September called **Labor Day. Labor** is another word for work. Without hard work nothing would have been built in America. On Labor Day we honor the workers who have made America strong.

At Sea Life Park in Hawaii, people explore the ocean floor and learn about plants, animals, and underwater currents. This capsule is used to take people deep into the ocean.

A Land of Freedom

Our country has always stood for freedom. We are proud that so many people have found a better life in the United States. Today, people still come to our country to find a better life. We are working to make tomorrow even better.

We are exploring in space and under the ocean. We are working to solve problems in our growing cities. We are trying to keep our country beautiful while we get the resources we need.

You are part of our country's future. You will help America stay strong, busy, and free.

Reading Check

1. Why did people come to the United States from Europe and other parts of the world?
2. What is labor?
3. What places are we exploring today?

SKILLS FOR SUCCESS

USING TIMELINES TO SHOW HISTORY

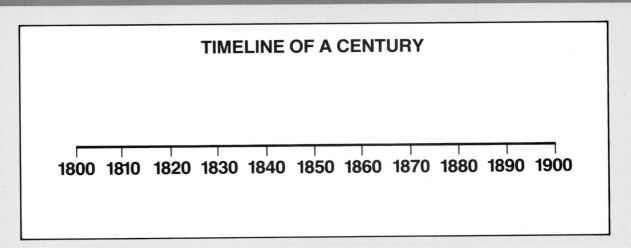

TIMELINE OF A CENTURY

1800 1810 1820 1830 1840 1850 1860 1870 1880 1890 1900

You know that you can put dates on a timeline. A timeline of your life might tell the year you were born and the year you started school. It would show other important dates in your life.

A timeline can also show a much longer amount of time. Reading timelines can help you understand the order of things in history.

The timeline above covers a **century.** A century is 100 years. The year 1900 is 100 years, or one century, later than the year 1800.

On the timeline above, each line stands for ten years. The year 1810 is ten years later than the year 1800. The year 1830 is 30 years later than the year 1800.

Remember that you read a timeline from left to right. The earliest date is on the left. The later dates are on the right.

A Timeline of American Firsts

A timeline shows important events. The timeline on page 244 shows when some important events first happened in America's history. The timeline covers two centuries, from 1800 to 2000.

Look at the space between 1800 and 1850 on the timeline. Find the 1830 entry. It says "**1830** Railroad." In 1830, a train made its first run on a railroad track in the United States.

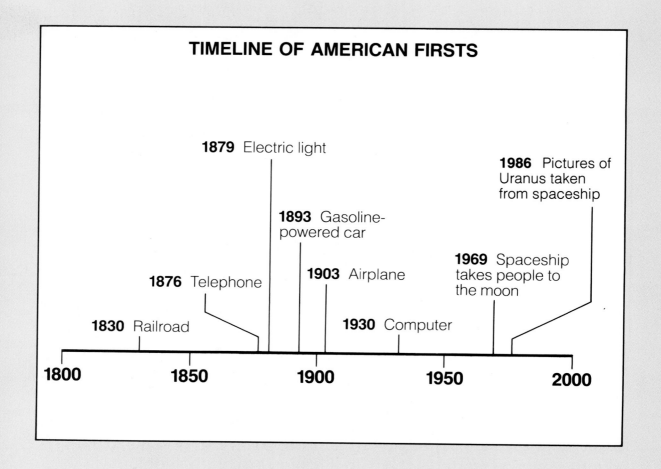

TIMELINE OF AMERICAN FIRSTS

1879 Electric light

1893 Gasoline-powered car

1986 Pictures of Uranus taken from spaceship

1876 Telephone

1903 Airplane

1969 Spaceship takes people to the moon

1830 Railroad

1930 Computer

1800 · 1850 · 1900 · 1950 · 2000

Now look at the space between 1850 and 1900. Find the first entry in that space. It tells you that the first telephone in our country was used in 1876.

The second entry between 1850 and 1900 says "**1879** Electric light." There is one more entry in the space between 1850 and 1900. What does it say?

CHECKING YOUR SKILLS

Use the timeline on this page to answer these questions.

1. Which came first—the first gasoline-powered car or the first electric light?

2. Did the first airplane flight happen before or after the first telephone was used?

3. Could a person have used a computer in 1970?

4. Did the person who invented the computer use electric lights when he worked?

5. Were pictures of Uranus taken from a spaceship before or after people landed on the moon?

CLOSE-UP

STARS, STRIPES, SONGS, AND CELEBRATIONS

The United States is a big country. It is full of differences. The land itself is very different from one end to the other. People from all over the world have come to live here. They add to our country's differences.

Even though our people and communities are different, they are also the same. They are all American. They share certain things. These shared things help bring us together as a nation.

Our Country's Flag

Our flag is one of the most important things we share. Our country's flag is a **symbol.** A symbol is anything that stands for something else. Our flag stands for the people, the government, and the ideas of our country. We have flags in our schools and in many other places.

I pledge allegiance to the flag of the United States of America and to the republic for which it stands, one nation under God, indivisible, with liberty and justice for all.

Our flag is a symbol of our country.

245

Here, children learn how to fold our country's flag. The flag must be folded a certain way, and it must never touch the ground.

These words, the Pledge of Allegiance, are often said before public meetings or at schools. They are a way of showing respect and love for our country.

Our National Anthem

Singing is another way we Americans show respect for our country. When we get together for events like sports games or concerts, we often sing "The Star-Spangled Banner." This song is our **national anthem.** Our national anthem praises our country.

"The Star-Spangled Banner" was written by Francis Scott Key. He wrote the words during the War of 1812. This was a war between England and the United States. Key was being held prisoner by the English on a ship during a big battle. Through the night, the firing of guns kept on. Key could not tell who was winning.

When dawn came, Key saw the American flag still flying at the fort across the water. He knew then that the Americans had won. He was inspired to write the national anthem.

This flag inspired Francis Scott Key (above) to write our national anthem. The flag may now be seen at the Museum of History and Technology in Washington, D.C.

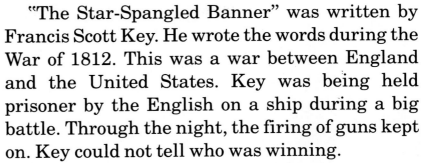

The Star-Spangled Banner

Oh, say, can you see, by the dawn's early light,
What so proudly we hailed, at the twilight's last
    gleaming?
Whose broad stripes and bright stars, through the
    perilous night,
O'er the ramparts we watched, were so gallantly
    streaming.
And the rockets' red glare, the bombs bursting
    in air,
Gave proof through the night, that our flag was
    still there.
Oh, say does that star-spangled banner yet wave
O'er the land of the free and the home of the brave?

247

The bald eagle is America's national bird.

Symbols of Our Nation

Our nation has many symbols. Our flag is one of them. The **Statue of Liberty** is another symbol. The Statue of Liberty was a gift from France. It was first seen by our nation on October 26, 1886. The statue stands in New York Harbor, facing the Atlantic Ocean. Many people have crossed that ocean to find freedom and a better life. The Statue of Liberty is a symbol of their hopes.

Look at the pictures on this page. They are all symbols of our country.

The Statue of Liberty was restored to mark its 100th birthday in 1986. On the right is the Capitol building in Washington, D.C.

We celebrate Martin
L. King, Jr.'s birthday
in January.

Americans Share Holidays

Americans share special holidays, too. Chapter 9 tells about many of these holidays. The Fourth of July, Columbus Day, and Martin Luther King, Jr.'s birthday are just a few of these holidays. On these special holidays, we can give thanks for the good things in our nation that we all share.

Fireworks blaze across the sky to celebrate our country's birthday on the Fourth of July.

249

USING WORDS

Use one of the words in parentheses to answer each question correctly.

1. Amerigo Vespucci was an _____. (explorer, Indian)
2. _____ in our country were not free until the Civil War. (Pilgrims, Slaves)
3. The land in America ruled by England was called the English _____. (reservations, colonies)
4. People in America wanted to start a new _____. (nation, Mayflower)
5. American Indians often had to live on _____. (reservations, labor)

REVIEWING FACTS

1. On what holiday do we remember the person who found America in 1492?
2. When and where was the first Thanksgiving?
3. Why do we remember July 4, 1776?
4. Why did the Civil War happen?
5. Why do we celebrate Labor Day?

THINKING CRITICALLY

1. Did all American Indian groups live in the same way? How were their ways of life different?
2. How are settlers different from explorers?
3. Why was being able to make their own laws important to the English colonists? How did they gain this right?
4. How did the people who came from other countries make America special? How do you think America would be different if they had not come?
5. Which of America's holidays is your favorite? Why?

⬤ PRACTICING SKILLS

Using Calendars Find a calendar for this year. Find the dates of these holidays.

1. Flag Day
2. Columbus Day
3. Thanksgiving

UNIT 4 REVIEW

WORDS TO REMEMBER

Number your paper from 1 to 10. Use the words below to fill in the blanks. Use each word only once.

buffalo
colonies
crossroads
explorers
freedom
gold pan
history
labor
manufactured
settlers

1. Our country has a long and proud _____.
2. Communities often began at _____.
3. The Plains Indians used the _____ for food, clothing, and shelter.
4. The Mexicans invented the _____.
5. Machines, cars, and computers are _____ goods.
6. Christopher Columbus and Amerigo Vespucci were _____.
7. People in Jamestown and Pilgrims in Plymouth were _____.
8. People in the English _____ wanted their own government.
9. Americans decided to fight for _____ from England.
10. The work that has made our country strong is _____.

FOCUS ON MAIN IDEAS

1. Where and why did communities begin in the past? Where and why do they begin now? What kinds of communities are we planning for the future?
2. Who came and started the community of Denver? How was their way of life different from that of the Arapaho Indians?
3. Why did the community of Jamestown do so poorly at first? How did the Pilgrims begin their community differently? How did these two groups of people meet their needs?
4. What did the Declaration of Independence tell people?
5. Why are people still coming to our country today? What do they hope to find?

THINK/WRITE

Imagine that you are an American Indian before the settlers came. One day you see boats coming onto the shore. People who look and dress differently get off the boats. Write a story telling how you would feel about these newcomers arriving in your land.

ACTIVITIES

1. **Drama** Choose something that happened in Denver's history. Work with other students to act this out. For example, you could act out making a tepee or panning for gold.

2. **Research/Oral Report** A penny has a picture of Abraham Lincoln on it. Look at some other coins and bills. Tell whose pictures are on them.

3. **Art** Think of what freedom in America means to you. Draw a picture that shows how you feel about being free.

4. **Remembering the Close-up** Look at the pictures on page 248. The bald eagle, the Statue of Liberty, and the Capitol are all symbols of our country. Choose one of these symbols and write a report telling why it is a symbol of our country.

 SKILLS REVIEW

1. **Using Pictures** Look at the picture below. Is it old or new? Name two ways that you can tell.

2. **Using Calendars** Look at the calendar on page 232 and answer the following questions.

   a. What month follows May?

   b. Christmas is December 25. Looking at this calendar, tell on what day of the week Christmas is.

   c. In which month is your birthday? Find this month on the calendar.

   d. How many months come before your birthday?

3. **Using Timelines** Make a timeline of your life. Show five things that have happened to you since you were born.

YOUR COMMUNITY

In this unit you have seen how communities begin and how they grow. You have also seen how our country began. Use the following activities to see how your own community started.

LEARNING ABOUT PEOPLE

1. Find out from what countries people in your community came. Maybe a street or lake in your community has a Spanish or French name. Maybe your town is named after a town in another country. Name one thing that shows how early settlers from other countries have made a difference in your community.

YOUR COMMUNITY'S HISTORY

2. Go to the library and find the following information.
   a. When your community was started
   b. Why people settled there
   c. Three important events in your community's history

Make a timeline showing the history of your community using this information.

3. Find out if there are any places of history near your community. Maybe your community is near the site of a Civil War battle. Perhaps a President's home is nearby. Write a paragraph about any place of interest near your community. Tell why it is important.

4. Find out what your community looked like long ago. Go to the library or talk to people who have lived in your community a long time. Find some old pictures of your community. Make a class scrapbook showing how your community has changed.

LEARNING ABOUT SETTLERS

5. Find out about the first settlers in your community. When did they first settle in your community? What crops did they grow? Draw a picture showing how they lived and worked.

Community Facts and Figures

City	Jun Tan	Caracas	Haifa
Country	China	Venezuela	Israel
Continent	Asia	South America	Asia
Population (estimated)	unknown	3,000,000	235,000
Interesting Fact	More people live along the Chang Jiang (River) than live in the United States.	Caracas was founded in 1567 by Spaniards looking for gold.	People have lived in the area near Haifa for 3,000 years.

AROUND THE WORLD

Long ago, people dreamed of sailing the seas and discovering new, exciting lands. Today, you can visit many parts of the world in only hours or days. You can travel to other countries, or you can read about them.

Look at the picture on page 254. The picture shows a community in the country of Austria. Austria is in Europe.

This community in Austria probably looks very different from your community. Yet in many ways, people in Austria and everywhere else are the same. People everywhere work to meet their needs. People everywhere live in communities and have fun together. In this unit, you will see how people live around the world.

Dar Es Salaam	London	Paris	Mexico City	Amsterdam
Tanzania	England	France	Mexico	The Netherlands
Africa	Europe	Europe	North America	Europe
900,000	6,765,000	2,176,000	9,191,295	715,000
Dar Es Salaam had six times more people in 1987 than in 1964.	London has almost been destroyed twice. Old landmarks were rebuilt.	Paris has one of the oldest universities in the world.	Mexico City is the second-largest city in the world.	Amsterdam has more than 100 canals that help drain the city.

Meeting Needs Around the World

Pretend you are taking a trip around the world. In this chapter, you will see different foods that people eat. You will look at the clothes that people wear. You will see some interesting buildings. You will discover how people meet their needs in different places.

Look for these important words:

Key Words
- grain
- sashimi
- feta cheese
- rice

- pasta
- shish kebab

Places
- Japan
- Uruguay

- Greece
- Finland
- Italy
- Turkey

Look for answers to these questions:

1. What foods do we get from animals?
2. What foods do we get from plants?
3. What kinds of food do people in hot, rainy climates often eat?
4. How do we get foods from other countries?

1. FOODS AROUND THE WORLD

We all need food to live. Food is a need that everyone in the world must meet. Not everyone eats the same kinds of food, though. People in different parts of the world often eat different kinds of food. They prepare and make food in different ways, too.

Where We Get Our Food

We get all our food from plants and animals. We get meat, eggs, and dairy products from animals. We get fruits, vegetables, nuts, and **grain** from plants. Grain is small, hard seeds from certain plants, such as wheat. People around the world use grain. They use grain to make bread, pastries, and cereal.

257

Foods From Animals

What people eat often depends on where they live. People who live near water often eat a lot of fresh fish.

Japan is a country of islands in Asia. Fish is an important food in Japan. The Japanese like to eat raw fish, called **sashimi** (SAHSH•uh•mee). They dip sashimi in different sauces. People in Japan eat a lot of cooked fish, too.

In places where there are rich grasslands, people often raise cattle for food. **Uruguay** (YUR•uh•gway) is in South America. In Uruguay, the grass grows to be as high as you are. There is enough grass for many cattle.

In **Greece,** many people raise goats and sheep. They use milk from these animals for cheese. This cheese is called **feta** (FET•uh) **cheese.**

Sashimi is a favorite food in Japan.

Raising cattle is important in Uruguay. The weather is mild, and cattle graze year round on the rich grassland.

258

Rice grows well in warm, wet Bali. Young rice is bright green. When it ripens, rice turns yellow and can be picked.

Foods From Plants

In some parts of the world, the climate is hot and rainy. Fruits and vegetables can grow all year long. So it is not surprising that people who live there eat many fruits and vegetables.

In countries where the weather is often cold, the growing season is short. In these countries, people often grow crops such as potatoes and beets. These crops grow well in cold weather. The main part of the plant grows under the ground, where it is not so cold. **Finland** is a country that grows a lot of potatoes. Potatoes are one of the main vegetables there.

Rice grows well in many parts of the world. Rice is a grasslike plant with seeds. It is a grain. Rice needs lots of water to grow. About half the people in the world eat rice as their main food.

People buy and sell potatoes at an outdoor market in Finland.

259

Together, meat and vegetables make up a shish kebab.

Pasta comes in many different shapes and sizes.

Special Foods Around the World

Every country has special kinds of food. **Italy** is known for **pasta** (PAHS•tuh). Pasta is noodles made from flour, water, salt, and eggs.

Shish kebab (SHISH kuh•BAHB) is a special food in countries such as **Turkey.** Shish kebab is made by roasting cubes of lamb, tomatoes, peppers, and onions on a long, metal rod.

Many years ago, some foods were only known in certain parts of the world. Yet many people now eat foods from all over the world. One reason is that people now travel more. Sometimes they move to other countries. When they move, people bring the foods of their countries with them.

There is another reason why different foods are eaten in more places now. Today, planes and ships can carry foods quickly around the world.

Reading Check

1. What do people use grain for?
2. Why do people in Finland grow potatoes?
3. How did airplanes change the foods we eat?

Look for these important words:

Key Words
- sarongs
- reflects
- cotton

Places
- Tibet
- Samoa
- Saudi Arabia

Look for answers to these questions:

1. How do clothes protect people from cold weather? Give examples.
2. How do clothes protect people from hot weather? Give examples.
3. In what ways are clothes around the world different? In what ways are they often alike?

2. CLOTHING AROUND THE WORLD

You have read about some different kinds of food around the world. There are many different kinds of clothing around the world, too. Now you will look at some clothing around the world.

Cold Weather Clothing

The man in the picture on the right lives in the Himalayan Mountains of **Tibet.** Tibet is in Asia and is now part of China. It gets very cold in Tibet. The man must wear a warm cap.

The cap is lined with fur. Even the earflaps are lined with fur. A warm cap is very important in the cold mountains of Tibet.

People must wear very warm clothing in cold climates. They wear heavy sweaters, coats, and furs. They often wear mittens and boots.

The ear flaps on this Tibetan cap can be turned down in very cold weather.

261

Warm Weather Clothing

In other parts of the world, people dress to stay cool in the heat.

The boys in the picture on the left live in **Samoa.** Samoa is an island in the Pacific Ocean. The weather in Samoa is very hot. The boys do not need shirts. They wear **sarongs.** A sarong is a piece of cloth wrapped around the waist.

It is even hotter in **Saudi Arabia** than in Samoa. Yet people in Saudi Arabia cover themselves with clothes. The sun is so hot there that people must wear headdresses and long white robes to stay cool. The color white **reflects,** or throws back, the sun's rays. This kind of clothing also protects people from the sting of desert sands.

The people in both Samoa and Saudi Arabia are dressed to stay cool in hot weather.

The picture on the left shows a silk-printing factory in England. Some of the colorful cotton that is made in India is shown on the right.

Using Different Materials for Clothing

The kind of clothing people wear sometimes depends on where they live. People often make clothing from materials they can get nearby.

People in many countries of the world grow **cotton.** Cotton comes from a plant. People use soft white cotton to make clothing.

People in China have made the cloth called silk for many thousands of years. Silk is spun by silkworms, which feed on the leaves of the mulberry tree.

Special Clothing Around the World

People around the world wear clothing for the same reasons. They wear clothing to protect them from the weather. They wear special clothing to do certain jobs. They wear clothes because they look nice or are fun to wear.

People wear very special clothes sometimes. In the pictures on this page, people are wearing clothing for special events.

Transportation makes it a lot easier to send clothing materials around the world. That is one reason clothing is becoming more alike around the world.

People in Japan wear kimonos (kuh.MOH.nuhz) for holidays and festivals. On the right, people in Scotland wear skirts called "kilts" for a special dancing event.

How are these people in Japan and Scotland dressed alike? How are their clothes different from those on page 264?

Clothing is also becoming more alike because people know more about clothing in other countries. Newspapers and magazines show us the kinds of clothing people everywhere are wearing.

Look at the pictures on this page. Do the clothes in these countries look like the clothes you see people wearing in the United States?

Reading Check

1. How is the way people in Samoa dress different from the way people in Saudi Arabia dress?
2. What plant is grown for cloth in many countries around the world?
3. Why is clothing becoming more alike around the world?

Look for these important words:

Key Words
- salt box house
- shingles
- thatched roofs

Places
- Sweden
- Nova Scotia
- Egypt

- Ireland
- Thailand
- Nairobi, Kenya

Look for answers to these questions:

1. How do people decide what material to use in their shelters?
2. Why do shelters in Nova Scotia have very steep roofs?
3. Why are many Thailand houses built on poles?

3. SHELTERS AROUND THE WORLD

People all around the world live in shelters. Shelters keep out wind, rain, heat, and cold.

People often build shelters or homes from materials found near where they live. Shelters can be made from wood, brick, concrete, or stone. They can also be made from animal skins and other materials.

Using Wood for Shelters

There are lots of trees for lumber in **Sweden,** in northern Europe. People in Sweden use the lumber to build homes. People carve the wood trim into pretty shapes. Sometimes they paint bright designs inside and out. The picture on page 267 shows a house in Sweden.

Many houses in Sweden (left) and Nova Scotia (right) are built from wood.

Nova Scotia (NOH•vuh SKO•shuh) is in Canada. Look at the picture above of the house in Nova Scotia. Like the houses in Sweden, it is made of wood. It is called a **salt box house.** Long ago, salt came in little boxes that looked like this house.

The house is covered with **shingles.** Shingles are thin pieces of wood laid over each other in rows. Look at how steep the roof is. It is steep for a reason. Large amounts of snow fall in Nova Scotia. The wooden shingles and the steep slant of the roof let snow slide off easily.

People around the world often use the same materials for building shelters. Yet you have just seen that a wooden home in Sweden is different from one in Nova Scotia. People around the world have different ideas of what they like. They have different ways of building shelters.

Using Other Materials for Shelter

Egypt, in northern Africa, is a country of deserts. In Egypt, people often build shelters from bricks made by mixing mud and straw. The bricks are dried in the sun. They make thick walls that keep the desert heat out.

Ireland, in Europe, is famous for its fields of emerald-green grass. Rocks and stones dot the fields. Farm families in Ireland sometimes live in stone houses with **thatched roofs.** A thatched roof is made from bundles of straw.

Another picture on this page shows a house in **Thailand** (TY·land), in Asia. This house is standing on poles above the water. Thailand has many rivers and a lot of heavy rain. When it floods, the houses on poles stay above the water.

The top left picture shows brick shelters in Egypt. On the bottom left is an Irish house with a thatched roof. On the right is a house built on poles in Thailand.

268

Some Shelters Are the Same

The shelters you have just read about are very different from one another. Some shelters around the world, though, look very much alike.

Shelters in very big cities often look alike. A business center in Toronto, Canada, might look much like a business center in **Nairobi, Kenya.** Yet these two cities are halfway across the world from each other.

How do these business centers in Toronto, Canada (left) and Nairobi, Kenya (right) look alike?

Reading Check

1. Why are many homes in Sweden made from wood?
2. Why do many people in Egypt use bricks to build shelters?
3. Why are shelters built in Ireland different from shelters built in Thailand?

SKILLS FOR SUCCESS

TIME, THE EARTH, AND THE SUN

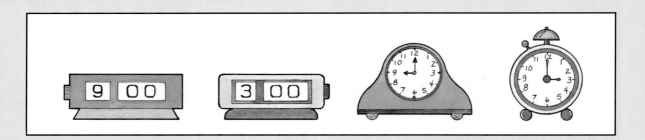

We use many words to say when we do things. In the "morning" we get up and eat breakfast. Around "noon" we eat lunch. In the "evening" we eat dinner. At "night" we go to sleep.

To tell the time more exactly, we use clocks. Each day is divided into 24 hours.

Morning is the time between sunrise and noon. The afternoon goes from noon until the sun starts to set. Then the evening begins. After a few hours, night comes. Night lasts until the sun rises again.

We call the hours between midnight and noon **A.M.** For example, 9 A.M. means nine o'clock in the morning. The letters stand for words that mean "before noon." We call the hours between noon and midnight **P.M.** These letters stand for words that mean "after noon."

Why We Have Day and Night

To explain day and night, we usually say it is light during the day and dark at night. From Earth, it looks as if the sun rises in the east. The sun seems to travel across the sky during the day. In the evening it seems to set in the west.

The sun does not really move at all. If you were on a spaceship far from Earth, you would be able to see what really causes day and night. You would see that the Earth slowly **rotates,** or turns around.

The Earth is always rotating. It takes the Earth 24 hours to spin completely around. We call those 24 hours one day.

As the Earth rotates, places on the Earth turn toward the sun and then away from it. When your community is turned away from the sun, it is night.

The picture on this page shows how the Earth rotates.

The Earth is a sphere, or ball. Light can shine on only part of it at a time. It is daytime on the part of the Earth facing the sun. It is nighttime on the part facing away from the sun.

Day and Night in Different Places

Look at the Earth in the picture below. The Earth is rotating in the direction shown by the arrows. Kansas City is moving toward the sun. That means the sun is about to rise in Kansas City, Missouri. It is already morning in Belém, a city in South America. It is still night in Anchorage, Alaska.

Kansas City will move all the way around as the Earth spins. When it returns to the same spot, 24 hours will have passed.

Anchorage and Belém are far apart from each other. You can see that they do not face the sun at the same time. When two places are that far apart, they have day and night at very different times.

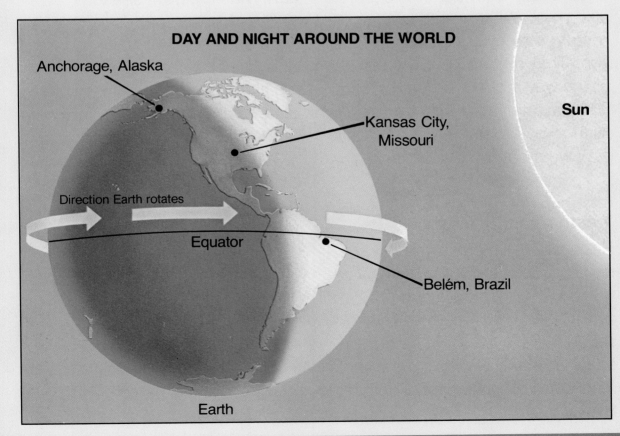

DAY AND NIGHT AROUND THE WORLD

Anchorage, Alaska

Kansas City, Missouri

Sun

Direction Earth rotates

Equator

Belém, Brazil

Earth

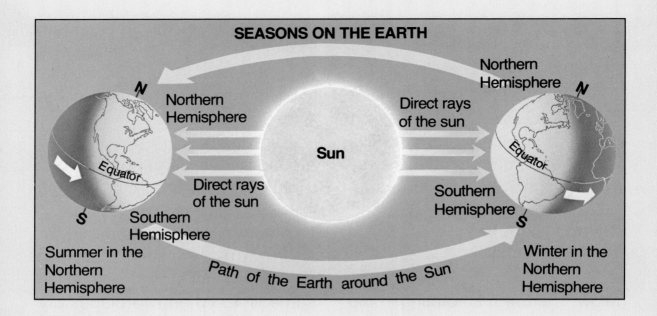

SEASONS ON THE EARTH

Northern Hemisphere
Direct rays of the sun
Sun
Direct rays of the sun
Southern Hemisphere
Summer in the Northern Hemisphere
Path of the Earth around the Sun

Northern Hemisphere
Direct rays of the sun
Equator
Southern Hemisphere
Winter in the Northern Hemisphere

Equator

The Earth Revolves

You have seen that the Earth rotates once every 24 hours. The Earth also moves in another way. It **revolves** (ree•VAHLVZ) around the sun. That means it slowly travels all the way around the sun. It takes 365 days for the Earth to revolve all the way around the sun. That is how we measure a year.

Weather and Seasons

Because of the Earth's shape, some parts of the world have more sun. Places near the equator get more sun. They are hot or warm most of the year. Places near the North Pole and the South Pole have less sun. They are quite cold all year long.

Many places on Earth are warm in summer and cold in winter. The Earth has different seasons.

Seasons happen because the Earth is tilted. We have summer when northern parts of the Earth are tilted toward the sun. We have winter when northern parts are tilted away from the sun.

CHECKING YOUR SKILLS

Tell or write the answers to these questions.

1. What do "A.M." and "P.M." mean?
2. Why do we have day and night?
3. How long does it take for the Earth to revolve around the sun?
4. Is it usually colder near the equator or at the North Pole?
5. Why do we have seasons?

CHAPTER 10 REVIEW

USING WORDS

Use one of the words in parentheses to complete each sentence.

1. People around the world use ____ to make bread and cereal. (cotton, grain)
2. People in Italy eat a lot of ____. (pasta, sashimi)
3. ____ is used to make clothing. (Cotton, Sarong)
4. Houses in Nova Scotia have ____. (thatched roofs, shingles)
5. ____ are made from bundles of straw. (Thatched roofs, Shingles)

REVIEWING FACTS

1. Why does what people eat often depend on where they live?
2. Why can people around the world eat many of the same foods?
3. Why does what people wear sometimes depend on where they live? Give two examples.
4. What are some clothes people wear in cold weather?
5. What are three materials people use to build shelters?

THINKING CRITICALLY

1. Many years ago some foods were known only in certain parts of the world. Explain why this has changed. Name a food from another country.
2. What kinds of clothes do people in your community wear in hot weather? How are these clothes different from clothes in Saudi Arabia?
3. People in Japan sometimes wear kimonos. Do people in your community ever wear special clothes? If so, why?
4. Pick a place in the world to live. Tell what the weather and resources nearby are like. What kind of shelter would you build? How would it be different from the shelter you now live in?

⬤ **PRACTICING SKILLS**

1. **Time, the Earth, and the Sun**
It is now daytime in your community. Look at a globe or a map of the world (see pages R8–R9). Name a place in the world where it is nighttime.

Living in Communities Around the World

People around the world live in communities. Communities around the world have governments and services. They have histories. In this chapter, you will explore some communities around the world.

274

Look for these important words:

Key Words
- plot
- beisbol
- subway

Places
- Jun Tan, China
- Caracas, Venezuela
- Haifa, Israel
- Mount Carmel

Look for answers to these questions:

1. What natural resources are important to Jun Tan, China?
2. How did the discovery of oil help Caracas, Venezuela, to grow?
3. Why is Haifa, Israel, a big transportation center?

1. COMMUNITIES USE NATURAL RESOURCES

In Unit 2 you read how natural resources are important to communities. You read about farmers using natural resources to raise crops in Merced, California. You saw how coal mining is important in Pikeville, Kentucky. You saw how important shipping is in Chicago, Illinois.

People in communities around the world use natural resources to make a living. There are farming, mining, and port communities around the world.

In the next pages, you will look at communities in the countries of China, Venezuela, and Israel. You will read about how important natural resources are to the people who live in these communities.

Food for millions of people is grown in many farming communities like Jun Tan, China. Here, workers care for the crops with hoes and other simple tools.

Jun Tan, China

Jun Tan is a farming community in eastern **China.** Jun Tan has the natural resources needed for farming. It has rich soil, plenty of water, and a good climate for farming.

The land in Jun Tan is owned by the government. Until recently, many families shared the land to be farmed. Now, however, individual families may rent the farmland from the government. Rent is paid by giving the government a certain amount of the crop grown.

In the past, the farmers were told by the state which crops to grow on their **plot.** A plot is a piece of land. Farmers had to give all their crops to the government. Now the farmers are allowed to grow any crop they choose. After the rent is paid they may sell what is left. They use the money to buy tractors and tools to help them grow food.

276

In parts of China, farming is still done with hand tools like hoes. Water buffaloes and other animals pull the plows. In other parts of China, machines like tractors are used. Some people even own their own machines. Others share.

Besides farming, the people in Jun Tan often do other jobs. One farmer might also be a carpenter. Another farmer might be a teacher or a bricklayer. Workers in the community make many of the goods they need.

Do you remember the community of Merced, California? Look back at pages 66–71 to remember. Jun Tan and Merced are both farming communities. Yet the ways people live and work in each place are very different.

The man below is a carpenter. He works at a workshop in Jun Tan, China.

Caracas, Venezuela

Caracas (kah•RAH•kuhs) is the capital city of **Venezuela** (ven•uhz•WAY•luh). Venezuela is on the north coast of South America.

Caracas began many hundreds of years ago. You can find buildings that are 400 years old in Caracas.

Caracas was not always as big as it is now. One important thing that helped it grow was the discovery of oil.

In 1922 oil was found in Venezuela. More and more people came to drill for oil. Many of them came to Caracas. Caracas grew very quickly. It is still growing.

Caracas is an old city, but finding oil made many new jobs for people. Money from oil was used to build new buildings.

This picture shows oil drilling in Lake Maracaibo, Venezuela's largest lake. Much of Venezuela's oil is found under this lake.

Money from oil has been used to build many new skyscrapers and freeways. Now Caracas is almost a brand new city. Yet because Caracas has grown so fast, it has had to face new problems. The city needed homes for the many people who moved there. The government of Venezuela built many apartment houses in the city. Today, however, the city still needs more homes.

A favorite sport in Caracas is **beisbol** (BAYZ.bahl). This word is a mix of Spanish and English. Can you guess what it means?

Do you remember the oil-drilling community of Midland, Texas? Look back at pages 98–104 to remember. Caracas is a lot older than Midland. That is one way the two communities are different from each other.

Haifa, Israel

The port city of **Haifa** (HY•fuh), **Israel,** is on a bay with mountains all around. The bay empties into the Mediterranean Sea.

The bay is deep enough for ocean-going ships. This makes Haifa a very important transportation center. Crops and goods are brought on trucks to Haifa from farms and factories. Then they are shipped from the harbor in Haifa to other places. Goods are shipped into Haifa, too. They are taken by trucks to other parts of Israel.

Haifa is a city of three parts. It is near a mountain called **Mount Carmel.** The lower part of Haifa, by the bay, is where all the shipping goes on. There cargo is loaded and unloaded, and goods

From high on Mount Carmel in Israel, you can view the city of Haifa and part of Israel's coast.

are stored in big buildings. The middle part of Haifa, covering the sides of Mt. Carmel, is where most of the businesses and stores are. The highest part of the city, near the mountaintop, is where most people live.

A long **subway** connects the three parts of Haifa. A subway is a train that is mostly underground. The people in Haifa say the subway links "upstairs" Haifa with "downstairs" Haifa.

Do you remember the American port city of Chicago, Illinois? Look at pages 114–121 to remember. Both Haifa and Chicago are important transportation centers. Crops and goods move into and out of these two communities.

Many people in Haifa use the subway to go from one part of the city to another.

Reading Check

1. Who owns the land in a Chinese farming community?
2. Why did Caracas grow so quickly?
3. How are the three parts of Haifa different?

SKILLS FOR SUCCESS

READING POPULATION MAPS

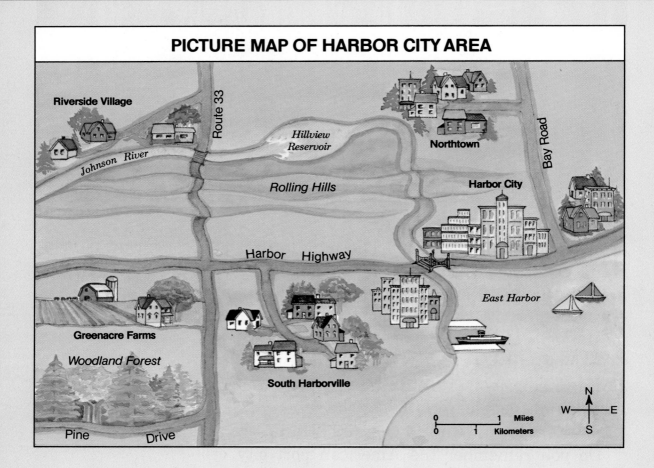

PICTURE MAP OF HARBOR CITY AREA

Maps can show where people live. They can show how many people live in different places.

Look at the picture map on this page. It shows Harbor City and the places around it. Many people live in Harbor City. Near the city are two suburbs.

On the left side of the map are farms and a small town, called Riverside Village. Few people live in this area. The farms are far apart from each other.

Using a Population Map

The same places can be shown on a **population map.** Population means how many people live in a place. Look at the population map on the next page.

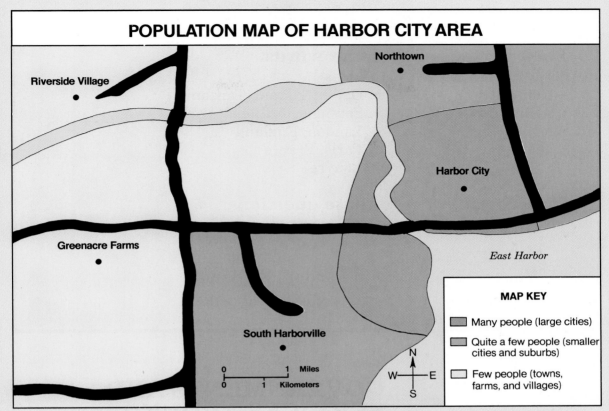

POPULATION MAP OF HARBOR CITY AREA

Northtown

Riverside Village

Harbor City

Greenacre Farms

East Harbor

South Harborville

Miles
0   1
0   1
Kilometers

N
W—E
S

MAP KEY

Many people (large cities)

Quite a few people (smaller cities and suburbs)

Few people (towns, farms, and villages)

Find the blue area on the map. Now look for blue in the map key. The map key tells you that blue areas are where many people live close together.

Find the same area in the first map. The picture map shows many large buildings here. Both the picture map and the population map of Harbor City show that this area is crowded.

Look at the map key again. What does the color yellow stand for? Find the yellow area on the map. Then find the same area in the picture. Is the yellow area farmland or the city?

CHECKING YOUR SKILLS

Use the maps to help you answer these questions.

1. Which city or town has the most people?

2. Which towns or cities have the smallest number of people?

3. Do more people live in Northtown or in Riverside Village? What other place has about the same number of people as Northtown?

4. Find the area that is south of Harbor Highway and west of Route 33. How many people live there?

Look for these important words:

Key Words
- bobby
- sculptures
- fort
- palace

Places
- Dar es Salaam, Tanzania
- Serengeti National Park
- London, England
- Paris, France
- Louvre

Look for answers to these questions:

1. Why is Dar es Salaam, Tanzania, an important city?
2. What do bobbies do in London, England?
3. How are services around the world alike?

2. GOVERNMENTS AND SERVICES AROUND THE WORLD

Communities around the world have rules and laws. This is true of countries, too. Every country has a government. Every country has a capital. Every country provides services to its people, too.

This picture shows a government building in the capital of Tanzania.

Dar es Salaam, Tanzania

Dar es Salaam (DAHR ES suh•LAHM) is in **Tanzania** (tan•zuh•NEE•yuh). Tanzania is a large country in eastern Africa.

There are many factories in and near Dar es Salaam. People make cement, glass, cloth, and footwear in the factories.

Dar es Salaam is the capital of Tanzania. Laws for the whole country are made there.

Some important laws in Tanzania have to do with the way land is used. There are many animals and much beautiful scenery in Tanzania. Farmers use some of the land to grow crops.

Some years ago, more food was needed in Tanzania. Lawmakers passed a law. They took some land from the **Serengeti** (ser•uhn•GET•ee) **National Park** and made it into farmland.

Lions, elephants, and zebras roamed freely on this land. The law let farmers fence off this land and use it for farming. The wild animals could not live on the land anymore.

At the same time, the lawmakers set aside some nearby land for the wild animals. They said that this land would be only for the animals, not for farms or factories. It is against the law to kill or trap any of the animals there.

By making these laws, the lawmakers tried to meet the people's need for food. They also tried to meet the animals' need for a place to live.

Gnu, (NOO) can run very quickly. Here, they graze on Tanzania's grassland.

285

Services Around the World

Communities all over the world provide services for people. There are police and fire departments, parks, schools, libraries, and museums in cities all over the world.

In **London,** the capital of **England,** a police officer is called a **bobby.** The bobbies of London do many of the same things police everywhere do. They direct traffic. They help people who are lost or who have problems. They make sure the laws are obeyed.

Paris, France, is one of the most beautiful cities in the world. Many people come to visit this city's gardens, parks, and buildings. Paris also has some of the best-known museums in the world.

A bobby stands guard near a government building in London, England.

The **Louvre** (LOO•vr) is an art museum in Paris. Many thousands of paintings can be seen here. Other works of art, such as **sculptures,** are also at the Louvre. A sculpture is a figure made from stone, clay, or metal.

The Louvre began as a **fort** long, long ago. A fort is a place for protecting soldiers. Soldiers lived inside the safe walls of the fort. Later the Louvre was used as a **palace,** a place for kings to live. Each king added more and more buildings to the Louvre. Today, if all the rooms of the Louvre were placed end to end, they would make a building 8 miles (about 13 km) long!

The Louvre, left, is one of the largest art museums in the world. Many sculptures, such as the one on the right, are kept in the Louvre.

Reading Check

1. What is the capital of Tanzania?
2. How is a bobby like a police officer in our country?
3. Why is the Louvre so big?

Look for these important words:

Key Words
- pyramid
- Aztec Indians
- sea level
- dikes

Places
- Mexico City, Mexico
- Amsterdam, The Netherlands

Look for answers to these questions:

1. Why is Mexico City both old and new?
2. Why isn't The Netherlands covered with water?
3. What are canals in Amsterdam used for?

3. THE HISTORIES OF TWO CITIES

Mexico City is the capital of **Mexico.** It lies in a mountain valley. It is on very high land.

Amsterdam is a city in western Europe. It is the capital of **The Netherlands.** Amsterdam is on low land near the sea.

Both of these cities have long, interesting histories. Over the years they have changed and grown.

Mexico City, Mexico

Mexico City is more than 600 years old. You can see Mexico City's past in the buildings in the picture on page 289. Do you see the stone steps? They are the steps of a **pyramid** (PEER•uh•mid) that once stood in this place. A pyramid is a building with flat sides that come to a point on

top. The **Aztec Indians** lived in Mexico City about 600 years ago. They built the pyramids.

Do you see the church behind the pyramid steps? That church is more than 400 years old. It was built by the Spanish. They came to Mexico City when the Aztecs already had a busy city.

In 1521, Spanish explorers fought against the Aztecs and won. Much of the beautiful Aztec city was destroyed. The Spanish took over the city and built a new city in its place.

Look again at the picture. Do you see the tall, modern buildings behind the church? Each year, many more are built in Mexico City.

Today Mexico City is a mix of the old and new. Its old buildings show its past. Its new buildings show its present and future.

This picture shows the famous Plaza of Three Cultures in Mexico City. There, you can find the steps of an Aztec pyramid, an old Spanish church, and modern buildings.

289

Cars travel along a dike in The Netherlands.

Amsterdam, The Netherlands

The Netherlands is a country in Europe. Much of The Netherlands is below **sea level.** Sea level is the level of the ocean.

You may wonder why lands below sea level are not covered with water. The answer is that huge **dikes,** or dams, hold back the sea. There are 1,500 miles (2,400 km) of dikes in The Netherlands. The dikes protect the land from flooding.

Workers build dikes around water-covered lands. Then they pump out the water and drain the lands. They pump the water into canals. The dry land that is left can be used for farming and to build communities.

Boats as well as cars can travel through Amsterdam. Boats travel on waterways called canals.

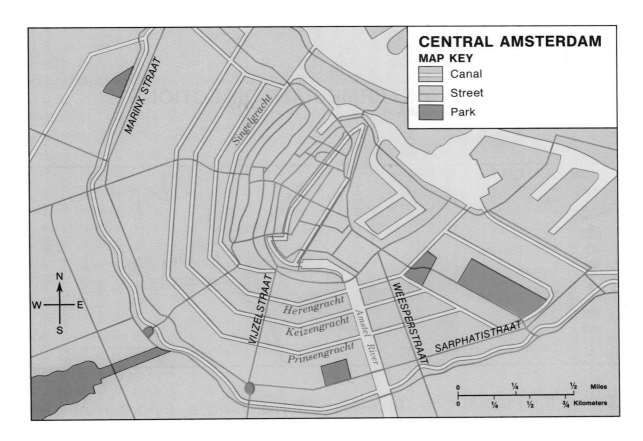

Amsterdam is a city of canals. Amsterdam was built on land that had once been under water. Dikes and canals were built so that people could use the land. Canals became important waterways. They were used to move goods to lakes and seas. Then the goods could go to other countries.

Amsterdam is still growing. The people of Amsterdam go on building canals. Amsterdam keeps growing and changing.

Reading Check

1. What group of people built the pyramids in Mexico City?
2. How do you think the Plaza of Three Cultures in Mexico City got its name?
3. Why are canals important in Amsterdam?

SKILLS FOR SUCCESS

USING INTERMEDIATE DIRECTIONS

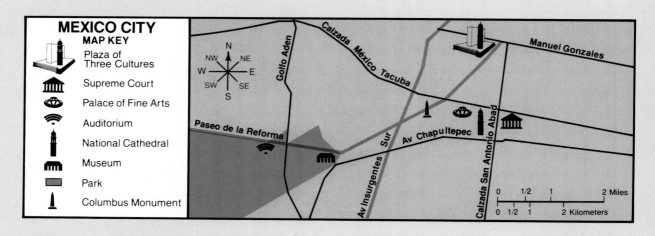

MEXICO CITY MAP KEY

Plaza of Three Cultures
Supreme Court
Palace of Fine Arts
Auditorium
National Cathedral
Museum
Park
Columbus Monument

Look at the map above. You can tell by looking at the compass rose that the auditorium is west of the museum. Yet if someone told you that the park is southwest of Columbus Monument, how would you find that direction?

You know which way is west because you have learned the four cardinal directions, north, south, east, and west. There are also four "in-between" directions, southeast, southwest, northeast and northwest. These are called **intermediate directions.** The intermediate directions lie between the four main directions.

To better understand intermediate directions, look at the compass rose. Find the line that passes halfway between south and west. The letters **SW** stand for southwest. The park is southwest of Columbus Monument.

CHECKING YOUR SKILLS

Use the map above to help you answer these questions.

1. What do **NE, NW,** and **SE** stand for?

2. What direction is the Plaza of Three Cultures from Columbus Monument?

3. If you went from the court to the Palace of Fine Arts, in which direction did you go?

292

CLOSE-UP

CELEBRATIONS AROUND THE WORLD

People everywhere enjoy the special excitement of holiday celebrations. Let's look at some celebrations around the world.

New Year's in China

New Year's in China lasts two weeks in January or February. It is the biggest, brightest celebration of the year.

New Year's is a time to visit family and friends. People hang good luck flags beside their doors. They wear new clothes to start the new year. All over China, there are dances, plays, parades, operas, and acrobats.

Masks and costumes are part of Chinese New Year's celebrations. On the left is a nighttime parade. On the right, costumed people walk on stilts.

Easter in Poland

On the other side of the world, in **Poland,** the biggest celebration of the year is Easter. Families spend days getting ready for the holiday. On Easter, the table is covered with food. There are beautiful Easter eggs, too.

Making Easter eggs is an art in Poland. The eggs are given as presents.

In Poland, people decorate Easter eggs in many different colors.

Pesach in Israel

In Israel, one of the happiest times of the year is **Pesach** (PAY·sahk), or "Passover."

Long ago, the people of Israel were kept as slaves in Egypt. They were treated badly. After many years these people were finally able to leave Egypt. They became free people again.

The people of Israel celebrate Passover for eight days. They retell the story of how the slaves became free. Families gather for special meals. The **Seder** (SAYD·ur) is one of these meals.

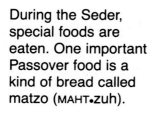

During the Seder, special foods are eaten. One important Passover food is a kind of bread called matzo (MAHT·zuh).

294

Brightly colored decorations and piñatas fill the puestos at Christmastime in Mexico.

Christmas in Mexico

The Christmas celebration in Mexico continues for more than a week. Nine days before Christmas, the **posadas** (poh•SAH•dahs) begin. Families and neighbors gather to act out a Christmas story. Sometimes families have the posada on only one night. But usually it is acted out every night until Christmas.

Meanwhile, the streets are filled with colorful Christmas stalls called **puestos** (PWAYS•tohs). There, people sell toys, rag dolls, and special foods and candies. Many of the things in the puestos are homemade. There are **piñatas** (peen•YAH•tuhs) in all different shapes and colors, too. These piñatas will be filled with candies and broken open on Christmas Eve.

Celebrations Travel Around the World

People in San Francisco celebrate Chinese New Year's with the "dragon dance."

Some of the celebrations from around the world also take place in the United States. Many Americans celebrate Passover in the same way people do in Israel. One of the largest Chinese New Year's celebrations in the world takes place in San Francisco, California. In different parts of our country, children break open piñatas at Christmas time.

The holidays you just read about are only a few of the many celebrations held around the world. Which celebration do you like best? Does your community hold any of these celebrations?

295

CHAPTER 11 REVIEW

USING WORDS

Number a sheet of paper from 1 to 5. Write **true** beside the number of each sentence that is true. Write **false** beside the number of each sentence that is not true. The underlined words give you a clue.

1. Families in Jun Tan, China, may rent a <u>plot</u> to farm.
2. A police officer in Paris, France, is called a <u>bobby</u>.
3. The <u>Louvre</u> is a museum in Paris, France.
4. The people of Amsterdam built <u>pyramids</u>.
5. There are many <u>dikes</u> near Amsterdam.

REVIEWING FACTS

1. What are two different ways of farming in China?
2. Why is Haifa, Israel, an important city?
3. What choice did lawmakers in Dar es Salaam, Tanzania, have to make about the land?
4. What can a person see at the Louvre in Paris, France?
5. Why are there many dikes in The Netherlands?

THINKING CRITICALLY

1. Why are natural resources important to Jun Tan, China, Caracas, Venezuela, and Haifa, Israel? How do people in these communities use resources?
2. Compare Pikeville, Kentucky, and Amsterdam, The Netherlands. How are they alike? How are they different?
3. Choose one of the countries you read about in this chapter. Tell how your food, clothing, and shelter would be different if you lived in that country.

● PRACTICING SKILLS

Reading a Population Map Look at the population map on page 283. Then answer these questions.

1. What do population maps show?
2. What kinds of areas have the fewest people?
3. What kinds of areas have the most people?

WORDS TO REMEMBER

Number your paper from 1 to 10. Use the words below to fill in the blanks. Use each word only once.

Aztec Indians
bobby
dikes
grain
palace
plot
reflects
rice
sea level
subway

1. The bread we eat is made from ____.

2. Many people in the world eat ____ as their main food.

3. The color white ____ the sun's rays.

4. A ____ is a piece of land.

5. A long ____ connects the three parts of Haifa.

6. A police officer in London, England, is called a ____.

7. The Louvre in Paris, France, was once a ____.

8. The ____ in Mexico City built beautiful pyramids.

9. The community of Amsterdam is below ____.

10. The ____ in Amsterdam hold back the sea.

FOCUS ON MAIN IDEAS

1. Sometimes what people eat depends on where they live. Give examples in three countries that show this.

2. Where is cotton grown? How is silk made? Why are cotton and silk important?

3. Why do shelters that are built from the same material often look different in different countries? Why do they often look the same?

4. Who owns the land in the farming community of Jun Tan, China? How has life changed for farmers in Jun Tan? What other jobs do people in Jun Tan have?

5. What happened to Mexico City when the Spanish explorers came? How can you tell that Mexico City is both old and new?

Think of a country you would like to visit. Find out more about that country in an encyclopedia. Write a report telling how that country is different from America.

ACTIVITIES

1. **Art** Make a class travel poster of people, places, and celebrations around the world. Cut out pictures from old magazines, or draw pictures. Paste the pictures onto a piece of construction paper.

2. **Visiting a Store** Visit a grocery store or clothing store with a parent or other grownup. Find three pieces of clothing or three kinds of food that come from other countries. Tell what country each thing came from.

3. **Making a Bulletin Board** Cut out or draw pictures of different types of shelters around the world. Include shelters from your own community. Display the pictures on the bulletin board. Under each picture, tell in which country it is found.

SKILLS REVIEW

1. **The Earth and the Sun** Look at pages 270–272 and answer the following questions.

   a. What is the difference between "A.M." and "P.M."?

   b. How long does it take the Earth to spin completely around?

   c. Explain why it cannot be daylight in Anchorage and Belém at the same time.

   d. How do we measure a year?

   e. Why is it warmer in Belém than it is in Anchorage?

   f. Why does the Earth have different seasons?

2. **Using Intermediate Directions** Use the map below to answer the following questions.

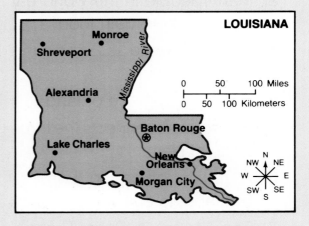

   a. If you went from Shreveport to Alexandria, which direction would you travel?

   b. Is Morgan City southeast or southwest of New Orleans?

YOUR COMMUNITY

You saw in Unit 5 how people in communities around the world live. You read about different kinds of food, shelter, and clothing. Now find out how these communities are like your own community.

LEARNING ABOUT YOUR COMMUNITY

1. Imagine you have a pen pal in one of the communities you read about in this unit. Write a letter to this pen pal. Tell your pen pal how your communities are alike and different. Ask your pen pal questions.

LEARNING ABOUT FOODS AROUND THE WORLD

2. Find out if there are any restaurants in your community that serve food from other countries. Maybe there is a Chinese or Mexican restaurant in your community. Name two restaurants and tell one thing they make. Tell how it is different from American food.

REMEMBERING THE CLOSE-UP

3. The Close-up told about celebrations around the world. Do you or people in your community celebrate the holidays you read about? Go to the library to find out about a holiday in another country. How do people celebrate this holiday?

4. You have read how New Year's is celebrated in China. Write a report telling how New Year's in China is like New Year's in your community. Tell how it is different. Are there any celebrations in your community like New Year's in China? If so, include them in your report.

LEARNING ABOUT CUSTOMS

5. People all over the world have customs. Some customs are things that people do at the same time year after year. Fireworks on the Fourth of July is a custom people in our country have. Name one local custom that people in your community have.

REFERENCES

FACTS ABOUT THE STATES

STATE (Abbreviations)	STATE CAPITAL	STATE POPULATION*	STATE NICKNAME	STATE BIRD	STATE FLOWER
Alabama (Ala., AL)	Montgomery	4,021,000	Yellowhammer State; Heart of Dixie; Cotton State	common flicker	camellia
Alaska (Alaska, AK)	Juneau	521,000	Last Frontier; Land of the Midnight Sun	willow ptarmigan	forget-me-not
Arizona (Ariz., AZ)	Phoenix	3,187,000	Grand Canyon State; Sunset State; Apache State	cactus wren	saguaro (giant cactus)
Arkansas (Ark., AR)	Little Rock	2,359,000	Land of Opportunity	mockingbird	apple blossom
California (Calif., CA)	Sacramento	26,365,000	Golden State	California valley quail	golden poppy
Colorado (Colo., CO)	Denver	3,231,000	Centennial State	lark bunting	Rocky Mountain columbine
Connecticut (Conn., CT)	Hartford	3,174,000	Constitution State; Nutmeg State	robin	mountain laurel
Delaware (Del., DE)	Dover	622,000	First State; Diamond State	blue hen chicken	peach blossom
Florida (Fla., FL)	Tallahassee	11,366,000	Sunshine State	mockingbird	orange blossom
Georgia (Ga., GA)	Atlanta	5,976,000	Empire State of the South; Peach State	brown thrasher	Cherokee rose
Hawaii (Hawaii, HI)	Honolulu	1,054,000	Aloha State	nene (Hawaiian goose)	hibiscus
Idaho (Idaho, ID)	Boise	1,005,000	Gem State; Spud State	mountain bluebird	syringa (mock orange)
Illinois (Ill., IL)	Springfield	11,535,000	Land of Lincoln; The Inland Empire	cardinal	native violet
Indiana (Ind., IN)	Indianapolis	5,499,000	Hoosier State	cardinal	peony
Iowa (Iowa, IA)	Des Moines	2,884,000	Hawkeye State	eastern goldfinch	wild rose
Kansas (Kans., KS)	Topeka	2,450,000	Sunflower State; Jayhawker State	western meadowlark	sunflower
Kentucky (Ky., KY)	Frankfort	3,726,000	Bluegrass State	Kentucky cardinal	goldenrod
Louisiana (La., LA)	Baton Rouge	4,481,000	Pelican State; Bayou State	brown pelican	magnolia
Maine (Maine, ME)	Augusta	1,164,000	Pine Tree State	chickadee	white pine cone & tassel
Maryland (Md., MD)	Annapolis	4,392,000	Old Line State; Free State	Baltimore oriole	black-eyed Susan
Massachusetts (Mass., MA)	Boston	5,822,000	Bay State; Old Colony	chickadee	mayflower
Michigan (Mich., MI)	Lansing	9,088,000	Wolverine State; Water Wonderland	robin	apple blossom
Minnesota (Minn., MN)	St. Paul	4,193,000	Land of 10,000 Lakes; Gopher State	common loon	pink & white lady's slipper
Mississippi (Miss., MS)	Jackson	2,613,000	Magnolia State	mockingbird	magnolia

*These population figures reflect the most recent available estimates.

STATE (Abbreviations)	STATE CAPITAL	STATE POPULATION*	STATE NICKNAME	STATE BIRD	STATE FLOWER
Missouri (Mo., MO)	Jefferson City	5,029,000	Show Me State; Gateway to the West	bluebird	hawthorn
Montana (Mont., MT)	Helena	826,000	Treasure State	western meadowlark	bitterroot
Nebraska (Nebr., NE)	Lincoln	1,606,000	Cornhusker State	western meadowlark	goldenrod
Nevada (Nev., NV)	Carson City	936,000	Silver State; Battle Born State	mountain bluebird	sagebrush
New Hampshire (N.H., NH)	Concord	998,000	Granite State	purple finch	purple lilac
New Jersey (N.J., NJ)	Trenton	7,562,000	Garden State	eastern goldfinch	purple violet
New Mexico (N. Mex., NM)	Sante Fe	1,450,000	Land of Enchantment; Sunshine State	roadrunner	yucca
New York (N.Y., NY)	Albany	17,783,000	Empire State	bluebird	rose
North Carolina (N.C., NC)	Raleigh	6,255,000	Tar Heel State; Old North State	cardinal	dogwood
North Dakota (N.Dak., ND)	Bismarck	685,000	Sioux State; Flickertail State	western meadowlark	wild prairie rose
Ohio (Ohio, OH)	Columbus	10,744,000	Buckeye State	cardinal	scarlet carnation
Oklahoma (Okla., OK)	Oklahoma City	3,301,000	Sooner State	scissortailed flycatcher	mistletoe
Oregon (Oreg., OR)	Salem	2,687,000	Beaver State	western meadowlark	Oregon grape
Pennsylvania (Pa., PA)	Harrisburg	11,853,000	Keystone State	ruffed grouse	mountain laurel
Rhode Island (R.I., RI)	Providence	968,000	Little Rhody; Ocean State	Rhode Island red	violet
South Carolina (S.C., SC)	Columbia	3,347,000	Palmetto State	Carolina wren	Carolina yellow jessamine
South Dakota (S.Dak., SD)	Pierre	708,000	Coyote State; Sunshine State	ring-necked pheasant	American pasqueflower
Tennessee (Tenn., TN)	Nashville	4,762,000	Volunteer State; Big Bend State	mockingbird	iris
Texas (Tex., TX)	Austin	16,370,000	Lone Star State	mockingbird	bluebonnet
Utah (Utah, UT)	Salt Lake City	1,645,000	Beehive State	seagull	sego lily
Vermont (Vt., VT)	Montpelier	535,000	Green Mountain State	hermit thrush	red clover
Virginia (Va., VA)	Richmond	5,706,000	Old Dominion; Mother of Presidents	cardinal	dogwood
Washington (Wash., WA)	Olympia	4,409,000	Evergreen State; Chinook State	willow goldfinch	coast rhodo-dendron
West Virginia (W. Va., WV)	Charleston	1,936,000	Mountain State	cardinal	rhodo-dendron
Wisconsin (Wis., WI)	Madison	4,775,000	Badger State; America's Dairyland	robin	wood violet
Wyoming (Wyo., WY)	Cheyenne	509,000	Equality State; Cowboy State	meadowlark	Indian paintbrush

*These population figures reflect the most recent available estimates.

ATLAS

CANADA

Seattle
Olympia ⊛
**WASHINGTON
(WA)**

Portland •
• Salem

Columbia River

Helena ⊛
**MONTANA
(MT)**

Missouri River

**NORTH DAKO
(ND)**
⊛ Bismarck

**OREGON
(OR)**

**IDAHO
(ID)**
• Boise

• Billings

**WYOMING
(WY)**
Casper •

⊛ Pierre
**SOUTH DAKO
(SD)**

Snake River

• Pocatello

Sacramento River

Sacramento ⊛

⊛ Carson City

**NEVADA
(NV)**

*Great
Salt
Lake*
Salt Lake
City ⊛
Provo •

**UTAH
(UT)**

Cheyenne ⊛

Platte River

**NEBRASKA
(NE)**

Denver ⊛
**COLORADO
(CO)**
• Colorado
Springs

**KAN
(K**

River

**CALIFORNIA
(CA)**

Las •
Vegas

Colorado

Colorado River

**PACIFIC
OCEAN**

Los •
Angeles

**ARIZONA
(AZ)**

Phoenix ⊛

Santa Fe ⊛
• Albuquerque

**NEW MEXICO
(NM)**

**OKLA
(O**

Okla

• Tucson

**TEXAS
(TX)**

Austin

MEXICO

ARCTIC OCEAN

Yukon River

**ALASKA
(AK)**

CANADA

Anchorage •

Juneau ⊛

R4

| 0 | 250 | 500 | Miles |
| 0 | 250 | 500 | 750 | Kilometers |

PACIFIC OCEAN

PACIFIC OCEAN

Kauai

Oahu
Honolulu

HAWAII (HI)

• Maui

Rio Grande

| 0 | 100 | 200 | Miles |
| 0 | 100 | 200 | 300 | Kilometers |

Hawaii

UNITED STATES OF AMERICA

CANADA

Lake Superior

MINNESOTA (MN)
neapolis • St. Paul

WISCONSIN (WI)

M I C H I G A N (MI)

Lake Michigan

Lake Huron

St. Lawrence River

MAINE (ME)
Augusta ⊛
• Portland

Burlington •
Montpelier ⊛

VERMONT (VT)

NEW HAMPSHIRE (NH)
Concord ⊛
Manchester •
• Boston

Lake Ontario

Milwaukee •
Madison ⊛

Lansing ⊛

Detroit •

Lake Erie

Albany ⊛

NEW YORK (NY)

Springfield •
Hartford ⊛

MASSACHUSETTS (MA)
Providence ⊛

RHODE ISLAND (RI)

CONNECTICUT (CT)

IOWA (IA)
• Cedar Rapids

Chicago •

Cleveland •

Bridgeport •

Newark •
⊛ Trenton
• New York City

ha
⊛ Des Moines

ILLINOIS (IL)
Springfield ⊛

INDIANA (IN)
Indianapolis ⊛

Fort Wayne •

OHIO (OH)
⊛ Columbus

PENNSYLVANIA (PA)
Harrisburg ⊛
Philadelphia •

NEW JERSEY (NJ)

Dover ⊛

DELAWARE (DE)

MARYLAND (MD)

Baltimore •
Washington D.C. ⊛
Annapolis ⊛

Missouri River

St. Louis •

ka
Jefferson City ⊛

MISSOURI (MO)

Louisville •
⊛ Frankfort

KENTUCKY (KY)

Wabash River

Huntington •

Ohio River

WEST VIRGINIA (WV)
⊛ Charleston

VIRGINIA (VA)
Richmond ⊛

Norfolk •

ATLANTIC OCEAN

⊛ Raleigh

NORTH CAROLINA (NC)
• Charlotte

Nashville ⊛

TENNESSEE (TN)

ARKANSAS (AR)

Memphis •

Tennessee River

Fort Smith •
Little Rock ⊛

River

Mississippi River

⊛ Columbia

SOUTH CAROLINA (SC)
Charleston •

• Atlanta

MISSISSIPPI (MS)

ALABAMA (AL)

• Birmingham

GEORGIA (GA)
• Columbus

Montgomery ⊛

⊛ Jackson

LOUISIANA (LA)

Baton Rouge ⊛

• Biloxi

Tallahassee ⊛

• Jacksonville

Houston

New Orleans •

FLORIDA (FL)

MAP KEY
National boundary
State boundary
( ) Postal abbreviation
⊛ National capital
⊛ State capital
• Large city

Gulf of Mexico

BAHAMAS

N
NW NE
W E
SW SE
S

0   100   200   300 Miles
0 100 200 300 400 Kilometers

CUBA

R5

LANDFORMS OF THE UNITED STATES

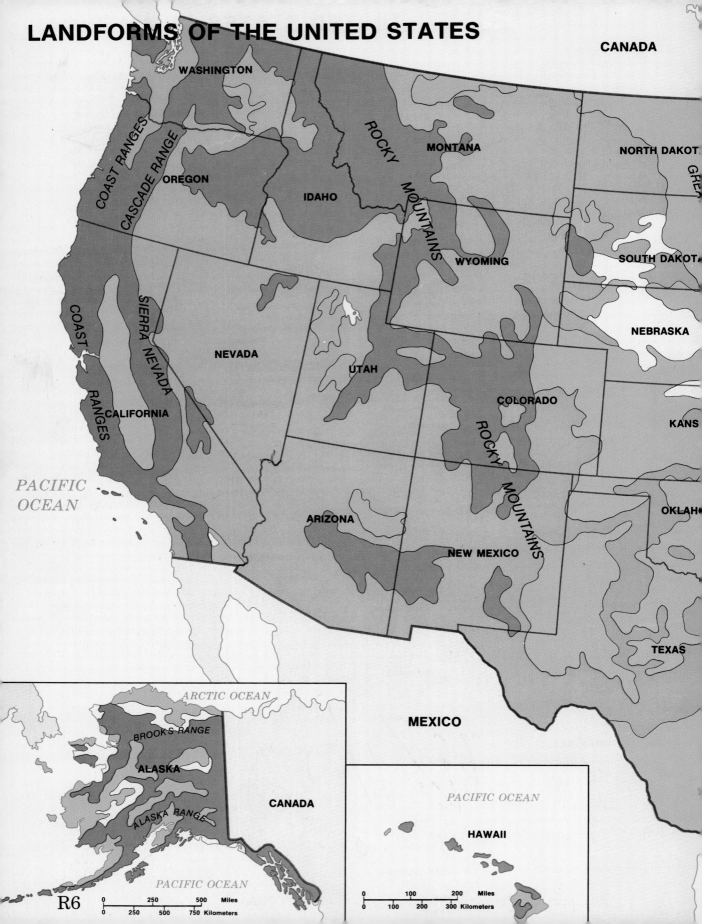

CANADA

WASHINGTON

COAST RANGES

CASCADE RANGE

OREGON

ROCKY MOUNTAINS

MONTANA

NORTH DAKOT

IDAHO

WYOMING

SOUTH DAKOT

GREA

COAST RANGES

SIERRA NEVADA

NEVADA

UTAH

COLORADO

NEBRASKA

CALIFORNIA

KANS

PACIFIC OCEAN

ARIZONA

NEW MEXICO

ROCKY MOUNTAINS

OKLAH

TEXAS

MEXICO

ARCTIC OCEAN

BROOKS RANGE

ALASKA

CANADA

ALASKA RANGE

PACIFIC OCEAN

HAWAII

PACIFIC OCEAN

R6

| 0 | 250 | 500 | Miles |
| 0 | 250 | 500 | 750 | Kilometers |

| 0 | 100 | 200 | Miles |
| 0 | 100 | 200 | 300 | Kilometers |

CANADA

Great Lakes

INNESOTA

WISCONSIN

M I C H I G A N

IOWA

ILLINOIS

INDIANA

OHIO

PENNSYLVANIA

NEW YORK

VERMONT

MAINE

NEW
HAMPSHIRE

MASSACHUSETTS

RHODE ISLAND

CONNECTICUT

NEW JERSEY

MARYLAND

DELAWARE

PLAINS

MISSOURI

KENTUCKY

WEST
VIRGINIA

VIRGINIA

APPALACHIAN MOUNTAINS

ARKANSAS

TENNESSEE

NORTH CAROLINA

SOUTH CAROLINA

MISSISSIPPI

ALABAMA

GEORGIA

LOUISIANA

FLORIDA

*ATLANTIC
OCEAN*

N
NW NE
W   E
SW SE
S

*Gulf of
Mexico*

BAHAMAS

MAP KEY

Mountains

Plateaus

Hills

Plains

National boundary

State boundary

R7

0   100   200   300 Miles
0   100   200   300   400 Kilometers

CUBA

THE WORLD

National boundary

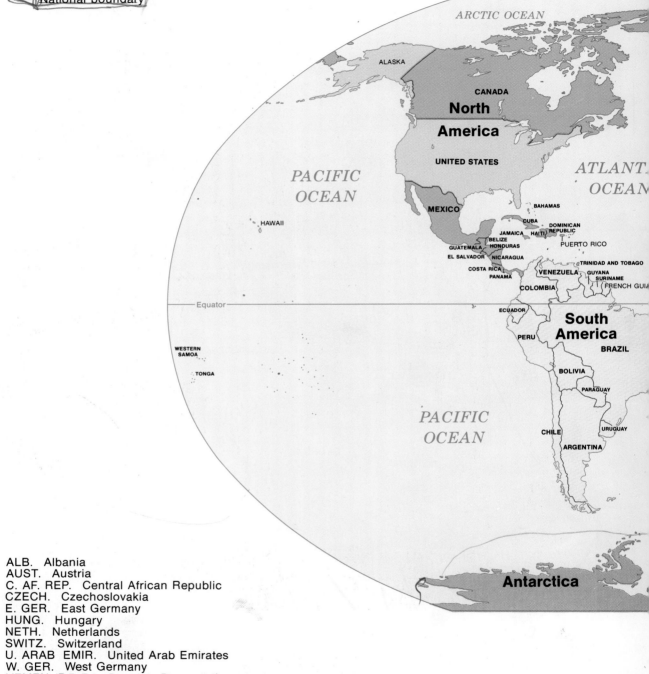

ARCTIC OCEAN

ALASKA

CANADA

North America

UNITED STATES

PACIFIC OCEAN

ATLANTIC OCEAN

MEXICO

BAHAMAS

CUBA

DOMINICAN REPUBLIC

JAMAICA   HAITI

BELIZE

GUATEMALA   HONDURAS   PUERTO RICO

EL SALVADOR   NICARAGUA

COSTA RICA

PANAMA

TRINIDAD AND TOBAGO

VENEZUELA   GUYANA

SURINAME

FRENCH GUIANA

COLOMBIA

HAWAII

Equator

ECUADOR

PERU

South America

BRAZIL

WESTERN SAMOA

TONGA

BOLIVIA

PARAGUAY

PACIFIC OCEAN

CHILE   URUGUAY

ARGENTINA

Antarctica

ALB. Albania
AUST. Austria
C. AF. REP. Central African Republic
CZECH. Czechoslovakia
E. GER. East Germany
HUNG. Hungary
NETH. Netherlands
SWITZ. Switzerland
U. ARAB EMIR. United Arab Emirates
W. GER. West Germany
YEMEN (P.D.R.) People's Democratic
   Republic of Yemen
YUGO. Yugoslavia

ARCTIC OCEAN

ICELAND

NORWAY
SWEDEN
FINLAND

SOVIET UNION (USSR)

UNITED
KINGDOM
England
IRELAND
DENMARK
NETH.
E.
GER.
W.
GER.
POLAND
CZECH.
HUNG.
Europe
FRANCE
SWITZ.
AUST.
ITALY
YUGO.
ROMANIA
BULGARIA
SPAIN
GREECE
TURKEY

MONGOLIA

Asia

N. KOREA
JAPAN
S. KOREA

PORTUGAL

MOROCCO
TUNISIA
LEBANON
ISRAEL
SYRIA
IRAQ
JORDAN
IRAN
AFGHANISTAN
CHINA
PAKISTAN

TERN
HARA
ALGERIA
LIBYA
EGYPT
SAUDI
ARABIA
U. ARAB EMIR.
NEPAL
BHUTAN
TAIWAN

MAURITANIA
MALI
NIGER
Africa
CHAD
SUDAN
YEMEN
YEMEN
(P.D.R.)
OMAN
INDIA
BANGLADESH
BURMA
LAOS

NEGAL
GUINEA
BURKINA
FASO
NIGERIA
C. AF. REP.
ETHIOPIA
SOMALIA
SRI LANKA
THAILAND
VIETNAM
KAMPUCHEA
PHILIPPINES

PACIFIC
OCEAN

LEONE
LIBERIA
IVORY
COAST
GHANA
TOGO
BENIN
CAMEROON
CONGO
GABON
UGANDA
KENYA
RWANDA
BURUNDI
ZAIRE
TANZANIA

MALDIVES

BRUNEI
MALAYSIA
SINGAPORE

INDONESIA

PAPUA
NEW
GUINEA

SOLOMON
ISLANDS

Equator

ANGOLA
MALAWI
ZAMBIA
MOZAMBIQUE
MADAGASCAR

INDIAN
OCEAN

FIJI

ATLANTIC
OCEAN

NAMIBIA
ZIMBABWE
BOTSWANA
SOUTH
AFRICA

Australia

NEW
ZEALAND

Antarctica

0   500   1,000   1,500   2,000 Miles
0   1,000   2,000   Kilometers

R9

Glossary

This glossary contains important social studies words and their definitions. Each word is pronounced as it would be in a dictionary. When you see this mark ′ after a syllable, pronounce that syllable with more force than the other syllables. The page number at the end of the definition tells where to find the word in your book.

add, āce, câre, pälm;   end, ēqual;   it, īce;   odd, ōpen, ôrder;   tŏŏk, pōōl;   up, bûrn;   yōō as u in *fuse*;   oil;   pout;   ə as a in *above*, e in *sicken*, i in *possible*, o in *melon*, u in *circus*;

check;   ring;   thin;   this;   zh as in vision.

A

address (ə·dres′) The location of something, usually the street number, community, state, and zip code of a building. (p. 42)

advertisements (ad·vər·tīz′-mənts) Information about things that are for sale. (p. 164)

aerospace (âr′o·spās) Having to do with air and space. (p. 214)

A.M. (ā·em) The hours between midnight and noon. (p. 270)

American Indians (ə·mer′ə·kən in′dē·ənz) The people who have been living in North and South America for thousands of years. (p. 47)

American Revolution (ə·mer′-ə·kən rev·ə·lōō′shən) The war America fought with England to become free (1775–1783). (p. 230)

authors (ô′·thərz) People who write books. (p. 28)

Aztec Indians (az′tek in′dē·ənz) Indians who lived in Mexico City more than 600 years ago. (p. 289)

B

banks (bangks) Places where people keep money. (p. 20)

bar graph (bär graf) A graph that uses bars of different heights to show amounts of things. (p. 105)

board of education (bôrd uv ej·ōō·kā′shən) A group elected by the members of a community to decide how the schools are to be run. (p. 180)

borders (bôr′dərz) Lines drawn on a map to show where one place ends and another begins. (p. 44)

boundaries (boun′də·rēz) Another word for *borders*. (p. 44)

buffalo (buf′ə·lō) A large, shaggy, wild ox. (p. 208)

business center (biz′nəs sen′-tər) Downtown, where most of the people in a community work. (p. 20)

butterfat (but′ər·fat) The cream that rises when milk is left standing. (p. 81)

by-products (bī′prod·əkts) Parts of a resource or product used to make other goods. (p. 91)

C

calendar (kal′ən·dər) A table showing the days, weeks, and months of the year. (p. 232)

canal (kə·nal′) A waterway made by people. (p. 118)

cannery (kan′ə·rē) A factory where foods are canned. (p. 74)

capital (kap′ə·təl) A place where rules for a state or country are made. (p. 38)

capitol (kap′ə·təl) A building where people meet to make rules for a state or country. (p. 43)

cargo (kär′gō) Goods carried on ships, trains, or planes. (p. 117)

cattle (kat′əl) Cows, bulls, and steers raised for meat. (p. 65)

century (sen′chə·rē) One hundred years. (p. 243)

citizen (sit′ə·zən) A member of a country. (p. 1)

city council (si′tē koun′səl) The lawmakers in a city. (p. 151)

city manager (si′tē man′ə·jər) A city leader who helps make sure things get done. (p. 151)

Civil War (siv′əl wôr) A war fought in America between the North and South (1861–1865). (p. 237)

claim (klām) To say that some-place is owned by a country. (p. 224)

climate (klī′mət) The usual weather in a place, year after year. (p. 59)

clinics (klin′iks) Places that give medical treatment. (p. 179)

coal (kōl) A dark brown or black mineral which gives off heat when burned. (p. 85)

coast (kōst) Land next to an ocean. (p. 124)

colonies (kol′ə·nēz) Places that are ruled by other countries. (p. 228)

community (kə·myōō′nə·tē) A town, city, suburb, or other place where people live and work together. (p. 1)

Congress (kon′grəs) The elected lawmakers from each state who make laws for the whole country. (p. 161)

Constitution (kon·stə·tōō′shən) The written laws for our country's government. (p. 231)

consumer (kən·sōō′mər) Someone who buys goods or services. (p. 138)

containers (kən·tā′nərz) Large steel boxes in which goods are packed for shipping. (p. 117)

continent (kon′tə·nənt) One of the main land areas of the world. (p. 15)

cotton (kot′ən) The white, fluffy part of the cotton plant used to make cloth. (p. 263)

courts (kôrts) Places where judges decide how people who break laws should be punished. (p. 152)

creamery (krē′mə·rē) A factory that makes milk ready for people to buy, and makes other dairy products from milk. (p. 81)

crime (krīm) Something that is against the law. (p. 170)

crop (krop) Any plant raised by a farmer. (p. 60)

crossroads (krôs′rōdz) Places where main roads meet. (p. 204)

D

dairy farm (dâr′ē färm) A farm where cows are raised for their milk. (p. 78)

dairy products (dâr′ē prod′-əkts) Things made from milk. (p. 78)

dam (dam) A wall built across a river or lake that controls water flow. (p. 111)

Declaration of Independence (dek·lə·rā′shən uv in·di·pen′dəns) A message written in 1776 that said the colonies no longer belonged to England. (p. 230)

derrick (der′ik) A tall tower that fits over an oil well. It holds machines for drilling, lifting, and pumping oil. (p. 102)

desert (dez′ərt) An area of dry land where few plants can grow. (p. 33)

detectives (di·tek′tivz) People trained to solve crimes. (p. 170)

dictionaries (dik′shən·âr·ēz) Books that list words in alphabetical order and tell their meanings. (p. 29)

dikes (dīks) Dams, or walls, that hold back water. (p. 290)

direction (də·rek′shən) Which way something is going or facing. North, south, east, and west are the main directions. (p. 10)

distance scale (dis′təns skāl) Something on a map that helps you find out how far one place really is from another. (p. 7)

drill (dril) Pieces of pipe used to make holes deep into the earth. (p. 102)

E

economics (ek·ə·nom′iks) How goods, services, and money are traded back and forth. (p. 139)

elect (ə·lekt′) To choose by vote. (p. 152)

election (ə·lek′shən) A time when people make choices by voting. (p. 158)

electricity (ə·lek·tri′sə·tē) Power used for lights, heating, and machines. (p. 91)

encyclopedias (ən·sī·clə·pē′dē·əz) Books that give facts in alphabetical order about many subjects. (p. 29)

energy (en′ər·jē) Power that makes things work. (p. 87)

equator (i·kwā′tər) A make-believe line around the Earth halfway between the North and South poles. (p. 13)

Eskimos (es′kə·mōz) Groups of people who have been living in the cold parts of Russia, Alaska, Canada, and Greenland for many hundreds of years. (p. 47)

explorer (iks·plôr′ər) A person who travels to new lands to discover things. (p. 223)

F

factories (fak′tər·ēz) Big buildings where goods are made. (p. 64)

family (fam′ə·lē) The people you live with, especially your parents, brothers, sisters, and other relatives. (p. 1)

farming community (färm′ing kə·myoo′nə·tē) A community where most of the people work on farms or with the resources from farms. (p. 69)

ferryboats (fer′ē·bōts) Boats that carry people and cars. (p. 126)

fertilizer (fûr'təl·ĭ·zər) Something added to the soil to feed plants and make them grow better. (p. 62)

flow chart (flō chärt) A chart that shows the order in which something is done. (p. 133)

fort (fôrt) A place for protecting soldiers. (p. 287)

freedom (frē'dəm) Not being under someone else's rule. Being able to make many choices about your life and government. (p. 229)

fresh water (fresh wô'tər) Water that does not have salt in it. The water in most lakes and rivers is fresh. (p. 109)

fuel (fyōol) Something that gives off heat when it is burned. (p. 93)

G

ghost towns (gōst tounz) Places where no one lives anymore. (p. 206)

globe (glōb) A model of the Earth. (p. 12)

goods (gŏodz) Things made by people. (p. 59)

government (guv'ərn·mənt) A group of people that makes laws and sees that they are followed. (p. 150)

governor (guv'ər·nər) The leader in a state government. (p. 160)

grain (grān) Small, hard seeds from certain plants, such as wheat. (p. 257)

grid (grid) Lines that cross one another. On a grid map, letters and numbers help you find things. (p. 175)

group (grōop) People who get together because they share the same needs and interests. (p. 1)

growing season (grō'ing sē'zən) The months in which crops can grow. (p. 63)

guide words (gīd wûrdz) Words at the top of a dictionary page that tell you the first and last words on that page. (p. 29)

H

harbor (här'bər) A protected place where ships or boats can stay. (p. 113)

harvest (här'vəst) To pick crops. (p. 62)

Hawaiians (hə·wä'yənz) The people who lived on the Hawaiian Islands before explorers came from Europe. (p. 50)

hazard (haz'ərd) A danger. (p. 173)

hemisphere (hem'ə·sfir) One of the halves of the Earth. (p. 46)

history (his'tə·rē) The story of the past. (p. 203)

homogenized (hō·mäj'ə·nīzd) Mixed in such a way that the butterfat in milk does not separate from the milk. (p. 81)

hospital (hos'pi·təl) A place where hurt or sick people can go for medical care. (p. 26)

I

income (in'kəm) The money a person earns. (p. 136)

industries (in'dəs·trēz) Big businesses. (p. 128)

intermediate directions (in·tər·mē'dē·it di·rek'shənz) The four directions between the cardinal directions. (p. 292)

R13

irrigation (ir·ə·gā′shən) Bringing water from another place to help crops grow. (p. 63)

island (ī′lənd) Land with water all around it. (p. 50)

J

judge (juj) A person who decides if laws have been broken and decides punishment if they have been broken. (p. 150)

L

labor (lā′bər) Work. (p. 241)

lake (lāk) A body of water with land all around. (p. 33)

landform map (land′fôrm map) A map that tells you about the shape of the land. (p. 96)

law (lô) A written rule that must be obeyed by all the people of a community, state, or country. (p. 149)

lawmakers (lô′mā·kərz) The people in government who make laws. (p. 150)

library (lī′brer·ē) A place where people can find books, magazines, and newspapers. (p. 27)

list (list) A way to order things by writing them down. (p. 76)

location (lō·kā′shən) Where something is. (p. 119)

lumber (lum′bər) Wood that is sawed and used to make goods. (p. 128)

M

majority rule (mə·jôr′ə·tē rool) The idea that if more than half of a group votes for something, the rest of the group has to go along with the choice. (p. 158)

manufactured (man·yoo·fak′-chərd) Made in factories. (p. 214)

map (map) A drawing of a place. (p. 6)

map key (map kē) Something that tells what the symbols in a map stand for. (p. 6)

mayor (mā′ər) The leader in a city or community government. (p. 150)

mine (mīn) A large hole or deep tunnel used to remove minerals from the earth. (p. 85)

mineral (min′ər·əl) A natural resource found in the earth. (p. 85)

model (mo′dəl) A small copy of something. (p. 4)

mountain (moun′tən) A large, raised part of the land. (p. 33)

N

nation (nā′shən) A country with a government of its own. (p. 229)

national anthem (nash′ən·əl an′thəm) Our national anthem is "The Star-Spangled Banner." (p. 246)

Native Americans (nā′tiv ə·mer′ə·kənz) Groups of people who were living in America before the European explorers came. American Indians, Eskimos, and Hawaiians are Native Americans. (p. 47)

natural resources (na′chər·əl rē′sôr·səz) Things found in nature that people can use. (p. 59)

needs (nēdz) Things we must have in order to live. (p. 22)

neighborhood (nā′bər·hŏŏd) A smaller part of a community, made up of the people who live or work near one another. (p. 1)

O

ocean (ō′shən) A huge body of salt water. (p. 13)

oil (oil) A mineral that is a dark, thick liquid, found deep in the ground. (p. 85)

P

pasteurized (pas′chə·rīzd) Quickly heated and then cooled in such a way that harmful germs are killed. (p. 81)

pasture (pas′chər) A field of grass and other kinds of plants that animals eat. (p. 41)

petroleum (pə·trō′lē·əm) Oil. (p. 99)

Pilgrims (pil′grimz) People from England who settled in Plymouth, Massachusetts, in 1620. (p. 226)

plains (plānz) Low, flat lands. (p. 96)

Plains Indians (plānz in′dē·ənz) Indians who lived on the Great Plains east of the Rocky Mountains. (p. 207)

plateaus (pla·tōz′) Lands that are usually high and flat. (p. 96)

plot (plot) A piece of land. (p. 276)

P.M. (pē·em) The hours between noon and midnight. (p. 270)

population map (pop·yoo·lā′-shən map) A map that shows how many people live in a place. (p. 282)

port (pôrt) A community where ships can dock. (p. 113)

President (prez′ə·dənt) The leader of our country. (p. 38)

private property (prī′vit prop′-ər·tē) Homes and businesses that belong to individuals. (p. 168)

producer (prə·dōō′sər) Someone who makes goods or gives services. (p. 137)

property (prop′ər·tē) Land, buildings, and other things people own. (p. 168)

property tax (prop′ər·tē taks) A tax on the land and buildings a person owns. (p. 185)

public property (pub′lik prop′-ər·tē) Zoos, parks, and other things that are open to everyone. (p. 168)

public transportation (pub′lik tranz·pər·tā′shən) Services that people pay to use to get from place to place. Buses and trains are two kinds of public transportation. (p. 179)

public works (pub′lik wûrks) A city department that provides such services as repairing roads, supplying clean water, and so on. (p. 177)

pyramid (pir′ə·mid) A building with flat sides that come to a point on top. (p. 288)

R

recreation (rek·rē·ā′shən) Things people do for enjoyment. (p. 182)

recycling center (rē·sī′kling sen′tər) Places where people bring old newspapers, cans, and bottles so they can be used again. (p. 89)

refinery (ri·fī′nər·ē) A factory where oil is made ready for different uses. (p. 104)

reservations (rez·ər·vā′shənz) Lands the government gave Indians to live on. (p. 236)

reservoir (rez′ər·vwär) A lake used for collecting and storing water. (p. 178)

resource map (rē′sôrs map) A map that shows where resources are located. (p. 64)

responsible (ri·spon′sə·bəl) Obeying rules and laws that go along with using community services. (p. 147)

revolves (ri·volvz′) The way the Earth moves slowly around the sun. (p. 272)

ripe (rīp) Ready to be eaten. (p. 71)

river (ri′vər) A long, flowing body of water. (p. 33)

rotates (rō′tāts) Turns around. The Earth rotates once every 24 hours. (p. 270)

route (rōot) A way to get from one place to another. (p. 122)

rural (rûr′əl) Near forests or farms. (p. 35)

S

sales tax (sālz taks) A tax people pay when they buy something. (p. 185)

salt water (sôlt wô′tər) Water that contains salt, as the water in the oceans. (p. 109)

savings (sā′vingz) The money people set aside for the future. (p. 137)

sawmill (sô′mil) A factory in a logging area where big saws cut logs into boards. (p. 128)

sculptures (skulp′chərz) Works of art made from stone, clay, or metal. (p. 287)

sea level (sē le′vəl) The level of the ocean. (p. 290)

services (sûr′vəs·əz) Jobs people provide for us, such as car repairs or haircuts. (p. 136)

settlers (set′lərz) People who come to a new place, especially to build houses and farms. (p. 225)

sewage (sōo′əj) Waste water from homes, businesses, and streets. (p. 178)

sewage treatment plants (sōo′əj trēt′mənt plants) Buildings where sewage is cleaned and treated. (p. 178)

shelters (shel′tərz) Homes, stores, and other buildings. (p. 22)

skim milk (skim milk) Milk that has had the cream taken off the top. (p. 82)

slaves (slāvz) People who were owned by other people. (p. 227)

suburb (sub′ərb) A community close to a city. (p. 35)

subway (sub′wā) A train that runs mostly underground. (p. 281)

Supreme Court (sə·prēm′ kôrt) The most important court in the United States. (p. 161)

symbol (sim′bəl) Something that stands for something else. (p. 6)

T

table (tā′bəl) A special kind of list, often using lines or boxes to arrange facts. (p. 77)

taxes (tak′səz) Money people pay to support their government and its services (p. 185)

tepees (tē′pēz) Cone-shaped tents in which some Indians lived. (p. 207)

timeline (tīm′līn) A line that shows a number of years and marks things in the order in which they happened. (p. 233)

town meeting (toun mē′ting) A meeting in which all the people in a town take part in its government. (p. 154)

trade center (trād sen′tər) A place where people buy and sell many goods. (p. 203)

transportation (tranz·pər·tā′-shən) Moving people or things from one place to another. (p. 112)

V

valley (val′ē) Low land between hills or mountains. (p. 67)

value (val′yo͞o) How much something is worth. (p. 135)

valves (valvz) Things used to control how fast a liquid flows. (p. 103)

volumes (vol′yo͞omz) Separate books that are part of a set of encyclopedias. (p. 30)

volunteer (vol·ən·tir′) A person who does something for free. (p. 187)

W

well (wel) A narrow, deep hole made in the ground to reach water, oil, or natural gas. (p. 85)

Y

yogurt (yō′gûrt) A dairy product that is thicker than milk and has a slightly sour taste. (p. 78)

Z

ZIP code (zip kōd) A set of numbers that helps the Post Office find an address more quickly. (p. 42)

Index

Page references for illustrations are set in italics.

R18